HUMANS AS A SERVICE

HUMANS AS A SERVICE

THE PROMISE AND PERILS OF WORK IN THE GIG ECONOMY

JEREMIAS PRASSL

Magdalen College
University of Oxford

OXFORD
UNIVERSITY PRESS

OXFORD
UNIVERSITY PRESS

Great Clarendon Street, Oxford, OX2 6DP,
United Kingdom

Oxford University Press is a department of the University of Oxford.
It furthers the University's objective of excellence in research, scholarship,
and education by publishing worldwide. Oxford is a registered trade mark of
Oxford University Press in the UK and in certain other countries

First Edition published in 2018

Impression: 1

Published in the United States of America by Oxford University Press
198 Madison Avenue, New York, NY 10016, United States of America

British Library Cataloguing in Publication Data
Data available

Library of Congress Control Number: 2017957869

ISBN 978-0-19-879701-2

Printed and bound by
CPI Group (UK) Ltd, Croydon, CR0 4YY

To Abi

Contents

Introduction

In the spring of 1770, a sensation was presented to the court of Maria Theresa in Vienna: nothing less than the world's first fully automated chess robot—the Mechanical Turk. Automata, or mechanical simulations, were a technical obsession of the time. This machine, however, was in a different league. Once activated, the Turk would recognize its opponents' strategy, pick up chess pieces, and make its own moves—surprisingly good ones, at that. Over the years, the Mechanical Turk mesmerized international audiences. It played Napoleon Bonaparte—and caught him cheating. Despite many attempts to reveal its secrets (even Edgar Allen Poe had a go), however, the technology enabling the Turk's magic prowess remained a mystery until shortly before its destruction in a nineteenth-century blaze.

Given that it would take another century-and-a-half until IBM's Deep Blue took on and defeated world chess champion Garry Kasparov in the 1990s, just how had Austrian engineer Wolfgang von Kempelen managed to create a chess robot in the eighteenth century? Well, as so often in life, if something sounds too good to be true, it probably is: crouching in a hidden compartment inside the Turk's chessboard was a human player, moving pieces around the board above. During pre-game presentations, the operator was quite literally hidden behind modern technology, moving around between whirring wheels, shiny dials, and complicated machinery as each side panel was opened in turn.[1]

★ ★ ★

Over two centuries later, Amazon CEO Jeff Bezos took to the stage at the Massachusetts Institute of Technology (MIT) to set out his vision for Amazon's future. He hadn't come to talk about selling books, groceries, or even drones; rather, the plan was to rent out 'Amazon's guts' and become the world's leading provider of 'web services'. Software developers requiring processing

Humans as a Service: The Promise and Perils of Work in the Gig Economy. First Edition. Jeremias Prassl. © Jeremias Prassl 2018. Published 2018 by Oxford University Press.

power and data storage would no longer need to buy expensive hardware to meet their needs; they could tap into Amazon's servers instead and pay a fractional price for the services required.

Amazon's mighty servers, however, weren't the only new product on offer that morning. Jeff Bezos revealed that the company's algorithms were still struggling with some fairly basic tasks—from working out how to categorize photographs to determining which products on its website had double listings. Amazon's solution? To develop an internal platform that outsourced these tasks to humans. Users around the world would log on, review the images, and help Amazon's algorithms to do their job.

There seemed to be no limit to what could be outsourced in this way, from transcribing podcasts to small programming jobs. The platform would create a new kind of 'microwork', whereby a 'crowd' of individuals could complete discrete tasks in minutes—and be paid pennies for it. The platform's name? Amazon Mechanical Turk (MTurk).

Welcome to the Gig Economy

Over the course of the past decade, Amazon's MTurk has been joined by a large number of competitors, both online and in the real world. An ever-growing number of start-ups are setting up online platforms and mobile 'apps' to connect consumers, businesses, and workers—often for jobs lasting no longer than a few minutes. What started out as a small niche for digital 'crowdwork' has grown into a global phenomenon. Some of the major players have quickly become household names—think 'ride-sharing' companies Uber, Lyft, Didi, and Ola, delivery apps Deliveroo and Foodora, or casual task platforms Helpling and TaskRabbit.

New platforms are cropping up in industries from transportation to domestic care, from professional services to manual labour. They are at the vanguard of what is often called the 'gig economy', evoking the artist's life in which each concert, or 'gig', is but a one-off task or transaction, without further commitments on either side.[2]

The rise of these companies has been meteoric—and is surrounded by intense public debate. Contradictions abound. To some, the 'Uber economy' is merely the latest instantiation of 'runaway capitalism... screwing' the workers;[3] to others, 'collaborative consumption' is key to a fundamental improvement in our working lives.[4] Journalists, regulators, and academics have quickly become interested in the gig economy. Most agree that we are witnessing a revolution—whilst bitterly contesting its nature. On the one hand, there are those who enthusiastically promote the gig economy as nothing less than a fundamental reinvention of labour markets, weaving 'a fascinating tapestry of innovation, one that provides an early glimpse of what capitalist societies might evolve into over the coming decades'[5]—a story of platforms facilitating 'the exchange of goods, services, or social currency, thereby enabling value creation for all participants'.[6]

Vociferous critics, on the other hand, castigate gig platforms for extending 'a harsh and deregulated free market into previously protected areas of our lives',[7] thus:

> forging an economic system in which those with money will be able to use faceless, anonymous interactions via brokerage websites and mobile apps to hire those without money by forcing an online bidding war to see who will charge the least for their labor.[8]

Humans as a Service

Back in 2006, Jeff Bezos had no such qualms. The CEO of one of the world's largest tech companies was excited by MTurk's business promise. In addition to books, groceries, and gadgets, Amazon would henceforth sell *work*:

> You've heard of software as a service—
> —Well, this is basically humans as a service.[9]

Humans have always provided services to their employers and customers, of course. As workers, however, they enjoy significant legal and economic protection in return, from minimum wage and unfair dismissal laws, to social security and pensions. Therein lies the attraction of 'humans as a service': like information technology (IT) infrastructure, large workforces are expensive to build and maintain. Servers need to be powered and cooled; workers need to be trained and paid wages—irrespective of peaks and troughs in consumer demand.

Once work itself becomes the service or commodity, however, such responsibilities can be avoided, lowering prices for consumers and increasing employers' profits. Lukas Biewald, CEO of MTurk's competitor platform CrowdFlower, makes the business case:

> Before the Internet, it would be really difficult to find someone, sit them down for ten minutes and get them to work for you, and then fire them after those ten minutes. But with technology, you can actually find them, pay them a tiny amount of money, and then get rid of them when you don't need them anymore.[10]

Sounds good—until you put yourselves in the shoes of the worker whose labour has become a service, to be bought and traded like any other commodity. Employers can dip into the crowd to meet their constantly changing staffing needs; workers are left without security or protection.

Rebranding Work

How did we get here? Legal systems across the world have long attempted to protect workers against such extreme forms of commodification. Nearly a century ago, when the United Nations' International Labour Organization (ILO) was founded, the High Contracting Parties agreed upon a series of guiding principles 'of special and urgent importance'. First amongst them? The idea that 'labour should not be regarded merely as a commodity or article of commerce'.[11]

In return for the economic benefits of control over their workforce, employment regulation imposes upon employers a number of protective obligations. It's a crucial trade-off: workers have to follow their employers' orders, and enjoy a basic level of stability and economic security in return. Genuinely independent service providers enjoy no such legal protection— but they are free to choose their customers, to set their prices, and to negotiate over terms and conditions. Work, in short, is legally protected; entrepreneurship is not.

Why, then, is it no longer 'really difficult' to get someone to work for you and then 'get rid of them when you don't need them anymore'? How can the gig economy sell *humans as a service* and ignore traditional employment law protection? Because, not unlike a modern-day Mechanical Turk, many platforms are ultimately designed to obscure the reality behind their business model. Carefully worded terms and conditions characterize platforms as matchmakers and workers as independent entrepreneurs, beyond the reach of legal regulation. Work is rebranded as entrepreneurship, and labour sold as a technology.

The Platform Paradox

According to most platforms' terms and conditions, their business model is to operate powerful software applications (apps) designed to match consumers who need a task done with entrepreneurs in search of their next 'gig'. The underlying quest is to remove as much 'friction' as possible from each interaction. Beautifully designed apps with clever functionalities offer swift introductions, and make the gig economy fun and easy to use for both parties: drivers and passengers can see each other on their phones before a trip has begun; if you need help assembling new furniture, an algorithm will swiftly find the best—or cheapest—available handyman in the vicinity.

Upon closer inspection, however, it quickly emerges that many platforms offer much more than mere matchmaking services: they are in the business of *digital work intermediation*. To deliver tightly curated products and services to customers, gig-economy operators actively shape the entire transaction by means of close control over their workforce: from setting terms and conditions and checking relevant qualifications, to ensuring proper performance and payment. Gig-economy apps do not only make it quick and easy to find workers and tasks; user ratings also provide quality control and feedback, and digital payment systems render the entire transaction cashless.

This is the 'platform paradox': gig-economy operators present themselves as marketplaces, even though, in reality, they often act like traditional employers. Instead of passive matchmaking, platforms rely on rating systems and algorithmic control to ensure that each aspect of the worker's task is completed in compliance with company policy and customer instructions.

Labour as a Technology

Technology is at the heart of this new and rapidly growing industry. The Internet facilitates communication at lightning speed—regardless of whether users are in the same neighbourhood or at different ends of the globe. Algorithms can crunch vast numbers of transactions in seconds, taking into account a near-unlimited number of relevant variables. Smartphones and tablets have put powerful processors in the palms and pockets of consumers and workers; GPS satellites accurately calculate their location and mobile payment mechanisms have made cash obsolete.

Technology, however, doesn't just enable gig-economy transactions; it also shapes our perceptions of what's going on behind the scenes. When we tap along through a well-designed app to pick a meal or watch a small car symbol inch closer on a map, it's easy for the lines between algorithms and humans to become blurred: both appear inextricably involved in getting the job done. Professor Lilly Irani of University of California San Diego was amongst the first to highlight how the gig economy's emphasis on technology leads us to perceive 'people as computational infrastructure ... In this world ... some become creators while others become computers.'[12]

Gig-economy platforms, in other words, make labour less visible, even where an element of physical interaction remains. In a world of *humans as a service*, Irani argues, workers are 'kept at a distance and organized for innovators' pleasures'.[13] As a result, 'stories of uneven rights, compensation and safety are not aberrations, but rather constitutive of the roles and ideologies of high-technology work'.[14]

Invisible though it might be, labour is central to the gig economy: without access to large pools of on-demand workers, it would be impossible for platforms and apps to deliver any of the gigs, tasks, and rides they offer. Jeff Bezos admitted as much when he spoke of using crowdworkers to deliver 'artificial artificial intelligence'—and brazenly named Amazon's new platform after the infamous eighteenth-century chess hoax.

Making the Gig Economy Work

Whilst its fraud has long been discovered, the Turk can still teach us an important lesson today: in thinking about the gig economy, it's crucial that we look beyond platforms' contractual terms and powerful technology. We will discover fascinating digital innovations and genuine entrepreneurship opportunities—but we must not let that mislead us into a world of technological exceptionalism. The gig economy's product, first and foremost, is work. Always remember the little chess player hidden away in his box. Beneath the shiny surface of our phones, tablets, and computers, behind the frictionless apps that allow us to order all kinds of products and services, someone, somewhere, is doing work.

The gig economy's hidden workers are the central focus of this book. If we are to understand the industry's implications for the world of work, however, we need to look further, and discover its promise for workers, consumers, and society at large—as well as the perils of insecure, low-paid work. The ultimate goal? Making the gig economy work for everyone: a sustainable business model in which we all get to enjoy the benefits of platform innovation—without reducing humans to a service.

It is crucial to note that nothing in this analysis suggests that we should shut platforms down. The gig economy has great potential: improved matching efficiency and its associated algorithms can add value to our economy, create job opportunities, and allow all of us to enjoy access to better products and services. For the industry to operate to everyone's benefit, however, we need to ensure that platforms can no longer arbitrage around existing rules and have to bear the full cost of their business model: employment law is the key to equal and equitable conditions for all.

As Jeff Howe, the journalist who coined the very language of 'crowd-sourcing', notes in the introduction to his enthusiastic book on 'the power of the crowd [to drive] the future of business', companies who 'view the crowd as a cheap labor force are doomed to fail'.[15] The promise of the gig economy is great—but we need to make sure it lives up to its full potential, for everyone. Humans must never become a service; platforms should.

Platforms as a Service

To this end, the book is loosely structured into three parts. We will, first, explore the reality of life and work in the gig economy, before attempting to chart solutions to the problems identified. Finally, we will take a step back to think about the broader implications of the gig economy for consumers, taxpayers, and markets at large.

Exploring the Gig Economy

The thorniest of these tasks comes first—and will take up most of the first four chapters. Chapter 1 sets the scene, looking at 'Work on Demand' in the gig economy and illustrating platform's role in digital work intermediation through several archetypical examples. The phenomenon might still form no more than a small part of labour markets—but it's no flash in the pan, given its rapid expansion into new tasks and industries. Looking at the economics of the gig economy, we discover competing drivers of value creation— only some of which (notably, increased efficiency in matching labour supply and demand) should be encouraged.

We then turn to linguistic matters, exploring how, despite their focus on commercial labour intermediation, platforms were originally cast in a different light, operating under the mantle of a 'sharing economy'. Superficial as this may seem, language matters. This is the central theme of Chapter 2, 'Doublespeak'.

Discussions of the gig economy to date have been characterized by a clash of narratives—'simple stories [that] distort multifaceted realities', in the words of Frank Pasquale:[16] platforms either promise to revolutionize the future of work to the benefit of all or represent a return to medieval feudalism. Each of these narratives is important in its own right—but, as we quickly discover, much more is at stake. With regulators around the world trying to work out how the gig economy should fit into existing legal structures, narratives play a powerful role in shaping regulation. At its crudest, this means that proponents portray the gig economy as a radically new and 'disruptive' industry, which governments would do well to leave alone. Opponents suggest that platforms' inherently exploitative practices should be banned altogether. Neither suggestion will detain us for long.

Matters become more interesting once we turn to the gig economy's two central claims in refuting traditional employment laws: entrepreneurship and innovation. There is plenty of evidence for elements of both when platforms' innovative use of technology and matching algorithms enable workers to embark on entrepreneurial careers. But the narrative does not hold true for *all* gig workers: given the vast heterogeneity of work, the reality is inevitably more complex.

Chapter 3, 'Lost in the Crowd', explores the entrepreneurship narrative, juxtaposing platforms' promises of autonomy, freedom, and self-determination with the sobering reality of algorithmic control. Gig work suggests flexibility, yet the business model often requires a tightly curated service. Life as a 'micro-entrepreneur', it turns out, is heavily conditioned by ever-watchful rating algorithms, which aggregate customer feedback and compliance with platform guidelines to exercise close (albeit often indirect) control. Failure to comply can have drastic results—up to, and including, sudden, unexplained 'deactivation'.

In many instances, algorithms will also assign work—and determine rates of pay. Depending on consumer demand, this means that the promised flexibility of on-demand work can quickly turn into economic insecurity, as gig income is highly unpredictable from week to week. The promise of freedom similarly rings hollow for many—not least because of carefully constructed contractual agreements, which ban some gig workers from taking platforms to court. Instead of enjoying the spoils of successful entrepreneurship, a significant proportion of on-demand workers find themselves trapped in precarious, low-paid work.

The innovation narrative is similarly multifaceted, as we discover in Chapter 4. There is much that is innovative about the gig economy's reliance on modern technology—but in so far as work is concerned, the business model is ancient. This is the 'Innovation Paradox'. Many platforms' business models are built around large workforces competing over relatively low-skilled tasks, controlled by powerful intermediaries. The future of work, it turns out, is a blast from the past. From eighteenth-century outwork to nineteenth-century dock labour, there is ample historical precedent for this organization of work—and the resulting working conditions.

And it is not only in history that we can find similar models: technology apart, gig work fits neatly into a broader trend of fissurization, from temporary agency work to supply-chain outsourcing, which has been growing in our labour markets for several decades. On closer inspection, an even more fundamental problem with the innovation narrative emerges: supposedly innovative elements of platforms' strategies might, in fact, simply be aimed at entrenching existing operators against future competitors.

Charting Solutions

Against this backdrop, Chapter 5 turns to how we should regulate work in the on-demand economy. To the extent that 'disruption' has become tech-speak for breaking the law, the time has come to 'Disrupt the Disruptors'. Most on-demand gigs, tasks, and rides are work, rather than entrepreneurship—and should be recognized as such. In a first step, this means that the industry needs to be brought within the scope of employment law. Legal systems across the world have learned to respond to employers' attempts at mischaracterizing work as independent entrepreneurship by focusing on the reality of the underlying relationship instead. In more complex, multilateral scenarios where customers and platforms share control, a further question crops up as to who the responsible employer should be.

Once within the scope of employment law, workers will enjoy access to a basic floor of rights—from minimum wage entitlements to discrimination protection. Given the intermittent nature of gig-economy work, however, this will not always be enough to rebalance the scales and to counteract gig workers' inequality of bargaining power vis-à-vis their platforms. We need to develop existing standards in response to the specific challenges of pre-carious work—from portable ratings and higher wage levels for flexible hours, to rethinking social partner involvement. In concluding, one of gig work's most pervasive—yet fundamentally misleading—myths is tackled head-on: there is no inherent incompatibility between flexible work and employment protection.

A Broader Perspective

Having tackled the narrow questions of employment law, the final chapter takes a step back and looks beyond the implications of on-demand work: what does the rise of a gig economy mean for consumers and for markets at large? A growing body of evidence suggests that, both as consumers and as taxpayers, all of us are potentially liable to pay for the real cost of platforms' services. Consumers increasingly find that the promised bargain of better services for lower prices unravels when things go wrong and platforms refuse responsibility. On the tax front, the fragmentation of payments and tax collection leads to serious underpayment and enforcement problems. The proliferation of low-cost labour might even end up disincentivizing investment in research, development, and working conditions that foster genuine innovation.

In all of these scenarios, employment law can play a crucial role in 'Levelling the Playing Field'. Chapter 6 returns to questions of consumer protection and tax enforcement to show how characterizing gig-economy 'micro-entrepreneurs' as workers and platforms as their employers closes down avenues for exploiting regulatory arbitrage, corrects negative externalities, and avoids asset misallocation.

At a fundamental level, the gig economy's problems—for workers, consumers, taxpayers, and markets—are all driven by a single issue: by presenting themselves as mere intermediaries rather than powerful service providers, platforms can shift nearly all of their business risk and cost onto others. Regulatory arbitrage, externalities, and asset misallocation all skew the playing field in favour of platforms and impose cost on everyone else. Despite much doublespeak to the contrary, the application of employment law in the gig economy is not a question of enforcing burdensome rules to thwart innovation. Businesses can compete on a level playing field only if existing employment laws are equally applied and consistently enforced. Ensuring the full application of employment law is crucial if we want to realize the promise of the gig economy—without being exposed to its perils.

I

Work on Demand

In June 2006, tech journalist Jeff Howe noticed that the Internet was reshaping the boundaries of work. The long-standing distinction between employees working for large companies and amateurs engaging in their craft as a hobby had become increasingly blurred:

> Hobbyists, part-timers, and dabblers suddenly have a market for their efforts, as smart companies in industries as disparate as pharmaceuticals and television discover ways to tap the latent talent of the crowd. The labor isn't always free, but it costs a lot less than paying traditional employees. It's not outsourcing; it's crowdsourcing.[1]

Crowdsourcing, he subsequently explained, is the 'act of taking a job traditionally performed by employees and outsourcing it to an undefined, generally large group of people in the form of an open call'.[2] Its rise from nowhere has been little short of meteoric: a mere decade later, recourse to the crowd has begun to permeate our daily lives. In cities around the world, consumers can hail Ubers instead of traditional taxis, order their food through Deliveroo, request handyman assistance from TaskRabbit, and outsource small digital tasks on Amazon's Mechanical Turk (MTurk). Welcome to the gig economy.

The ramifications are far-reaching. Traditional companies are replaced by platforms; their long-term employees recast as independent entrepreneurs. The platform economy, Professor Orly Lobel of the University of San Diego argues, is 'not only a paradigmatic shift for business, but also for legal theory'.[3] Such bold claims raise a number of issues: are they true? And, in any event, what is this idea of 'on-demand work' in the 'gig economy'?

In this chapter, we set out to explore how the gig economy works: we will meet some of the most important platforms, and illustrate their central role in shaping transactions between consumer and workers. This digital work intermediation is key to understanding the gig economy: platforms'

Humans as a Service: The Promise and Perils of Work in the Gig Economy. First Edition. Jeremias Prassl. © Jeremias Prassl 2018. Published 2018 by Oxford University Press.

sophisticated algorithms connect workers and customers, and exercise ongoing control over the ensuing relationships. We then chart the astonishing variety and global growth of the gig economy, with a particular emphasis on the underlying business model: how do platforms make money? Finally, we turn to the broader impacts of digital work intermediation: how do platforms go beyond mere matchmaking to shape the experiences of workers and consumers? The potential advantages of gig work are manifold, from the flexibility to choose when and where to work, to the ability to offer innovative and affordable services. But a life of intermittent, short-term 'gigs' also has its downsides, from economic insecurity to a lack of traditional employment protection.

Understanding the Gig Economy

Whether you are looking for food delivery from a nearby restaurant or a lawyer to help with a complicated property dispute, it's likely that there'll already be 'an app for that'. An exhaustive list, let alone description, of gig-economy platforms would far exceed the pages of this book—and be outdated before it could be printed. Despite their public prominence, platforms such as Uber, MTurk, and TaskRabbit are but the tip of an iceberg. Each business model has been copied and developed by a vast number of rival start-ups: Uber faces competition in the United States from Lyft, Didi in China, Ola in India, and a host of local taxi apps across the globe. Whereas TaskRabbit tackles all sorts of odd jobs, a growing number of operators focus on particular industries, such as restaurants: food-delivery rivals Deliveroo and Foodora had expanded to more than ten countries by 2016.[4] And MTurk faces competition online, whether it's Fiverr for quick jobs or platforms such as Upwork for higher-skilled work, including digital design and programming.

A further complication arises from the fact that gig-economy brands and business models vary across countries and operators. New platforms are launched and old ones dispatched into bankruptcy on a daily basis. Even well-established operators seem to reinvent themselves constantly: a platform might experiment across different cities with its customer pricing, the commission it charges, and how workers are assigned to particular tasks. Indeed, even the descriptions in this chapter will have to resort to generalizations and are by no means future-proof: changes to the business model require little more than a software update.

To grapple with the constant evolution of the on-demand economy, several academics have attempted to come up with a taxonomy of gig-economy work. One of the leading authors in this field is Jan Marco Leimeister of Kassel University in Germany. Together with his team, he has developed an extensive classificatory scheme of crowdsourcing and crowdwork. This distinguishes, for example, between 'internal' and 'external' crowdwork, depending on whether on-demand workers are employed by the platform operator or not. The latter category is then subdivided into a series of 'archetypes', including categories such as 'Microtask', where 'tasks are predominantly simple and repetitive', or 'Marketplace platforms', through which 'more long-term and complex jobs are given into crowd'.[5]

This understanding of *crowdwork* as a purely digital form of on-demand labour, whereby tasks can be completed behind a computer anywhere, is usually contrasted with *gigwork*, whereby tasks mediated through a platform have to be completed offline—think food delivery or cleaning.[6] The axes along which the field could be organized are nearly unlimited. Whether work is completed online or offline is one possible dimension, but it isn't the only differentiation by any means: think, for example, about the difference between task-specific platforms (Lyft, Deliveroo) versus generalist operators (Fiverr, TaskRabbit), or differences in who sets the price of each task (the platform, in some cases; the consumer or even the worker herself, in others).[7] In reality, all gig-economy platforms' business models overlap and intersect— with several crucial commonalities, including the use of algorithmic rating mechanisms, and a notable fondness for coming up with new names and labels.

Digital Work Intermediation

Even more importantly for present purposes, the gig-economy platforms' business model is universally based on near-instant recourse to a large pool of on-demand workers: the 'crowd', looking for their next 'gig'. The gig economy's promise to deliver speedy services at low cost is premised on the availability of a large supply of workers who can easily be matched with consumer demand. Behind the language of 'gigs', 'tasks', and 'rides' sits a much more sophisticated business model: the digital intermediation of work.

At first glance, platforms are but a small cog in the gig economy, pairing consumers looking for a particular service with a suitable entrepreneur willing to complete the task. Algorithms take into account a wide range of relevant factors, from the quality of previous work and current availability to geographic location, and optimize each match—before charging a small fee for the service.

Upon closer inspection, however, the platform's role goes far beyond mere match-making: it offers *digital work intermediation*. To deliver tightly curated products and services to customers, gig-economy operators actively shape the entire transaction by means of close control over their workers. We will explore the mechanisms behind this control in Chapter 3; suffice it to say here that whilst elements of work in the on-demand economy might not look like traditional '9-to-5' jobs with a single employer, the reality of work is often a far cry from the freedom and independence of genuine entrepreneurship. As a result, the services offered to consumers are considerably more than a simple one-off match, from quality monitoring to payment facilitation.

How does this work in practice? We will encounter a host of different platforms over the course of the coming chapters: there is a near-limitless variation of business models out there. To get a sense of digital labour intermediation, however, let's begin by exploring three archetypical operators to see the myriad ways in which platforms' algorithms shape the relationship between customer and worker.

Uber is 'Everyone's Private Driver' in cities across the globe. Its app offers customers ('riders') multiple types of service (such as UberX at the economy end of the spectrum and UberLUX for premium cars), depending on location.[8] Other platforms, such as TaskRabbit, offer a much broader range of services. Accessed through an app or website, the company advertises help with jobs ranging from moving home and furniture assembly, to cleaning and small repair works, in nearly 40 US cities, as well as London.[9] Digital remote work, finally, is the third gig-economy archetype. MTurk was one of the earliest operators in this field, connecting consumers and businesses ('Requesters') with workers ('Turkers') across the globe. Despite the variety of services on offer, each platform operates as a digital labour intermediary: matching consumer demand with workers from its pool—and exercising close control over the entire relationship.

Gig-economy services can be accessed with hitherto unimaginable ease (and often at much cheaper prices) once consumers have registered their personal and credit card details with a platform. Rather than heading out to the streets in search of a taxi, you can simply order a 'ride' at the touch of a button in any city in which Uber drivers are active, selecting a desired pick-up location and category of service. The app connects the rider with a close-by driver, whose location can be monitored via the app. Information, including the driver's name, photo, and car details, is shared with the rider to ensure easy identification. Once in the car (or beforehand, if the customer wants a price estimate), the rider enters her destination; an algorithm automatically works out the route.

On TaskRabbit, consumers choose a task category, and specify when and where the work should get done. An algorithm matches each request with a shortlist of 'Taskers' for the customer to engage, providing information about their experience and hourly rates. Sometimes, a 'Quick Assign' feature might also be available, allocating tasks to the first available worker. Details about the flat to be cleaned or items to be delivered are then arranged through the app.

On MTurk, jobs are broken down into so-called human intelligence tasks (HITs): a wide range of low-complexity, low-skill tasks, from identifying objects in photographs and extracting product details from receipts, to completing surveys and transcribing audio or video clips. Requesters upload these tasks to the platform and set a price (rarely more than a couple of US cents), time frame, and required worker qualifications.

The platforms, finally, also handle all payment transactions and provide feedback through worker (and sometimes consumer) ratings. Upon completion of each task, MTurk Requesters can approve or reject the work; payment is processed by the platform, with Amazon deducting a commission of 20–40 per cent, with a minimum of half a cent per hit.

An Uber passenger can simply jump out of the car at her destination— the price is determined by the app and payment processed through the card on file. The platform retains a commission of 20–25 per cent (depending on the city) and pays the rest to the driver. After each ride, passengers and drivers are invited to rate each other through a five-star system, the cumulative results of which become their 'ratings' displayed before future rides.

TaskRabbit similarly handles invoicing and payment on the basis of how many hours a task took to complete. Each Tasker can set her own hourly rates, to which the platform adds its commission (30 per cent, at the time of writing) and a 'Trust & Support Fee' of 7.5 per cent to fund worker vetting, customer support, and the platform's US$1 million insurance guarantee should 'something unexpected happen during the task'.[10] After completion of the task, clients and workers both leave feedback, with the client rating each worker out of five stars in response to a number of questions. A cumulative rating, together with any public review comments, will be displayed on Taskers' profiles to guide future customers.[11]

How Big Is the Gig Economy?

The platform economy, breathless futurologists assure us, is the future of work: with 'freelancing [as] the new normal',[12] it will fundamentally reshape the organization of businesses, the economy, and our working lives. Not everyone agrees. Frank Kalman, editor of *Talent Economy* magazine, is 'not buying it'.[13] The gig economy, he argues, represents a tiny fraction of our labour markets, goes against the grain of corporate work culture, and imposes a host of hidden coordination and transaction costs on traditional businesses. In short, 'gig work is likely to remain a small part of the overall labor force, both from an economic perspective and a cultural, performance and management perspective'.[14]

How big, then, is the gig economy? Depending on where we look, we are faced with wildly different numbers—especially when trying to determine what proportion of the overall workforce are engaged in the gig economy.[15] Very little, some argue: economists Lawrence Katz of Harvard University and Alan Krueger of Princeton University, for example, estimated in 2016 that a mere 0.5 per cent of the US workforce worked for on-demand platforms—that is, no more than 800,000 workers.[16] US Senator Mark Warner, meanwhile, cites a much larger (if hardly credible) range of estimates: 'I've seen it range from 3 million to 53 million.'[17]

The truth lies somewhere in between those extremes. Indeed, a more realistic consensus (at least as regards industry size) appears to be emerging at the time of writing. Several studies using a range of methodologies, from traditional surveys to an analysis of bank accounts to determine where income is derived from, have homed in on a figure of approximately 4 per cent of the working-age population both in the United States and the UK.[18] A report by the RSA, a UK think tank, published in spring 2017 similarly estimates that there are currently 1.1 million gig workers in the UK and that approximately '3 per cent of adults aged 15+ have tried gig work of some form, which equates to as many as 1.6 million adults'.[19]

From an overall labour-market perspective, these numbers don't necessarily sound like a major concern—until we consider the fact that most serious attempts at measuring the size of gig work in the broader labour market tend to understate its extent. Current statistical measures often fail to take into account the full scope of gig-economy work, not least because they tend to focus on primary income sources; workers supplementing their income with gig-economy work are thus likely to be excluded from official statistics.[20]

The gig economy is also an increasingly global phenomenon. Digital work, in particular, can easily be outsourced across borders. In January 2017, colleagues at the Oxford Internet Institute published the results of an intensive three-year study into online gig work across the globe. Their conclusion is clear: platform work 'is becoming increasingly important to workers living in low- and middle-income countries'.[21] Their detailed analysis of gig work in Kenya, Nigeria, South Africa, Vietnam, Malaysia, and the Philippines paints an already-familiar picture:

> [R]egions like Sub-Saharan Africa and Southeast Asia, in particular, can capitalise on this digitally-mediated work opportunity. New sources of work are especially needed as the youth-to-adult unemployment rate hits historic peaks and average wages remain significantly lower in emerging economies than in developed economies... [But there are] also concerns such as downward pressure on pay, long hours, discrimination, and lack of social contact for some.[22]

From London to Cape Town, New York to Hanoi, the opportunities and threats we observe mirror the tensions we will encounter throughout this book.

Explosive Growth

Despite our problems in pinning down the exact size of the gig economy today, given its clear—and global—growth trend (the figures cited above will, in all likelihood, be long outdated by the time you read them), on-demand work is likely to become an ever-more-salient topic in years to come.[23] The industry is booming. As Micha Kaufman, CEO of task platform Fiverr, noted as early as 2013:

> [A] revolution is taking shape—an entirely different kind of economy. The labor force of new entrepreneurs, which we call the Gig Economy, is growing rapidly around the world and could soon represent as much as 50 per cent of the US workforce.[24]

Whether it's the range of tasks offered and industries affected, turnover, or the numbers of consumers and workers, whichever way you measure the gig economy, growth rates are enormous.[25] Growing consumer demand is a key factor driving industry growth: as more and more tasks become available through online apps, both individual consumers and business users will come to rely on on-demand work.[26] Home-cleaning platform Handy, for example, grew to bookings worth US$1 million *per week* within two years of its launch.[27] Uber's app has proved similarly popular with consumers. Founded in San Francisco in the spring of 2009, less than a decade later Uber was operating in nearly 600 cities across 81 countries—providing more than 15 million journeys around the world on New Year's Eve 2016 alone.[28]

This explosive growth is fuelled by eye-watering amounts of venture capital investment: whereas a mere US$57 million was invested in on-demand platform start-ups in 2010, four years later that sum had risen to more than $4 billion. By 2017, investors had poured more than $12 billion into Uber alone—giving the company a valuation of nearly $70 billion.[29]

Why is the gig economy so attractive to investors? To answer this question, we need to return to the platforms' business model and take a deeper look at the underlying economics. In a world of digital work intermediation, how do the intermediaries actually make their money? And why are many operators valued so highly by venture capital firms and other sophisticated investors?

The Economics of the Gig Economy

Delving into the figures, we quickly discover a number of possible explanations. Some argue that the gig economy creates value through the platforms' faster matching of consumer demand and worker supply, relying on clever algorithms and sophisticated rating systems to grasp otherwise wasted business opportunities. Another school of thought is more critical, suggesting that regulatory arbitrage and negative externalities are at the core of most platforms' valuations.

Matching and Intermediation

We have already seen how the dominant story behind the gig economy's commercial success is one of platforms' vastly superior matching opportunities, unlocking and creating surplus value in the economy. Platforms then reap a small percentage of this added value through their fees. There is undoubtedly a core of truth to this: faster matches greatly improve the functioning of product and service markets.

Economics Nobel Laureate Christopher Pissarides was amongst the first to formalize this model in the employment context.[30] Imagine a labour market in which some firms are looking for workers in one city and individuals are looking for jobs in another. It will be hard for either party to find out about the other, leaving jobs unfilled and workers unemployed. These 'search frictions' are wasteful and leave everyone worse off. Through technological innovation, from location tracking and user ratings, to sophisticated algorithms that match consumers and workers, whether purely online or in the real world, platforms have drastically reduced this friction: using Amazon's MTurk, an economist in Australia can quickly find a student in the United States to help her to organize data in a large spreadsheet.

Even better, matching isn't the only market friction removed by the platform. In an open-market transaction with an independent entrepreneur, consumers would have to spend significant amounts of time and effort to find out information about the service provider's background and experience, control the quality of the work, and negotiate prices. This is the real value of digital work intermediation: gig-economy operators also provide information about how reliable a worker is, take care of invoicing and payments, and provide a (digital) infrastructure within which the entire exchange can take place.

With transaction cost so drastically reduced, the narrative continues, the traditional firm as described by Ronald Coase becomes obsolete; instead, we move into a hybrid world between markets and hierarchies. According to Coase's theory of the firm, companies exist because the control exercised by an entrepreneur-coordinator over her workforce and other factors of production is much cheaper than the cost involved in going out to the market and haggling over each individual transaction.[31] On the other hand, once an app has taken all of the hassle out of such transactions, Coase's entrepreneur will no longer need to strike long-term bargains with workers, let alone invest in assets; she can replace her workforce with an external crowd, ready to complete individual tasks as and when required.

Better matching and lower transaction cost undoubtedly unlock value: the economist finishes her job more quickly, the student earns some extra income—and Amazon charges a few US cents' commission for its matching and intermediation service. So far, so good: the Internet is used to facilitate transactions between strangers that could otherwise not have taken place. That story, however, fails to answer a fundamental question: why are sharing-economy platforms worth so much? How can start-up businesses that simply rely on matching supply and demand via the Internet quickly be valued in the millions or billions and lay claim to an economic revolution? Digital matching services, online marketplaces, and classified sites such as Craigslist and Gumtree have, after all, been around for nearly two decades— and are valued at much lower prices.

Regulatory Arbitrage

Professor Julia Tomassetti is highly critical of the suggestion that platforms' primary value creation is achieved through better matching and lower transaction cost: 'What happens when we actually subject the Uber narrative to scrutiny under Coasian theory? It does not hold up. From the Coasian perspective, Uber does not write the epitaph of the firm.'[32] Platforms, she argues, speak the language of markets—but they operate like old-fashioned employers, relying on technology to exercise tight control over their workforce.

Tomassetti doesn't deny that gig-economy platforms have dramatically lowered transaction cost in comparison with established competitors. Lowering transaction cost alone, however, cannot account for platforms' phenomenal valuations and claims to disruptive innovation: there is, despite all claims to the contrary, little that is genuinely novel as far as platforms' production processes are concerned. Uber follows the basic lines of a traditional taxi firm; TaskRabbit, those of a labour-outsourcing agency. The key to understanding the business model, Tomassetti points out, is a different one: platforms are but the latest example of 'postindustrial corporations'.[33] They seek 'to maximize profit, but not necessarily through productive enterprise. Rather, [they] may create shareholder value by other means, like asset manipulation, speculative activity, and, most pertinent here, regulatory arbitrage.'[34]

What does that mean? Victor Fleischer's seminal work defines *regulatory arbitrage* as 'the manipulation of the structure of a deal to take advantage of a gap between the economic substance of a transaction and its regulatory treatment'.[35] Firms, in other words, may try to structure their business so as to hide what is actually going on from regulators and evade the law. His first example of a 'pervasive' arbitrage technique? '[F]iring employees and re-hiring them as independent contractors to avoid employment regulation.'[36]

In that sense, then, employment law—or rather *the evasion* of employment law—is at the core of the gig-economy business model. Recourse to large pools of on-demand workers is 'the economic substance' of platforms' transactions. Employing a large workforce creates responsibilities—which impose cost on people-intensive business models. In return for the benefits of control over their workforce, employment regulation places a financial burden on employers, ranging from social security contributions, minimum wage laws, and sick leave, to health and safety regulations and union bargaining. Stable employment relationships are also associated with indirect cost, because the risk of fluctuations in demand cannot be offloaded onto individual workers: a bus company's drivers ply their routes and receive wages regardless of whether passengers are on board or not.[37]

Regulatory arbitrage in the gig economy takes many forms: think about ride-sharing platforms' insistence that taxi regulation does not apply to their business, for example. Portraying workers as independent entrepreneurs and refuting their employment status, on the other hand, is a consistent theme throughout: shareholder value is created by denying workers their legally mandated rights. Classifying workers as independent contractors allows platforms to offer services without having to pay for their cost. Responsibility for assets, remuneration, insurance, and tax, as well as the risks of fluctuating demand, are devolved to individual micro-entrepreneurs. The potentially enormous gains from this financial arbitrage are at the core of gig-economy business models. In the words of one financial adviser, 'adverse determinations in these matters may subject [the platform] to additional compensation expenses or taxes in certain jurisdictions, which could have a material adverse effect on its ability to operate its business'.[38]

Regulatory arbitrage also leads to negative externalities: the social cost of platforms' activities are higher than their private cost. Think, for example, of a number of ride-sharing cars roaming the streets whilst looking for the next passenger. We have already seen that platforms usually try to have as many workers as possible available at any given time. This is enticing to consumers, who can quickly catch a ride in whichever car is closest—whilst the drivers suffer precisely because supply is designed far to outstrip demand. The platforms' algorithms have trapped workers in a low-productivity environment in order to fulfil orders as quickly as possible, whilst ignoring the costs incurred by the other drivers looking for a job—from the cost of their time and petrol, to the environmental implications of having a large number of cars polluting away. Classic economic theory spells out the implications:

if a service provider doesn't have to bear the full range of costs created by her product or service, she will end up offering too much of it. The platform always wins, even if individual workers—and indeed society at large—lose out.

Cash Burn

On the basis of what we have seen so far, gig-economy shareholders should be able to rejoice and reap considerable profits: growing demand can be met without capital investment or other downside risks. In reality, however, most operators have been sustaining high losses. According to transportation industry analyst Hubert Horan: '[I]n the year ending September 2015, Uber had GAAP [Generally Accepted Accounting Principles] losses of [US]$2 billion on revenue $1.4 billion, a negative 143% profit margin... 2016 GAAP losses would easily exceed $3 billion.'[39] Numbers are less extreme for other platforms, but the underlying struggle for profitability is the same. TaskRabbit, for example, had long aimed to turn a profit by the end of 2016—and promptly 'backed away from that claim' when the time came, whilst continuing to insist that it would 'get there soon'.[40]

Horan suggests that subsidies funded by venture capital are a major factor behind these losses:

> Uber passengers were paying only 41% of the actual cost of their trips; Uber was using these massive subsidies to undercut the fares and provide more capacity than the competitors who had to cover 100% of their costs out of passenger fares. Many other tech startups lost money as they pursued growth and market share, but losses of this magnitude are unprecedented.[41]

As gig-economy platforms become mature market players, mounting losses raise a difficult question: will they ever be profitable? Or has regulatory arbitrage camouflaged a different model altogether, leading to a misallocation of capital? Writing for the *Financial Times*, Izabella Kaminska was amongst the first to raise these concerns as part of her long-running investigation of Uber's financials:

> If Uber is cheap it is not because it has out innovated the incumbent cab market, which at the end of the day has access to exactly the same ride-hailing technology. To the contrary, it's because investors have failed to recognise that the source of its greatest innovations is and always has been cheap money.
>
> Indeed, from egregious undercutting tactics based on promotional giveaways to turning a blind eye to exploitative labour practices thanks to the

cheap funding of aggressive lobbying campaigns aimed at changing legal frameworks or the reckless flooding of the market with huge amounts of spare capacity, none of it would be possible without access to cheap financing.[42]

If Kaminska is correct, we are still left with one final question: assuming that the rapid growth of gig-economy platforms has really been fuelled by little more than a combination of regulatory arbitrage and cheap venture capital, why are savvy investors competing to invest? What is behind their willingness to burn unprecedented amounts of cash?

Network Effects and Monopoly Power

It is common for start-up businesses to lose money early on, of course—not least by subsidizing products so as to gain market share. This is particularly important in industries in which investors hope to harness so-called network effects—that is, where all users of a particular service gain if additional consumers adopt it.[43] Think about the growth of a ride-sharing platform in a new city, for example. If a large number of consumers are using a particular app to hail taxis, it will become more attractive for drivers to sign up to that app. A large available pool of drivers, in turn, will make it easier and cheaper for consumers to find their next ride, further increasing the incentives for new drivers to join—and so on. It is unsurprising that gig-economy platforms will often try to kick-start this process by investing significant amounts of cash in subsidies for drivers as well as passengers.

Hubert Horan, however, is sceptical that this is the entire story. Cash burn, he suggests, is not merely about harnessing network effects, but rather a step in platforms' quest for monopoly power. Focusing once more on Uber as the most pointed example, he explains the links:

> [M]ost critically, the staggering $13 billion in cash its investors provided is consistent with the magnitude of funding required to subsidize the many years of predatory competition required to drive out more efficient incumbents. Uber's investors did not put $13 billion into the company because they thought they could vanquish those incumbents under 'level playing field' market conditions; those billions were designed to replace 'level playing field' competition with a hopeless battle between small scale incumbents with no access to capital struggling to cover their bare bone costs and a behemoth company funded by Silicon Valley billionaires willing to subsidize years of multi-billion dollar losses. Given Uber's growth to date, investor expectations that monopoly rents justifies the current level of subsidies and financial risks appears quite plausible.[44]

This account stands in stark contrast with the idea that the rise of gig-economy platforms will lead to increased competition, with lower prices and higher quality as the result: in the expensive pursuit of network effects, some platforms' goal may well be to smother competition, rather than to encourage it.

Individual operators will always vary in the extent to which their business model combines the factors thus set out. Whichever way we approach the question, however, the underlying economics don't appear to stack up—a quandary to which we return in the final chapter. Faster matching, digital work intermediation, and assorted rating algorithms have the potential to create much economic benefit. Regulatory arbitrage, externalities, and lacking profitability despite considerable cash burn, on the other hand, should give us all pause for thought.

The Promise—and the Perils—of On-Demand Work

For the time being, however, most of us appear to pay scant notice to these economic controversies. Businesses and consumers alike are turning to the gig economy to find rides across town, get errands and odd jobs sorted, and crowdsource work online, whilst a seemingly ever-increasing pool of workers competes to meet the demand. As a result, both consumers' and workers' day-to-day experiences of life and work in the gig economy have increasingly been subjected to public scrutiny—with decidedly mixed results.

Looking on the Bright Side of Life

Senior industry executives argue that, in times of financial crises and rising unemployment, gig-economy platforms 'are glimmers of hope...the force that saves the American worker'.[45] Viewed thus, the gig economy offers incredible opportunities to workers: it provides flexible work, and a chance to earn additional income as and when needed,[46] without the regimented working day and overbearing boss typical of traditional work. It can be a real lifeline for groups traditionally excluded from the labour market, from homebound workers to those with criminal convictions. Anyone can easily find work through digital intermediary platforms such as Fiverr or Amazon's

MTurk, where an online account is all that's required to start earning money.

Many workers agree—and are happy to share why they enjoy working in the gig economy. Uber's website, for example, features a series of 'Driver-Partner Stories':

> Mothers and fathers. Teachers and students. Artists and athletes. Uber driver-partners come from all walks of life. Whether they drive with Uber to support their passion, or just to earn extra cash in their spare time, meet Uber partners from around the world and learn what moves them.[47]

Their stories are genuinely inspiring: the flexibility and additional income of gig work allow many to pursue their goals and fulfil long-held dreams. Meet Yoseph, who emigrated from Ethiopia to New Haven, Connecticut, and fits in Uber driving around his university classes: 'What Yoseph loves most about driving in New Haven is meeting riders. "Yale attracts all kinds of interesting people".'[48] Or 'rockstar mom and Uber Partner, Christine, who drives to balance marketing for the family business and being in the stands for all of her son's baseball games'. Her advice? 'Do it!'[49] And then there's Loren: artist, Seattle school bus driver, adventurer. 'Uber has allowed her to work flexible hours whenever she wants to "and if you need to take a nap or get groceries you just turn off the blue button and come back to it whenever you want".'[50]

It is not only workers who are better off. Consumers, too, profit from the rise of the gig economy. Previously unaffordable services are suddenly available at the touch of a button. Anyone who has hailed an Uber or commissioned a survey on MTurk will be familiar with the ease and satisfaction that comes from speedy and low-cost service delivery. Studies of consumer preferences for ride-sharing platforms reveal the joys of cheaper pricing, wider choice, and easier access.[51]

There's nothing that seems impossible with the help of gig-economy platforms—even if that means organizing a kid's birthday party 'on one of the top rated beaches in all of SoCal!':

> With about 40 expected guests for her son's 8th birthday beach party, a Client in Los Angeles was, understandably, looking for a little assistance... Luckily, TaskRabbit was able to connect her with Tasker Rain F. Rain has experience working with kids, and she's also an accomplished event planner and staffer—the perfect combo for this task. She did it all with a smile and, with her help, the party was a big success![52]

The benefits extend to society at large: the gig economy allows us to tap into otherwise wasted time and assets, driving economic growth. Platforms create jobs in a world of rising unemployment, provide extra revenues to workers, and formalize work in traditionally problematic sectors. Their matching algorithms can foster 'greater trust between strangers…a cornerstone of transactions, technology being the other'.[53]

The rise of gig work might also have more indirect and unexpected benefits to society: a study by Jessica Lynn Peck of the City University of New York argues that the introduction of Uber has a clear effect on incidents of drink-driving: since the platform's arrival in New York City in May 2011, she estimates, there has been a 25–35 per cent decrease in alcohol-related collisions.[54] On-demand work might even benefit the environment: a 2010 study of car-sharing in North America suggested that for each shared vehicle, 9–13 cars could be taken off the road.[55]

The Dark Side of the Moon

Just as there is much to be lauded and enjoyed about the on-demand economy, however, there is also cause for concern. A growing number of articles, policy reports, and academic writings present another—darker—picture. The gig economy, this line of thinking suggests, cynically exploits workers—and might also be harmful to consumers and the public at large.

Until the UK's general election in the early summer of 2017, Frank Field MP chaired the House of Commons Work and Pension Committee, overseeing a major enquiry into gig-economy work. The evidence before the Committee was troubling. In a private report subsequently submitted to Transport for London, he urged the regulator to address 'three evils' and 'insert a much needed floor into the bottom of this particular area of the labour market':

> We are troubled to note that the practices described to us by drivers working with Uber would appear to fit the Victorians' definition of 'sweated labour'. In 1890, a House of Lords Select Committee deemed labour to be 'sweated' when earnings were barely sufficient to sustain existence; hours of labour were such as to make the lives of the workers periods of almost ceaseless toil; and conditions were injurious to the health of the workers and dangerous to the public.[56]

An analysis of drivers' submissions suggested that drivers were 'at risk of taking home less than a third of the National Living Wage', even though they had to 'stay on the road for extended periods of time to make a living' and did 'not have the freedom to determine their own working patterns'.[57]

The US National Employment Law Project (NELP) has been a similarly vocal critic of gig-economy work, highlighting 'micro wages' and exploitative working conditions.[58] Unpredictable consumer demand makes flexibility illusory; invasive data collection denies users privacy; workers are increasingly isolated and left to compete against each other. The NELP's report into the on-demand economy cites an online posting by a frustrated crowdworker:

> Horrific. Digital sweat shop, slave wages, sometimes NO wages. You will be asked to jump through an absurd number of hoops for less than minimum wage. If you have a college degree and are either a professional writer, or a professional in the field you are writing about, don't even lower yourself to this. It only kills your professional self worth.[59]

A survey by the UK's Chartered Institute of Personnel and Development (CIPD) further warned of the overall lower financial resilience of gig-economy workers, nearly half of whom said that they could only 'afford to live for either less than one month or for up to two months without falling behind on paying key bills or living expenses if they lost their income due to unforeseen circumstances'.[60] Psychologists increasingly highlight the dangerous public health implications of low-paid, insecure work.[61]

These concerns are nothing new: scholars have long argued that technology is a major driver of labour-market inequality, giving rise to a 'cyberproletariat'.[62] Labour sociologist Professor Ursula Huws wrote about 'the making of a cybertariat' several decades before the advent of the gig economy.[63] Rapid technological advances, however, mean that many of these trends have found their sharpest edge yet—with worries about consumer and broader societal welfare similarly on the rise.

Consider the promise of better service at cheaper prices, for example—a picture increasingly contradicted by quality concerns about gig-economy products and services. It's not difficult to see why quality might suffer: '[T]o be hyper-affordable these are not necessarily on a par with established and leading competitors.'[64] Prices, too, are often more expensive than consumers are led to believe: dynamic algorithms allow platforms to increase prices in line with demand and a wide range of other factors—up to many multiples of the underlying cost.[65]

As regards society at large, it is hard to deny the overall gains of increased economic activity—but how equally are these distributed? Commentators are concerned about the entrenchment of a two-tiered labour market. As *The Economist* has noted, gig-economy entrepreneurs:

> have created a plethora of on-demand companies that put time-starved urban professionals in timely contact with job-starved workers, creating a sometimes distasteful caricature of technology-driven social disparity in the process; an article about the on-demand economy by Kevin Roose in *New York* magazine began with the revelation that the housecleaner he hired through Homejoy lived in a homeless shelter.[66]

Other concerns extend to the future of a competitive market economy at large. Consider, for example, the RSA's worry that:

> [A] small number of sharing platforms have been able to scale their networks to an extent where they are beginning to show signs of monopoly power in influencing the price, output, and investment of an industry, as well as in limiting the entry of new competitors.[67]

Some gig-economy platforms are not simply nimble start-ups; they could pose a real threat of cornering markets and becoming entrenched monopolies.

What Is Going On?

Turning to the empirical evidence behind these competing accounts, we reach a counter-intuitive conclusion: there is truth in both. How can that be? Because of the vast heterogeneity underpinning gig-economy work, in tasks, as well as working conditions. This diversity is one of the key themes emerging throughout the book.[68] We cannot think of gig work as a single, homogeneous category, tempting though it might be to do so, particularly when looking for 'the solution' to concerns about on-demand work.

Perhaps unsurprisingly, a recent World Bank report found that the heterogeneity of work translates into starkly different worker experiences:

> A part-time Filipino online worker reported earnings of [US]$3–4 per hour on oDesk (rebranded as Upwork), performing tasks such as transcription, data entry, and basic administrative services. In contrast, an experienced Nigerian online freelancer reported earnings of $20 per hour for software development and website design. At the high end, online freelancers consulting on patents or venture capital can earn more than $40 per hour.[69]

A detailed study by consulting group McKinsey in the autumn of 2016 divided gig-economy workers into four categories: *free agents*, who 'derive their primary income from independent work and actively choose this working style'; *casual earners*, who choose to rely on gig work to supplement their income; *reluctants*, who 'derive their primary income from independent work but would prefer traditional jobs'; and the *financially strapped*, who 'would prefer not to have to do side jobs to make ends meet'.[70] Overall, the report suggests, a majority of the gig workforce falls into the first two categories, engaging in gig work as a preferred choice. The report's authors nonetheless observe that:

> the magnitude of the problem is still striking. Scaling up the results of our survey suggests that 50 million Americans and Europeans are independent out of necessity, and more than 20 million of them rely on independent work as their primary source of income.[71]

Even more importantly, the study found that low-income households were much more likely to depend on insecure and unpredictable independent work—as opposed to higher-income households, for whom it was a matter of choice.[72] Freedom of choice, it turns out, is also a key factor in determining whether a gig worker will enjoy her job: 'Not surprisingly, those who work...because they feel their circumstances have forced them into it report much lower levels of satisfaction.'[73]

Quantitative empirical evidence on the broader impacts of the on-demand economy 'is very partial and inconclusive—in many cases, it is simply anecdotal and often presented by stakeholders in the current controversies'.[74] As a result, it is crucial that in discussing the gig economy we keep both its promise and perils in mind. Subsequent chapters will delve deep into the industry to explore why workers' and consumers' experiences can vary greatly; for now, it is time to explore the broader implications of the competing stories we have encountered—for they are crucial building blocks in shaping narratives about, and thus the legal regulation of, the gig economy.

2

Doublespeak

'Political language has to consist largely of euphemism, question-begging and sheer cloudy vagueness', wrote George Orwell in 1946. 'When there is a gap between one's real and one's declared aims, one turns as it were instinctively to long words and exhausted idioms, like a cuttlefish spurting out ink.'[1] The historical context of his remarks was very different, of course, and today's idioms are often newly minted rather than exhausted—but the underlying warning is as important as it was 70 years ago.

Gig work presents both great opportunities and serious problems. This complex reality, however, is rarely brought up in public discourse. Intense lobbying efforts are afoot and the political stakes are high: as regulators grapple with the rise of the on-demand economy, gig-economy doublespeak aims to shape our understanding of the industry—and, more importantly, its legal regulation.

To understand the gig economy, it is crucial that we look behind the language of innovation and technology, of sharing and collaborative consumption, of 'gigs' and 'tasks'. In the first instance, we will focus on arguments that the gig economy should not be regulated at all: platforms are cast as digital Davids fighting Goliaths entrenched by regulation. We can discern multiple iterations of this approach, with varying degrees of sophistication. At its crudest, this is the story that the law stands in the way of innovation and should leave 'disruptive' businesses well alone.

At a more sophisticated level, we encounter different proposals for new forms of regulation, united by a common theme: instead of relying on the democratically legitimized regulatory institutions of the state, we should 'develop more rational, ethical, and participatory models of regulation—models in which users and providers are equally invested and responsible for enacting the regulations in question'.[2] This narrative, however, need not detain us long: even a brief look demonstrates that the claim to disruptive

Humans as a Service: The Promise and Perils of Work in the Gig Economy. First Edition. Jeremias Prassl. © Jeremias Prassl 2018. Published 2018 by Oxford University Press.

technology often amounts to little more than a justification for ignoring established regulatory regimes—or simply breaking existing laws.

Consistent attempts at rebranding work, on the other hand, deserve much closer scrutiny. Initially, this strategy centred mostly on casting the emerging model as a social movement away from economic activity—or, at the very least, as fundamentally distinct from traditional work. Reality, however, is quickly catching up: most commentators today are clear about the industry's commercial focus and courts are increasingly content to ignore sophisticated contractual attempts to recast employees as independent contractors. The gig economy's claims of genuine entrepreneurship and innovation, on the other hand, pose a much more significant challenge: if true, they would leave little space for traditional employment regulation.

Shaping Narratives

The stakes are high: in 1971, Nobel Prize-winning economist George Stigler enumerated the many advantages of shaping economic regulation in favour of an industry, highlighting the extent to which key players would go to 'capture' their regulators and ensure favourable treatment.[3] Such influence, he noted, can take many forms, from bribes to the prospect of lucrative jobs. The most important ingredient, however, is 'asymmetric information', whereby the firms to be regulated hold significantly more relevant information than their regulators.[4]

Industry narratives are a crucial tool in shaping these information asymmetries. It is hard to regulate that which we don't understand, or perceive to be novel and different. This makes it important for any industry to create a particular, benevolent picture of its activities and their impact on society on which regulation will be based: no politician could—or should—disagree with fostering genuine entrepreneurship and innovation.

It is unsurprising, then, that most platforms employ a number of advisers and strategists to shape their public relations and political communications. A host of industry-representative groups and lobbying outfits working on behalf of the on-demand economy have sprung up—with varying degrees of transparency.

Sharing-economy critic Tom Slee points to Peers.org as a particularly interesting example of such lobbying efforts, 'appropriating the language of collective action and progressive politics for private financial gain'.[5] The platform describes itself variably as a 'member-driven organization to support the sharing economy movement', 'the world's largest independent sharing economy community', and an organization aiming 'to support workers by making the sharing economy a better work opportunity'—yet the reality appears to be somewhat different.[6]

Following an early promotional call, Andrew Leonard of *Salon* wondered:

> So the obvious question is, who does Peers represent? Natalie Foster [the organization's then director] described Peers as a 'grassroots organization' aiming 'to grow the sharing economy.' But some probing questions from a Bloomberg reporter on the call quickly established that 'grassroots' might not be the best word to describe Peers. Foster eventually admitted that Peers was launching with 22 partners, among whom were a number of companies operating in the sharing economy space.[7]

Like many Silicon Valley ventures, Peers.org has undergone several pivots, or changes in its business model, and whilst the language is still that of 'helping sharing economy workers', at the time of writing it serves essentially as an entry portal to on-demand work, advertising a host of platforms and offering related services—notably, insurance.[8] Portable benefits include health insurance, retirement savings plans, and even company contributions to benefits, whereby the 'Companies you work for can contribute to the cost of your benefits—per job completed, sale made, ride given'—which feature, however, was 'coming soon'.

Other outfits are somewhat more transparent, at least as regards their membership. Examples include tech:NYC:

> a nonprofit member organization that represents New York City's technology sector... [and] advocates for policies that underscore a regulatory environment that supports the growth of technology companies and technology talent in NYC; promote inclusion and diversity; and create access for all New Yorkers to connectivity, technology tools, and training.[9]

Sharing Economy UK, a trade body launched in March 2015, is even clearer in its aims. The organization describes itself as set up to work 'closely with Government, representing the sharing economy community, and lobbying for changes to protect consumers and sharing economy businesses'.[10]

Keeping Regulators at Bay

There is nothing surprising about such lobbying efforts in and of themselves, of course: every industry seeks to create positive public perceptions of its

activities. Gig-economy doublespeak, however, raises a much more fundamental point. Its narratives are not mere marketing tools; they are designed
to cultivate particular political and regulatory responses. At its most extreme,
a complete absence of regulation is called for: existing legal regimes are por-
trayed as harmful to consumers and workers, entrenching established and
overbearing competitors against nimble, disruptive start-ups.

Can this narrative stand up to scrutiny? There is a core of truth in the
radical argument against certain kinds of legal interference, to the extent
that some platforms operate in heavily regulated industries such as urban
transportation. On the other hand, it's less clear whether this can be extrapolated to the gig economy at large: some players have quickly become
Goliaths themselves, the majority of on-demand platforms don't operate in
heavily regulated industries, and the very notion of 'disruption' might have
taken on an entirely new meaning.

Disruptive Davids

The Book of Samuel tells the story of the Israelites' battle against the
Philistines. The mighty Goliath had been haranguing Saul's troops for 40 days
when a young shepherd named David, with but a few fights against wild
beasts to his name, stepped forward to take on the giant. Armed with nothing
more than a sling and a few rocks, he smote the armour-clad enemy.[11]

In the eyes of many Silicon Valley investors, this is the very template for
the growth of on-demand economy apps and platforms: nimble start-ups,
destined to disrupt big business, and succeeding in the face of excessive red
tape and bureaucratic regulatory fervour. The weapons are unmatched and
the chances of success appear small, but to the victor, the spoils—David, of
course, went on to become the king of Israel.

If religious analogy seems overblown, bear with me: we will repeatedly
encounter the zeal of the sharing economy's messiahs, as well as their pro-
phetic visions of future economies and labour markets. Many platforms
even have their very own founding myth. In the case of TaskRabbit, technology magazine *Wired* reports that the idea of 'neighbours helping neighbours' was born on:

> [a] wintry night in February 2008, when Busque, a 28-year-old engineer at
> IBM in Cambridge, Massachusetts, realized that she needed dog food for her
> yellow lab, Kobe. She wanted nothing more than to get someone else to
> trudge outside in the snow. 'I thought, wouldn't it be nice if there were a place

online you could go,' she says. 'A site where you could name the price you were willing to pay for any task. There had to be someone in my neighborhood who was willing to get that dog food for what I was willing to pay.'[12]

Most big technology businesses, you might say, have such stories: from Steve Jobs' garage, in which Apple was born, to Mark Zuckerberg's dropping out of Harvard to set up Facebook. That's true—but things become more difficult when we come to platforms' tales about their operations and their place in society. Seen in that light, founding myths are often part of a broader narrative designed to shield on-demand businesses from regulatory crosshairs by painting them as small players at the fringes of regulated business activity.

Writing in libertarian magazine *Cato Unbound*, Matthew Feeney eloquently sets out the case against regulating on-demand platforms:

> Sharing economy companies have highlighted the over burdensome nature of many of the regulations that govern transportation, accommodation, and other industries... regulators should resist the urge to impose old regulations on new innovative companies or to write new regulations that could encourage cronyism and stifle growth. Sharing economy competitors deserve the chance to compete, and regulators can help them do this by deregulating the industries the sharing economy is disrupting. The forces of a free market, not regulatory bodies, should decide which providers survive and which ones fail.[13]

This, then, is a story in which government regulation entrenches the interests of big business, denies innovative start-ups the chance to compete, encourages cronyism, and stifles growth—whilst the co-founder of a company valued in the tens of billions of dollars can boast to the *Financial Times* that he is 'a natural born trust-buster'.[14]

Regulatory Battles

The argument against regulation comes in different guises, from outright rejections of state interference to calls for new and radically different regulatory models. The former approach can be key to platforms' rapid expansion, particularly in the transportation industry, in which many operators relied on a strategy of 'asking forgiveness, not permission'. Details vary between jurisdictions and across different cities, but the fundamental question tends to be the same: should the same regulatory and licensing regimes apply to traditional transport operators and platforms such as Uber and Lyft? Historically, national and local regulators have imposed a large number of requirements on taxi companies, from licensing caps and price control, to driver background checks and general access conditions. Platforms argue that their operations are fundamentally different and thus should not be subject to the same requirements.

This quickly led to high-profile clashes with regulators and incumbent businesses around the world: from protracted legal battles before a London court over language testing and heated political fights with Mayor Bill de Blasio in New York, to Uber cars being torched in Nairobi and the French police arresting the company's executives on allegations of operating an 'illicit' taxi service. In Germany, a 2015 court order even banned certain Uber services and, in the spring of 2017, the company announced that it would pull out of Denmark in response to new taxi regulations.[15]

Even those who do not reject regulation outright tend to emphasize the benefits of 'experimentation first, regulation later'. New York University Stern Business School's Arun Sundararajan, for example, posits that 'history suggests that different types of economies require different approaches to regulation...it is neither possible nor economically viable to simply adopt existing rules and apply them to a new economy'.[16] The argument that existing regulation has ossified beyond repair, however, has powerful detractors—including Cambridge Professor Simon Deakin, who has argued that if 'technology can evolve, so can the law'.[17]

As regards the emphasis on regulatory experimentation, various scholars have advocated that we adopt an 'innovation law perspective' in support of 'permissionless innovation', whereby 'experimentation with new technologies and business models should generally be permitted by default...[and] problems, if they develop at all, can be addressed later'.[18] Such approaches, however, fail to take into account the powerful limitations that past decisions can impose on today's and tomorrow's choices. Put differently, regulation's path dependence weighs strongly in favour of careful thought first and brash disruption second.

A third school of thought, finally, acknowledges that some regulation will continue to be necessary—whilst insisting that the on-demand economy itself is best placed to provide it: '[R]egulation, often interwoven with the provision of trust, doesn't always have to originate with the government. In other words, history reveals that regulation can take on myriad forms, governmental and otherwise.'[19] In a short essay on 'Self-regulation and innovation in the peer-to-peer sharing economy', Molly Cohen and Arun Sundararajan have advocated such a 'reallocation of regulatory responsibility to parties other than the government': '[P]latforms should not be viewed as entities to be regulated but rather as actors that are a key part of the regulatory frame-work in this arena.'[20]

Upon closer inspection, several problems with this approach quickly become apparent. First, as Cohen and Sundararajan themselves note, clear conflicts of interest might emerge in certain regulatory areas.[21] Second, as we have already seen and will discuss in detail in Chapter 6, there is a strong tendency for certain platforms in the on-demand economy to emerge as near-monopolists in their particular market. In those situations, self-regulation is likely to lead to self-*interested* regulation. An early insight into the sort of self-regulation we might expect can be gleaned from Sharing Economy UK's Code of Conduct, to which its members must sign up—and the most explicit constraint in which appears to be an obligation to ensure that a platform's contact information is clearly visible online.[22]

The New Goliaths

Most calls for complete deregulation—or at least industry self-regulation—are premised on the need to foster small start-up innovation. This is a prob-lematic assumption for a number of reasons. Whilst increased competition is indeed desirable and new platforms are founded (and dispatched into bank-ruptcy) all the time, many of the key actors in the on-demand industry have quickly become Goliaths themselves; others never faced incumbent-friendly regulation in the first place. There is often little that is genuinely disruptive or innovative about most platforms' business models; instead, 'dis-ruption' has increasingly become code for something different altogether: breaking the law.

As regards challenges to entrenched economic interests, if existing regu-lation simply serves as a barrier to entry and protects incumbents, an increase in competition should be welcomed by workers and consumers alike. Many will benefit from easier access to labour and service markets: think of poten-tial London cabbies who no longer need to spend years studying the streets of London for 'The Knowledge' exam. Ask any consumer who has had to communicate with grumpy Parisian taxi drivers or has struggled to hail a yellow cab on a rainy Friday afternoon in Manhattan for proof of the con-sumer value of these new services.[23]

Professor Orly Lobel of the University of San Diego has suggested that, in looking at the legal regulation of the platform economy, we should dis-tinguish between *hard* cases (in which public welfare is at stake) and *easy* cases (in which legal regulation inhibits competition and creates barriers to entry). Questions of employment law, she notes, are hard cases—but the same is not true for traditional taxi regulation:

> Laws that do not promote welfare but rather protect entrenched interests are easy cases…Attempts at extending permit requirements—what industry interests often call 'leveling the playing field' between ridesharing companies and taxi companies, or between other platform companies and the businesses they disrupt—are generally harmful to the evolution of the platform and to competitive markets more broadly.[24]

Most platforms, however, never face such problems: they simply don't operate in heavily regulated environments. In that sense, ride-sharing apps are a red herring; assembling flatpack furniture, completing online questionnaires, and delivering takeout food are rarely regulated to the same degree as local taxi markets. Indeed, as far as employment law is concerned, whether a platform operates in a heavily regulated industry such as transportation or in an entirely unregulated field (think home cleaning) will usually be an irrelevant question.[25]

Even the very notion of platforms as small, disruptive Davids struggles to stand up to scrutiny. Brhmie Balaram, a senior researcher at the UK's Royal Society of Arts, has challenged the picture of nimble start-ups seeking to compete against big business: '[A] small number of companies in the sharing economy are overtaking traditional industry giants' to become entrenched monopolies themselves.[26] In fact, it's not even a question of David venturing out to smite a lion or a bear: the modern version of the biblical tale would see David buying out the wild animals' shares or assets rather than taking them on in open competition, as happened when ride service Lyft bought car-pooling operator Hitch and vehicle-servicing platform Cherry.[27]

The Goliaths need not worry any longer either, for similar reasons: on the rare occasion that a genuine clash looms, today's combatants appear to prefer sharing their tents, eschewing head-on combat. Following a drawn-out battle that cost both companies billions of dollars in subsidized travel for passengers and drivers, Uber announced in August 2016 that it had sold its entire Chinese operation to competitor Didi Chuxing, in return for a stake of nearly 20 per cent in its erstwhile rival. The immediate result? Beijing passengers were quick to take to social media and complain of a near doubling of the cost of rides, as discount codes and other subsidies were swiftly withdrawn.[28]

Disruptive Innovation?

In any event, some proponents of the sharing economy argue, society still reaps major benefits from growth driven by platforms' innovative disruption of existing business models. Picking up a few stones and hurtling them along in a little sling is, after all, a much less capital-intensive way of going about the business of slaying your enemies than heavy armour and swords, regardless of how many foot soldiers are at it.

Not quite, replies the Harvard Business School guru behind the theory of disruptive innovation. In December 2015, Clayton M. Christensen took to the pages of the *Harvard Business Review* to declare that 'Uber's financial and strategic achievements do not qualify the company as genuinely disruptive—although the company is almost always described that way.'[29] Disruptive innovation, according to Christensen and his co-authors, needs to 'originate in low-end or new-market footholds' and takes a while to catch up in terms of quality (which is 'how disruption drives prices down in a market')—neither of which could be said of Uber.

Not that this would discourage proponents of this radical narrative: doublespeak continues to infiltrate public discourse, reconfiguring existing notions and management-speak as required—up to, and including, the theory of disruption.

In its original, virtuous, version, Christensen described 'a process whereby a smaller company with fewer resources is able to successfully challenge established incumbent businesses'.[30] Contrast this with the observations by technology writer and one-time host of technology start-up competition 'TechCrunch Disrupt' Paul Bradley Carr:

> The original Silicon Valley meaning of a disruptive company was one that used its small size to shake up a bigger industry or bloated competitor. Increasingly, though, the conference stage was filled with brash, Millennial entrepreneurs vowing to 'Disrupt' real-world laws and regulations in the same way that me stealing your dog is Disrupting the idea of pet ownership. On more than one occasion a judge would ask an entrepreneur 'Is this legal?' to which the reply would inevitably come: 'Not yet.' The audience would laugh and applaud. What chutzpah! So Disruptive! The truth is, what Silicon Valley still calls 'Disruption' has evolved into something very sinister indeed.[31]

In sharing-economy doublespeak, ignoring regulation might come to be seen as a virtue of the highest order, with platforms' law-breaking likened to that of resistance heroes ranging from Mahatma Gandhi to Rosa Parks. Professors Frank Pasquale and Siva Vaidhyanathan have attacked these comparisons and suggested a darker analogy, arguing that today's:

> 'corporate nullification' follow[s] in the footsteps of Southern governors and legislatures [during the civil rights battles] in the United States who declared themselves free to 'nullify' federal law on the basis of strained and opportunistic constitutional interpretation... [W]hen companies... engage in a nullification effort, it's a libertarian-inspired attempt to establish their services as popular well before regulators can get around to confronting them.[32]

At its most extreme, the argument that deregulation fosters innovation in a world of 'crowd-based capitalism' casts governmental regulation as irrelevant at best and as a destructive constraint on promising innovation at worst. In reality, it often amounts to little more than an attempt at ensuring maximum profitability for particular platforms at the expense of competitors, consumers, and society at large.

Whilst there is a core of truth in the argument for increased competition, it is unlikely that many will fall for the broad extrapolation in favour of complete deregulation. The narrative required to support this stark position paints a misleading picture of key actors, misapplies traditional notions of disruptive progress, and, at its worst, operates as a thinly veiled excuse for breaking the law until regulators can catch up.

Platforms, however, have had more success in shaping perceptions of work in the gig economy. With employment law acting as a key restraint across the industry, the real prize for corporate doublespeak has been in selling platform-based work as innovative entrepreneurship.

Rebranding Work

In the early summer of 2016, Mike Ashley, the boss of major UK retailer Sports Direct, found himself summoned before a Parliamentary Select Committee in the UK to answer a series of questions about the working conditions in one of his major warehouses. Not only had staff been employed through outsourcing agencies and on so-called zero-hours contracts, which do not guarantee any work from one day to the next; they were also subject to an arbitrary 'six-strike policy' under which even the smallest infringement could lead to dismissal and had been paid below the National Minimum Wage.

The conclusions of the resulting report are damning:

A spotlight has been shone on the working practices and business model of Sports Direct. What the spotlight revealed was extremely disturbing. Workers at Sports Direct were not being paid the national minimum wage, and were being penalised for matters such as taking a short break to drink water and for taking time off work when ill... Serious health and safety breaches also seem to have occurred. For this to occur in the UK in 2016 is a serious indictment of the management at Sports Direct.[33]

Contrast this with the announcement, just over a year earlier, that US Representatives Eric Swalwell (Democrat) and Darrell Issa (Republican) had launched a 'bipartisan Sharing Economy Caucus, which will bring attention to this booming sector and its impact on our society and economy'.[34] The Californian Representatives were joined at the launch event by a range of industry lobbyists and experts, including Arun Sundararajan of NYU's Stern School of Business, and David Estrada, Lyft's Vice President for Government Relations.

Their conclusions?

This Caucus will explore the opportunities made possible by the sharing model, and how Congress can foster innovation and address challenges posed by this emerging sector... Americans increasingly rely on the sorts of innovative services the internet has made possible—services that bring Americans together while providing a new measure of convenience by providing opportunities to conduct business in more efficient ways... [We] will focus on these pioneering industries and ensure Congress is taking all of the necessary steps to facilitate, rather than hinder, the next great idea.[35]

As we will see in Chapter 3, the reality of work in the on-demand economy is often even more precarious than the underpaid, at-will contracts offered by Sports Direct. Ride-sharing drivers struggle to make the minimum wage once they have accounted for the cost of running their cars, workers are deactivated for refusing to accept particular tasks, and many find themselves working long shifts far beyond health and safety limits. Why, then, is it that Mike Ashley was (rightly) subjected to parliamentary humiliation, whereas the sharing economy is celebrated by its very own cross-party caucus in the US Congress? Why the contrast between a promise of regulatory investigation by the UK tax authorities for Sports Direct and of help 'before you start to hit regulatory barriers in Washington' for Lyft & Co.?

Because of the power of language in rebranding work and shaping regulatory responses. Zero-hours work is criticized for worker exploitation, low wages, and insecurity; the gig economy is lauded for fostering innovation and entrepreneurship.

Language Matters

We no longer talk of 'work'. The enthusiastic language of 'gigs', 'tasks', 'rides', 'lifts', 'hustles', 'hits', and 'favours' has begun to replace the traditional vocabulary of the labour market.[36] The on-demand economy comes with its very own vocabulary in an attempt to escape existing regulation. Language is a crucial ingredient in shaping our understanding of on-demand work—casting platforms as community actors, rather than economic operators, and rebranding employment as freelance entrepreneurship.

Peers, Neighbours, Friends

In the early days of the gig economy, observers were faced with a discourse of 'collaborative consumption',[37] peer-to-peer sharing, and neighbours helping neighbours: 'Rideshare with Lyft. Lyft is your friend with a car, whenever you need one.'[38] The persistence with which work in the on-demand economy has been labelled as anything but work—or even recognizable economic activity—is astonishing, with at least one US delivery platform taking this trend to its logical extreme and referring to its product as 'Favors', delivered by 'Runners', who are enticed to be 'Heroes'.[39]

By 'rebranding...labor as a kind of good-will effort toward others, rather than an old-fashioned exchange of work for remuneration',[40] on-demand platforms are hoping to avoid the regulatory obligations that most jurisdictions impose on ordinary employers and on businesses generally. Who, after all, could disagree with a bit of informal and friendly neighbourly help, let alone suggest that the state should regulate it? Most people would be hard-pressed to think of a general business regulation that should legitimately apply to my heading across town to drop off a few bottles of beer at a friend's barbecue.

The stakes, according to this narrative, could not be higher:

> [E]conomic sharing has long been central to human civilisation by strengthening the social fabric of communities, improving levels of wellbeing across society and promoting social equity. The critical question facing humanity today is whether we choose to support and scale up national and local systems of sharing, or whether we allow them to be further undermined and dismantled by those who are ideologically opposed to putting sharing at the centre of policymaking.[41]

For the vast majority of platforms, however, 'informal sharing' or 'peer-to-peer collaboration' is about as alien a concept as 'promoting social equity' and 'strengthening the social fabric of communities' might be to Uber's abrasive co-founder Travis Kalanick—for the whole point of informal community assistance is that it cannot be scaled up and monetized.

It can be hard to escape the jargon—and it's even more important not to be fooled into fuzzy thinking by a communal or 'sharing' spirit: the gig economy means business. Writing in the *New York Times*, Natasha Singer expresses her problems with the industry's twisting of language, from 'sharing' and 'peer', to the 'people' and 'collaborative' economy. What she objects to 'is the terminology itself and how it frames technology-enabled transactions as if they were altruistic or community endeavors'.[42] Sarah O'Connor at the *Financial Times* agrees:

> If there is one phrase that makes me wince more than the 'sharing economy' it is the 'collaborative economy'... What exactly is being shared here? Who is collaborating with whom? Freelancers on Upwork are no more sharing their skills with the world than I am sharing mine with the *Financial Times*.[43]

This is not to say that a few smaller platforms—including France's BlaBlaCar, which coordinates intercity car journeys and pegs drivers' earnings to estimated fuel consumption,[44] or Canada's BlancRide, which connects urban commuters[45]—have not experimented with genuine peer-to-peer services designed to cover costs, rather than to return significant profits. The reality of the vast majority of businesses in the on-demand economy, however, is one of for-profit corporations, 'taking a more and more intrusive role in the exchanges they support to make their money and to maintain their brand'.[46]

Passive Platforms, Freelancing Entrepreneurs
Even when the economic motives behind a platform's operation are clear, terminology can still play an important role—first and foremost in recasting employees (who enjoy recourse to a series of protective standards, from minimum wage laws to anti-discrimination norms) as independent freelancers and entrepreneurs (who can be engaged without having to offer such protection). The resulting narrative is clear: what's on offer for Taskers, Turkers, Driver Partners, Roo-women and-men, and other on-demand employees are entrepreneurial hustles, gigs, tasks, and rides...rather than old-fashioned work. Platforms, in turn, are not powerful labour intermediaries, but merely passive matchmakers.

In the spring of 2017, a set of internal Deliveroo guidelines were leaked to several London newspapers. The UK food-delivery platform had drawn up an extensive list of 'vocabulary guidelines' for staff interactions with its couriers. Over six pages, the memo lists a long number of 'dos and don'ts', complete with sample phrases. Workers are not to be hired and issued with a uniform; rather, they are 'onboarded' and sold an 'equipment pack' (which the company will repurchase when the worker is sacked). They sign a document setting out performance targets—to be referred to as a 'supplier agreement', rather than a contract of employment. The couriers aren't paid for their work; rider invoices are processed instead. And when things go wrong, no one gets fired: 'We are terminating your Supplier Agreement due to your failure to meet Service Delivery Standards.'[47]

Deliveroo is not alone in this strategic dissimulation. TaskRabbit's US website provides a list of 'Feature Tasks', illustrated with the picture of a happy young Tasker in her bright green TaskRabbit T-shirt and accompanied by the suggestion: '*We'll* help you get them done.' Whether it's 'Delivery Service' ('*We'll* safely transport anything from couches to documents to take-out food'), or even 'Organizing Closets' ('*Let us* help you clean up your closet and get things organized'), the message to the consumer is clear: we, the company, will offer these great services, whilst 'You live life'.[48]

The contractual fine print tells a rather different story. Before being able to create an account, all potential users must agree to TaskRabbit's terms of service. This contract purports to set out the platform's business model:

> The TaskRabbit Platform only enables connections between Users for the fulfillment of Tasks. Company is not responsible for the performance of Users, nor does it have control over the quality, timing, legality, failure to provide, or any other aspect whatsoever of Tasks, Taskers, Clients, nor of the integrity, responsibility, qualifications or any of the actions or omissions whatsoever of any Users. Company makes no representations about the suitability, reliability, timeliness, or accuracy of the Tasks requested and services provided by Users identified through the TaskRabbit Platform whether in public, private, or offline interactions.[49]

What a contrast: the images and slogans suggest a tightly curated product, delivered by an integrated operation under a single brand; the legal arrangement purports to set up nothing more than a series of contracts between independent buyers and sellers in an online marketplace. The platform's role is reduced to a brief (algorithmic) introduction, without any ongoing responsibility or involvement.[50]

As Izabella Kaminska was quick to point out in the *Financial Times* when the Deliveroo guidelines first surfaced, examples of hideous corporate-speak abound in today's business world, from euphemistic CEO missives to misleading product descriptions. 'The gig economy, however,' she argues, 'has taken such abuse to an entirely new and dubious level...language has become a weapon to be used in direct defiance of employment regulation.'[51] References to the 'Roo' or Rider Community, instead of a fleet of delivery couriers, are designed to defeat employment law through the contractual reclassification of workers as independent contractors—with less and less success.

Cuddly terminology as well as the fictional language used in gig platforms' contracts are increasingly coming under attack. When faced with Uber's strenuous denial of employer status in the autumn of 2016, an employment tribunal in London ruled that the ride-sharing platform's 'resorting in its documentation to fictions, twisted language and even brand new terminology' merited 'a degree of scepticism'.[52] The judge could not 'help being reminded of Queen Gertrude's most celebrated line: *The lady doth protest too much, methinks.*'[53] And whilst the Shakespearean flourish might be lacking in other jurisdictions, more and more courts around the world are similarly refusing to be fooled by carefully designed contractual euphemisms.

Shaping Regulation

Should we take this as an encouraging sign that there isn't much to worry about? Not quite. The language of sharing and collaborating, of freelancing and partnering, might not distract us for long—new labels alone cannot defeat existing regulation—but broader narratives of innovation and technology are much more powerful. Genuine entrepreneurs have little, if any, recourse to employment law. Rebranding old-school labour intermediation as an exciting new technological innovation thus poses a fundamental challenge to existing regulatory structures: if the gig economy is a radically new way of organizing work, old-fashioned employment law should no longer apply.

Entrepreneurship and Innovation

In these accounts, the on-demand economy is key to transforming work for the future: gone are the days of monotony and tedium in a 9-to-5 job, controlled by the watchful eyes of an overbearing boss in return for nothing more than a meagre pay-cheque at the end of each month. In the gig economy, every worker will be able to enjoy the stimulating diversity, grapple with the exhilarating challenges, and reap the vast financial rewards of entrepreneurship.

It gets even better: micro-entrepreneurship in the gig economy is characterized as a tool for inclusive growth in times of secular stagnation, bringing more and more citizens into gainful economic activity. Given the
flexibility of platform work ('You choose, not your boss!'), making a bit of
money on the side has become easier than ever—for everyone:

> students who want to supplement their incomes; bohemians who can afford
> to dip in and out of the labour market; young mothers who want to combine
> bringing up children with part-time jobs; [and] the semi-retired, whether
> voluntarily so or not.[54]

TaskRabbit founder Busque is one of the key proponents of this view:
'[P]roviding people with the tools and resources to set their own schedules,
be their own bosses and say how much they want to get paid is incredibly
empowering. It has huge implications for the global labour force.'[55] Shelby
Clark, founder of Relay Rides, agrees: 'Providers in the peer economy really
value the independence and flexibility; for lots of people, it has been trans-
formational... You meet great, interesting people. You have great stories.'[56]

Micro-entrepreneurship promises to unlock the value of idle or under-
used assets and skills, enthuses Nick Grossman of gig-economy investor Union
Square Ventures: 'Someone on Sidecar doing the same commute they do on
a daily basis and picking up a rider, it's really free money for the driver and
reduced cost for the rider.'[57] Perhaps best of all, we are told that the gig
economy offers precisely the sort of work environment today's labour force
wants: flexible work, on an informal basis, and the ability to work 'anywhere' using digital technology have all ranked highly in recent global surveys conducted by major professional services firms.[58]

No wonder, then, that Matt Hancock, one of the UK's former junior
ministers for business, was so euphoric in his foreword to a government-
commissioned review:

> The sharing economy is an exciting new area of the economy. Digital innov-
> ation is creating entirely new ways to do business. These new services are
> unlocking a new generation of microentrepreneurs—people who are making
> money from the assets and skills they already own, from renting out a spare
> room through Airbnb, through to working as a freelance designer through
> PeoplePerHour. The route to self-employment has never been easier.[59]

Rethinking Employment Regulation
What does this mean for employment law? Once more, we see a range of
proposals based on tales of entrepreneurship and innovation—from a complete

rejection of employment law to a watering down of existing laws through new, less protective, categories.

Policymakers grappling with the on-demand economy aren't short of potential blueprints. The last years have seen everything from legislative denials of employment status and arguments in favour of new 'third status' employment laws, to regulatory safe harbours and industry self-regulation. Whilst these proposals differ in just how far we should depart from existing laws, they all share a fundamental scepticism of existing regulation: are existing laws a straitjacket holding back innovative new business models? Why should we let employment law put fetters on entrepreneurial freedom?

At the extreme end of this spectrum is legislation that simply stipulates that employment law does not cover gig-economy workers. Some countries are more receptive to this narrative than others. In the United States, for example, platforms have been lobbying lawmakers behind the scenes at the state and local levels, drafting and supporting favourable bills, whilst attacking those that do not stick to the playbook. Industry efforts to create so-called ride-sharing laws are a good case study. Details vary across jurisdictions, but one common goal emerges: to deny workers' employment status and ensure that platforms are defined as mere intermediaries.

In June 2016, free-market think tank R Street's map of state-level legislation listed only five US states that had not enacted some form of transport network company (TNC) regulation.[60] At first glance, these measures set out a balanced approach, permitting on-demand platforms to operate and subjecting them to basic standards, from driver verification to insurance requirements.

Upon closer investigation, however, it becomes clear that new legislation frequently favours platforms' interests. As a Reuters investigation in late 2015 highlighted, key industry players were often closely involved in drafting the laws—many of which contain provisions designed to classify drivers as independent contractors, beyond the scope of state-level employment law protection.[61]

In some cases, this is achieved through explicit carve-outs. In Ohio, for example, the relevant Act stipulates that 'drivers are not employees [for purposes of key labour standards] except where agreed to by written contract',[62] and in Indiana, 'an Act to amend the [State] Code concerning insurance' discreetly stipulates that TNC drivers are similarly to be seen as independent contractors by law.[63] Other states have included less direct provisions to similar effect. In Texas, legislation stipulates that a TNC 'does not control, direct, or manage' its drivers, thus denying a key element in most employment law tests,[64] and in North Carolina, a 'rebuttable presumption exists that a TNC driver is an independent contractor and not an employee'.[65]

Similar lobbying efforts are by no means limited to the United States. A *European Agenda for the Collaborative Economy*, published by the European Commission in the summer of 2016, seemed to echo many of the industry's positions. The non-binding guidance issued to the then 28 EU member states stopped short of denying sharing-economy workers' employment status, but suggested that only platforms that controlled the price of services, set contractual terms, *and* owned 'key assets used to provide the underlying service' should be classified as service providers.[66]

Even those uncomfortable with the legislative classification of gig-economy workers as independent contractors eschew employment status. At the least radical end of the spectrum, we find proposals to create a 'third' employment status for gig-economy workers, located between the traditional categories of employee and independent contractor. Building on the notion that on-demand economy platforms represent a genuinely novel form of work, deserving of its own legal status and regulatory apparatus, Seth Harris, a former Deputy US Secretary of Labor, and Alan Krueger, a Princeton economist who has repeatedly collaborated with on-demand platforms, have argued in favour of the statutory introduction of a third, intermediate category to capture gig-economy workers. Their 'independent worker' would be entitled to some protection, including collective bargaining rights and elements of social security provision, whilst being denied recourse to basic standards such as wage and hours protection.[67]

Would the introduction of such a status be helpful? Not necessarily. Platforms would immediately be relieved of some of employers' most costly obligations—whilst continuing to litigate over independent worker status. As an exasperated US district judge noted, the task of determining worker status is often akin to being 'handed a square peg and asked to choose between two round holes'.[68] Adding a third round hole is unlikely to solve any classification problems. Indeed, several European jurisdictions, including Germany, Italy, Spain, and the UK, have long recognized intermediate worker categories without resolving any of the fundamental classificatory problems. If anything, more confusion is introduced—as became evident during recent UK litigation against Uber, with legal arguments focused on the third category recognized under English employment law.

A slightly stronger pushback against existing regulation underpins calls for so-called regulatory safe harbours, said to ensure that on-demand economy platforms can innovate outside the law. A proposal championed by Seth Harris and Alan Krueger, amongst others, is the idea that companies:

> are loath to [offer worker benefits] because offering benefits to workers would raise the risk that their work relationships would be adjudged employment by a court... To overcome this inefficient predicament, we propose that intermediaries be covered by a safe harbor provision such that pooling independent workers for purposes of providing benefits would not be legally interpreted as an indication of employee status.[69]

This notion of a regulatory 'safe harbour', however, is deeply flawed: it requires us to accept the argument that current regulation stops platforms from treating their workers decently and providing benefits because they are worried that this would lead to employee classification—and thus legally mandate the very rights a platform claims it *might* otherwise provide out of its own goodwill.

Scrutinizing the Narratives

In the last chapter, we began to explore contradictory accounts of the reality of on-demand economy work. On the one hand, we saw how the gig economy can present real opportunities: gone are the bosses of old, whilst individual entrepreneurs enjoy access to new markets, flexibly earning additional incomes. On the other, we also encountered a number of problems: instead of genuine autonomy and entrepreneurial freedom, workers might face a host of bosses in the form of customer ratings, algorithms, apps, and tasks, all clamouring for immediate and constant attention—without the regular pay, insurance, and pensions that traditional employers had to provide.

Rather than reflecting this heterogeneity, however, public discourse as shaped by the industry focuses on a consistently positive narrative. This, we saw, is not only a question of clever marketing. For nearly all platforms, the idea that they are providing technology to facilitate micro-entrepreneurs' businesses—rather than telling their workforce what to do—is the *sine qua non* of their business model. Tales of digital disruption, innovation, and entrepreneurship are crucial to this endeavour. Narratives shape regulation.

This, then, is the ultimate goal of sharing-economy doublespeak: to question whether the law in general, and employment regulation in particular, is still relevant in regulating the contractual relationships formed between platforms, their users, and their workforce. It's a manoeuvre presented in various guises, and with various degrees of intensity and sophistication—yet it is consistently centred on two narratives: first, that collaboration and sharing are entirely new disruptive models, far from economic activity deserving of regulatory interference at all ('neighbours helping neighbours'); and second, that the possibilities now available to individuals all over the world have created a new class of entrepreneurs, thriving in the rough-and-tumble of innovative open markets.

The former, crude story of collaboration and digital disruption has little truth to it. We have seen how most of the big regulatory battles between the Davids and Goliaths (or, rather, the Goliaths and Goliaths) of the sharing economy thus far have been fought in traditionally heavily regulated domains, such as taxis and transportation services—that is, industries in which previous incumbents may well have captured their regulators just as much as the on-demand economy is now trying to. As a result, we should be wary of platforms' attempts to translate lessons from these conflicts (which may well result in significant improvements for consumers, as many a Parisian or New Yorker will confirm) into a broader narrative about successful disruption: the vast majority of on-demand economy businesses operate in much less regulated environments.

Many of the potential alternative regulatory models discussed over the past few pages, on the other hand are significantly more sophisticated than the purist libertarianism we encountered at the outset. They too are based on the idea that only a break with existing models can lead to a 'broader innovation-enhancing solution' in support of genuine entrepreneurship.[70] Whilst we may rightly be sceptical about grand claims of digital disruption, however, we should not be too quick to discount the promises of innovation and entrepreneurship. If the platform economy represents a genuine new model delivering the benefits of entrepreneurship for all, then there is something to the case against employment classification and traditional regulatory models more broadly.

Let's take a closer look, beginning with the reality of work in the on-demand economy.

3

Lost in the Crowd

The *Freedom Economy Report 2016* by sharing-economy advocates Spera sets out a compelling vision for work in the on-demand economy: 'It is not just about a "gig" or "sharing a resource." It is about freedom, autonomy, and self-determination. And there has never been a better time to seek out, obtain, and enjoy this freedom than right now.'[1]

This narrative of entrepreneurship and opportunity chimes with the sharing-economy doublespeak we have already encountered. Remember Leah Busque waxing lyrical about how her TaskRabbit platform is fostering a new generation of entrepreneurs, 'with the tools and resources to set their own schedules, be their own bosses and say how much they want to get paid'?[2] Even better, it would appear, are the incredible financial rewards: in May 2014, an Uber press release picked up by news outlets all over the world suggested that drivers operating its cheapest service (UberX) were earning a median income of US$74,191 in San Francisco and $90,766 in New York.[3]

The entrepreneurship claim is central to the on-demand economy: who wouldn't relish the opportunity to swap the drudgery of monotonous, low-paid jobs for the excitement and rewards of the start-up world? Most platforms contractually insist that they are not service providers, but mere marketplaces facilitating transactions between independent entrepreneurs and their customers. Platforms 'do not want to be viewed as employers, and thus continually reinforce this by distancing themselves from the responsibilities that traditional businesses would take on in order to protect their workers or consumers'.[4]

At first glance, platform work blurs the traditional lines of business organization, whereby consumers buy goods and services from companies competing in the market, who in turn employ workers to manufacture or produce what is desired.[5] Regulation has long been shaped around this

Humans as a Service: The Promise and Perils of Work in the Gig Economy. First Edition. Jeremias Prassl. © Jeremias Prassl 2018. Published 2018 by Oxford University Press.

consumer–employer–worker triangle, which is precisely what the notion of the on-demand worker as an independent 'micro-entrepreneur' is designed to 'disrupt'. A complete lack of employment protection (and the significant cost savings that come with it) is crucial to on-demand, 'asset-light' operations' offers of cheap and abundant services.

It is not difficult to find instances of genuine entrepreneurship in the gig economy: think of a plumber using TaskRabbit to grow her business. When we look at platform work as a whole, however, the entrepreneurship narrative is much more difficult to sustain. In this chapter, we explore key elements of the entrepreneurial claim—freedom, autonomy, self-determination—and find that whilst they are true for some workers, others can quickly become lost in the crowd.

Many platforms' business models are explicitly premised on tight control over their workforce, subject to constantly changing and increasingly onerous terms—the very antithesis of facilitating entrepreneurship. In consequence, for a large number of workers, the reality of life as a Tasker, Driver-Partner, or Turker is more reminiscent of Victorian labourers' daily grind than the glamour of Silicon Valley: long hours for low wages, constant insecurity, and little legal protection—with no chance of a future upside.

Life as a Micro-Entrepreneur

Frederick Taylor's 1911 *Principles of Scientific Management* promised to improve the efficiency of businesses across the world by means of close monitoring of workers, an emphasis on rigid control over discreet tasks, and ever-changing adjustment of pay structures in response to individual output.[6] In reality, this translated into long dull hours under strict control and little pay, dehumanizing workers as drones on long assembly lines. The world's first management theory turned out to be unworkable in practice, as harsh and exploitative conditions drove large workforces to organize and revolt.

Today, Taylorism is back in full swing, resurrected under the guise of the on-demand economy, with technology and algorithms providing a degree of control and oversight of which even Frederick himself could not have dreamed. Instead of entrepreneurial autonomy, the vast majority of on-demand workers labour under strict platform supervision and control. Self-determination is but a distant dream, with frequent changes to platforms' business models making it impossible to plan ahead, and the notion of enjoying freedom rings hollow for more and more workers who have become locked into the system. And just as Taylorism threatened to dehumanize workers and slash their basic working conditions at the advent of the last century, so does the on-demand economy today: '[I]t's too hot to clean. Let Taskers handle the housework while you work on your summer tan.'[7]

Autonomy?

Most platforms' fine print suggests that they are merely in the business of what economists call 'matching': according to its terms of service, TaskRabbit 'provides an online venue where individuals or businesses who need something done... and individuals or businesses who are willing to perform such tasks... can connect with each other',[8] whilst Uber's terms and conditions similarly define the company as 'a technology platform that enables users... to arrange and schedule transportation and/or logistics services with third party providers of such services'.[9]

To help users find a perfect match, platforms rank service providers through a system of points or stars. Scores are calculated—ostensibly—on the basis of previous consumers' anonymous feedback following each task, with the resulting rating displayed to future users before the next 'gig' commences.

Entrepreneurs should, in principle, welcome an open and transparent rating mechanism, which helps them to overcome what economists call the 'lemons problem'. When hiring a worker over the Internet, it's nearly impossible to know how good they will be, with negative consequences for all involved. Good workers will be underpaid and bad ones overpaid, with firms potentially unwilling to hire anyone.[10] A rating mechanism allows individual entrepreneurs to signal the quality of their services and differentiates them from the crowd—thus providing access to better jobs, at higher pay.

As Tom Slee has argued, however, on-demand economy ratings might have little value in this regard.[11] Drawing on a range of empirical studies, he concludes that:

> [R]eputation systems fail in their basic task of distinguishing high quality or trustworthy offerings from lower-quality or untrustworthy offerings. There is no evidence that an Uber driver or a Handy cleaner with a rating of 4.9 is better in any way than someone with a rating of 4.6.[12]

Reputation algorithms, he argues, should instead be seen as:

> a substitute for a company management structure, and a bad one at that. A repu-
> tation system is the boss from hell: an erratic, bad-tempered and unaccountable
> manager that may fire you at any time, on a whim, with no appeal.[13]

Rather than merely signalling quality, then, the real point of rating algorithms is to control workers—both on a day-to-day basis and by locking
them into a particular platform's ecosystem.

How can a simple rating mechanism be so powerful? By not being quite
as simple: instead of merely aggregating consumer feedback, platform operators rely on constant algorithmic monitoring to ensure tight control over
every aspect of work and service delivery. Additional elements—from compliance with platform policies to how quickly and often a worker accepts
new tasks—are factored into the equation, with any deviation sanctioned in
real time.

Algorithmic control is exercised in myriad ways, often eschewing direct
orders or explicit instructions.[14] Alex Rosenblat and Luke Stark's study of
Uber's control mechanisms demonstrates how crowdwork conditions can
easily be 'shaped by the company's deployment of a variety of design decisions and information asymmetries via the application to effect a "soft control"
over workers' routines'.[15] Even though instructions are 'carefully designed
to be indirect, presumably to avoid the appearance of a company policy',[16]
they are incredibly powerful:

> Individualized metrics... foster a 'highly individualized sense of responsibility
> for one's own job stability', even though drivers have limited control over how
> passengers interact with the rating system or how Uber assesses it. By design,
> systematic accountability for the whole interactive process is downloaded
> onto individual drivers.[17]

In a 2015 case, US District Judge Edward M. Chen made a similar point,
finding that:

> Uber's application data can... be used to constantly monitor certain aspects of
> a driver's behavior. This level of monitoring, where drivers are potentially
> observable at all times, arguably gives Uber a tremendous amount of control
> over the 'manner and means' of its drivers' performance.[18]

Even though specific approaches vary wildly across different platforms and
time, the goal is often the same: rather than simply 'matching' well-informed
workers and customers, most platforms are digital work intermediaries, in

the business of tightly managing a large, invisible workforce. Nearly every aspect of on-demand work is shaped by the rating algorithms' constant hovering over each worker like a modern-day Panoptes, the all-seeing watchman of Greek mythology: from vetting potential entrants and assigning tasks, to controlling how work is done and remunerated, and sanctioning unsatisfactory performance—often without any transparency or accountability. As Judge Chen put it, citing Michel Foucault, 'a state of conscious and permanent visibility... assures the automatic functioning of power'.[19]

Algorithmic Management

'On the Internet,' a 1993 New Yorker cartoon suggested, 'nobody knows you're a dog.' In the on-demand economy, it seems that platforms want to know everything about their users—and their dogs. Control begins at the moment a potential worker registers with a platform, with most operators demanding extensive information and screening individual workers' credentials before activating their accounts in a process significantly more intrusive than merely signing up to yet another online service. It is not uncommon for platforms to demand copies of users' official identity documents and financial information, alongside a host of other details.[20]

Once a user is activated, platform control becomes even more intense, limiting the promised freedom to choose work, hours, and pay: workers are forced to accept low-paid and unpleasant tasks, must work long hours to earn and maintain good ratings, and may find that their actual take-home pay is well below minimum wage levels.

As regards task assignment, platforms employ a range of strategies to ensure that jobs are accepted as quickly as possible. Ride-sharing platforms, for example, often keep their drivers in the dark about passengers' destinations until the trip has begun. As independent entrepreneurs, drivers should be free not to accept unprofitable work—such as a short local ride after a long wait in an airport queue. In reality, however, many platforms require drivers to maintain high average acceptance rates of offers received whilst their app is activated and impose strict limitations on how many rides can be cancelled. Any attempt to focus on high-priced rides is controlled by the platform's algorithms: '[D]rivers are penalized for rejecting lower paid work in favor of higher paid work, which is illustrative of another constraint on their "freedom" as independent entrepreneurs.'[21]

For some time, Uber also instigated brief deactivation periods of up to 10 minutes as an immediate sanction for a driver's repeated refusal to accept unprofitable rides.[22] When a worker is ready to quit, algorithmic control is similarly quick to step in, with Rosenblat and Stark reporting how the app prompts drivers with an enticing pop-up message accompanied by the surge-price icon: 'Are you sure you want to go offline? Demand is very high in your area. Make more money, don't stop now!'[23]

Even in situations where workers are given more leeway in bidding for work or customers can freely choose amongst different workers' profiles, it is important not to underestimate the indirect control a platform's rating algorithms can exercise over workers' tasks—and thus their work and pay. Most platforms will provide some sort of preliminary ranking or personalized recommendations; others limit the amount of work for which freelancers can bid.[24]

Through a combination of technology and human factors, platforms also exercise firm control over most aspects of how, and to what standard, work is done. Once a driver has accepted an Uber request, for example, she will be directed to the passenger and onwards to the required destination through her version of the Uber app; customers can complain if a different route was chosen and they feel disadvantaged in consequence. Drivers are also 'reminded' to 'offer passengers bottled water, chewing gum, snacks, mints and phone chargers', to 'dress appropriately', and to carry bags and hold open doors for passengers. The platform's control extends as far as the music to be played during the ride: through corporate partnerships, drivers must enable passengers to use music apps to set their own background music. Rival provider Lyft exercises similar control over the 'ride experience'—even though it appears to have given up on some of its more curious requirements, including pink moustaches and drivers welcoming their passengers with a fist-bump.[25]

Where a platform does not specify the work to be done, it will still often control the way in which tasks are performed—whether through detailed stipulations such as TaskRabbit's bright green T-shirts featuring the company logo or through general conditions of use.[26] Amazon's Mechanical Turk (MTurk) insists that users 'specifically acknowledge and agree' to a range of conditions, including, for example, 'not [to] use robots, scripts or other automated methods to complete the Services'.[27]

Technology is once more key to this tight control. Upwork clients can check up on their workers through a so-called work diary: whenever a freelancer is engaged on a job paid by the hour, the platform's software captures regular screenshots of her screen, counts keystrokes and records work completed to enable clients' monitoring whether the freelancer is working for the whole of the time that she has billed for. Following a recent software update, Uber's app now taps into the GPS, gyrometer, and acceleration sensors in each driver's iPhone to detect drivers' speeding or abrupt braking.[28]

Crucially, however, algorithmic control often does not extend to protecting workers or facilitating their entrepreneurial choices. Whilst some platforms let workers rate customers, the scores are either not displayed at all or have little bearing on a consumer's ability to use the service.[29] As a result, on-demand workers can be exposed to illegal, dangerous, unethical, and emotionally downright brutal work—which must nonetheless be performed in a prompt, friendly, and cheerful manner to avoid low ratings.

Time pressure for many delivery services, for example, can be so high that it's impossible to complete tasks without breaking at least some rules of the road. Postmates' solution to illegal parking? An 'explicit suggestion that it's okay to break the law if that's what you've got to do to get the order done on time'.[30]

On other occasions, workers have been threatened with punishment for standing up to dangerous working conditions:

> I had a client a couple of months ago who wanted me to do his laundry. I did it and there was something kind of nasty on his stuff... I realized this nasty stuff was actually cat diarrhea all over his laundry... [The client] always posts that it's four loads of laundry and every time I did his laundry it filled 10 or 15 double loading washers. It was a mountain of laundry and it was all covered in cat diarrhea.
>
> The third time this happened, I actually called TaskRabbit and I said, 'Look this is what's happening. Plus I'm allergic to cats and it actually says that in my profile.' I said, 'I think I should get paid more than $25 for doing this.' TaskRabbit was actually very polite and said 'Yes, yes that sounds horrible. Thanks for letting us know, we'll have a word with him.'[31]

The worker's complaint, however, seemed not to deter the client. When she demanded a higher price in response to his next request for a few loads' washing, things went wrong: 'I got an email from TaskRabbit shortly thereafter saying that I was unprofessional. They said if I did that again, I was fired.'[32]

Other tasks might even expose workers to serious mental harm. In determining the quality of uploaded content, websites including Facebook and

YouTube increasingly rely on crowdworkers to determine whether content is inappropriate or offensive. Platforms such as CrowdFlower proudly advertise their ability to 'cut costs without sacrificing quality' in real-time content moderation:'[E]ach image submitted to the site is assessed by three reviewers whose judgments are automatically crosschecked to determine the best response.'[33] That doesn't sound too difficult—until you realize that the images in question will often include extreme pornography, 'brutal street fights, animal torture, suicide bombings, decapitations, and horrific traffic accidents'.[34]

How can we reconcile these conditions with many a worker's public account of her happy experiences, including those we encountered in earlier chapters? There are two possible explanations: first, remember the heterogeneity of platform work and on-demand workers. Someone whiling away spare hours and enjoying a programming challenge on CrowdFlower whilst earning a bit of extra income—and thus with the possibility of walking away at any point—will derive significantly more joy from gig work than another person forced to cobble together a living through a series of low-paid, precarious jobs. Second, remember the ever-watchful algorithm, able to detect any form of deviation: as Andrew Callaway points out in the context of (un)happy Uber drivers:

> [A]s a passenger, you're going to be rating your interview subject... That can have some implications as far as how honest drivers are when their passengers ask about how much they like it. Depressing workers don't get high ratings. Nobody wants to feel guilty about using an app they like.[35]

The Wages of Entrepreneurship

The reach of algorithmic control is by no means limited to controlling the work itself. Workers' pay is determined in a variety of ways across different platforms, from customers' specifying how much they are willing to pay for a particular job and workers' bidding for tasks, to fully automated central pricing such as Uber's dynamic algorithm, which determines remuneration for distance and time on the basis of factors such as individual city pricing levels, or even demand specific to a particular location and time through so-called surge pricing.[36] Some platforms also permit their customers to reject completed work (and thus avoid having to pay for it) and, whilst no or little reason is often given, platforms may refuse to get involved with any resulting disputes.[37]

Even where platforms do not set a wage rate, they still exercise significant control over how much the worker is paid. Many operators insist that no cash changes hands directly between consumers and workers in order to keep full control over all aspects of fees, invoicing, and pay-outs. Most platforms also determine when and how workers are paid their wages—sometimes in draconian ways: the majority of MTurk workers outside the United States can redeem their income only as an Amazon.com gift card, to be used exclusively on the company's online portals.[38]

Control over wage levels is central to the on-demand business model: costs to consumers must be kept low, whilst maximizing platform income. CrowdFlower's CEO once admitted in an interview that his company paid most workers no more than US$2–3 per hour[39]—and this is by no means an isolated incident: a worrying proportion of on-demand economy workers appear to be paid well below minimum wage levels. New York University Stern Business School's Panos Ipeirotis suggests that the average hourly wage for workers on Amazon's MTurk is $4.80 (2012), whereas Irani and Silberman have calculated a more realistic rate of $2.

In one sense, low wages could simply be seen as a result of standard market forces:

> The competitive nature of digital platforms...along with the very low barriers to entry/exit and the absence of wage ceilings or floors means that wages in [the on-demand] market are set at a level that is very close to what economists call the 'competitive market rate'—ie, the one that matches demand and supply for a given service.[40]

Upon closer inspection, however, it turns out that on-demand economy wages are often designed to be artificially low, directing a surplus of labour to compete over a limited number of tasks, with platforms taking a percentage of the resulting earnings, whilst workers are left to pick up the bill for any expenses. The oversupply of workers in particular acts as a real double whammy in so far as income is concerned: because demand for many gig services is relatively insensitive to supply, having too many workers compete for any given task will depress wage rates—and decrease individuals' chance of finding work, even at the lower price.

The very element of manipulating supply by forcing workers constantly to compete against each other for the next task goes a long way towards achieving low wage levels. Uber, for example, has been reported to contact drivers with promises of 'high demand' and 'big weekends' in particular cities or location. Even the highly skilled are subject to these forces, particularly where work can be completed online and is thus open to global competition. On UpWork's predecessor platform ODesk, over three-quarters of workers had at least an undergraduate degree—yet even those working full-time might earn only US$750 per month.[41]

Wage rates are further depressed by platforms' ever-increasing share of earnings. Actual commission rates vary dramatically, both across time and different platforms. As a general rule, most platforms will take 15–30 per cent of the worker's wage depending on often-complicated formulae. Amazon, for example, takes 20 per cent of the amount paid by the Requester to the Turker as commission, or 40 per cent commission for large tasks with 10+ individual 'Human Intelligence Tasks' (HITs). Given its minimum cut of half a cent per HIT, however, the commission often amounts to no less than 50 per cent of a worker's wage: in a 2010 study, a full quarter of HITs available on the platform were found to have a reward of US$0.01.[42] In consequence, wages are low and reports of high earners are often overstated: Pew Center research suggests that only 8 per cent of workers earn more than $8 per hour.[43]

Even where competition is localized because of physical service delivery, wages are pushed down by platforms' refusal to pay workers between tasks and their insistence that workers shoulder the vast majority of costs associated with their work. Whether cycling around town between deliveries or wading through a long list of online gigs to identify those for which she is eligible, a worker will be paid only for time actually spent serving a particular client—not unlike workers at branches of Burger King in the UK in the 1990s, who were infamously paid only for the minutes during which they flipped burgers or operated tills.[44] And it is not only the costs of 'idle' time that are shifted onto workers; in the gig economy, they are also responsible for everything from providing tools, such as their cars or computers, to paying for upkeep and running cost.

This fact is consistently excluded from platforms' official statistics and promotional materials, despite its huge impact on actual take-home pay. In their analysis using the platform's own data, Hall and Krueger find that mean hourly earnings for UberX drivers across the United States range from US$15.60 to $29.65 per hour—significantly more 'than their general-population driver counterparts'.[45] That doesn't sound too bad—until you remember that, '[o]f course, Uber's driver-partners are not reimbursed for driving expenses, such as gasoline, depreciation, or insurance'.[46]

Once all costs are subtracted, hourly wages quickly fall, often to far below minimum wage levels. Spot checks of New York Uber drivers reveal take-home pay of as little as US\$3.99 per hour or even a net financial loss (against a minimum wage of \$10.50).[47] Similarly, UK trade union GMB has calculated that top-rated and -paid Uber drivers in London will earn no more than £5.68 per hour (thus clearly below the UK's minimum wage of £7.50) once their expenses are taken into account.[48]

Given the high fixed cost of buying a car or computer compared to these low wages, it is unsurprising that many on-demand workers are prone to working long hours. Low pay is a key instrument to ensure that workers put in the extended shifts required to keep a large workforce available around the clock. To serve customers as quickly as possible, platforms need to keep a constant surplus supply of workers available—thus lowering the wages of each individual worker, who in turn needs to work even longer hours to make a living.

Some defenders of the sharing economy argue that the low wages and long hours resulting from platform control are not necessarily a problem, because most tasks are simply undertaken to supplement a stable primary income.[49] As Six Silberman, one of the leading experts on Amazon's MTurk has noted, however, this is far from the truth:

> [Many of] the narratives offered by researchers and employers to justify low pay—e.g., that most workers who rely on Turking income live in 'developing' countries with low costs of living; that most 'developed'-country workers work mainly to pass time; that crowd work is easy and workers relatively unskilled and uneducated; and that workers freely choose to participate in AMT and can easily choose other work if they find the pay too low—are inaccurate.[50]

Sanctions

This brings us to the final ingredient of platforms' all-pervasive control: algorithmic ratings are backed up by a series of incentives and sanctions. Well-paid or otherwise attractive requests are reserved for those with higher ratings, whilst low ratings trigger a series of 'performance standard probations', with workers confined to low-value tasks—or simply fired ('terminated').[51]

Even where workers are not deactivated entirely, low ratings can still spell trouble. Some platforms link quality (and quantity) of work to some form of 'elite' status, which allows users access to better tasks and higher pay, or ensures preferential search listings:

> [After] watching friends get shunted into low-rated purgatory shortly after starting out, one worker said he took dozens of low-paying jobs primarily in order to get enough of a ratings buffer...workers with poor records don't get booted off, but they appear far down the list of options, so they get less work and get less for it.[52]

The conditions for elite status are usually obscure. Whilst some platforms specify factors including average scores and numbers of tasks, others refuse to disclose their criteria.[53] The power of ratings is such that workers will deliberately undercharge customers in the hope of soliciting a favourable rating: 'Some drivers report strategically ending a trip early, thus lowering the fare for the passenger, in the hopes of getting a higher rating.'[54]

Rating system's sanctions aren't just all-powerful; they often appear to operate in an entirely unpredictable and arbitrary fashion, and might, on occasion, be downright racist or sexist. Control is not only more powerful, but also:

> more arbitrary than in traditional employment where if there were issues with your standards you might have a discussion with your clients, or your manager might take action to help you improve, whereas with the gig economy your customers instantly stop turning to you. No one is checking the people that are giving the ratings which means it's much more difficult to know that the ratings are objective.[55]

This is a particular concern given the growing evidence that on-demand platforms' algorithms aggregate users' conscious or unconscious biases, leading to discrimination against groups including female and ethnic minority workers. As one anonymous driver highlighted in an interview with *The Guardian*: 'College students down-rate older drivers, male riders down-rate female drivers who don't flirt along, drivers with disabilities get deactivated.'[56]

Sanctions can come with little advance notice and it is often difficult for on-demand workers to understand why their ratings have fallen in the first place:

> It's a huge disappointment to be fired from your ride sharing job, and to make things worse, you're given little to no warning or explanation about your deactivation. Instead, when you try to log on to drive, you're greeted with an error message.[57]

Amazon similarly reserves the right to 'terminate this Agreement, [and] suspend access to the Site...immediately without notice for any reason', with reports suggesting that any income remaining in the workers account may be forfeit.[58]

In other situations, algorithmic control can be almost comically harsh. The *Sunday Times* reports that when Joseph MacDonald, a Boston-based former Postmates driver, was run over whilst on his delivery bike (by a rideshare driver, no less), he followed the company's instructions and emailed it about his accident. The response? MacDonald was 'told that since [he'd] turned down a job—because of the accident—[he] would not be paid the $15 an hour you usually get if you accept one job an hour'.[59]

Specific algorithms and business models will always continue to vary over time and across different platforms. Platforms' tight control over their invisible workforce, on the other hand, is quickly emerging as a clear constant—a far cry from the headline promise of autonomy.

Self-Determination?

The promise of self-determination fares similarly badly. Many platforms' business models are structured to make it nearly impossible for individual micro-entrepreneurs to control wage and work levels on a consistent or commensurate basis: '[W]ages in the gig economy are often very flexible and may change more promptly in accordance with rising or falling demand and supply.'[60]

It is not only the untrammelled operation of market mechanisms (which entrepreneurs have to face too) that makes self-determination a distant dream for many on-demand workers; platforms' deliberate choices and control also play a crucial role, as business models are constantly rejigged in order to extract maximum gains.

At its simplest (and most frequent), this means a change in the percentage of workers' wages retained by the platform. MTurk's commission was doubled from 10 per cent to 20 per cent in July 2015;[61] in June 2016, Upwork changed its commission model from a flat rate of 10 per cent across all jobs to a sliding-scale system based on freelancers' lifetime billings with each client.[62] Uber has similarly continued to experiment with varying the amount of commission payable, which is particularly harmful to part-time workers if the percentage retained falls with the number of trips offered.[63]

Another common tactic is for platforms to offer reasonably generous rates and subsidies to workers when they first enter a new city or territory, only to reduce fares and increase commission in subsequent months. As we will see in Chapter 6, the primary purpose of this often loss-making strategy is to buy market share, with a view to crowding out competitors and to harnessing network effects. It is also a useful tactic to lock a large number of workers into the platform, which helps to create political goodwill and to overcome initial fears and political opposition. As the *New York Times* reports, drivers in Dallas, Texas, were initially very supportive of Uber:

> [They] formed a tactical alliance with the company to help it gain the city's approval, which local cab operators resisted. [Uber driver] Mr. Alemayoh even sang Uber's praises in testimony before the Houston City Council, after the company asked him to speak there as part of its expansion efforts. 'I said it's fair to drivers to have Uber,' he recalled. 'I spoke on their behalf, they didn't pay me.' But the relationship began to sour in 2014, when the company decreed that drivers with cars made before 2008 would no longer be able to participate in UberBlack [a premium rate service].[64]

Terms and conditions continued to get worse—notably for drivers who had invested in luxury cars to take advantage of promised premium rates and who were now forced to offer their services at bargain-basement prices. At the same time, however, opposition appeared to have become futile:

> [T]he drivers had long since recognized that they were at the company's beck and call. Because of Uber's popularity, almost all their other sources of business had dried up. And Uber had earned the imprimatur of the City Council, which made the drivers politically expendable, too.[65]

On-demand workers across the world have similarly witnessed how initially reasonably generous platforms have 'started to tighten the rope'—or, in some cases, changed their business model altogether.

TaskRabbit's levels of remuneration vary dramatically, for example, as the platform continues to experiment with different remuneration models. A notable shift in 2014 saw a move away from the original auction-style mechanisms, through which Taskers could specify their offers for any given task, to an algorithm matching clients with a selection of workers for a job, displaying their relevant hourly rates. Numerous such models appear to have been tested, from customers setting their 'optimum price' to taskers offering their rates (with the platform then charging an additional service fee), or even preset 'Quick Assign' tasks, for which TaskRabbit's algorithms determine pay.[66]

Deliveroo attempted a similar move in the summer of 2016, when it began to switch its workers away from a guaranteed hourly pay structure (£7 in London) with small bonuses (£1 per delivery) to a riskier model paying £3.75 per delivery, and abandoned scheduled shifts in favour of free choice. Couriers were up in arms: Deliveroo's busiest periods coincide with London rush-hour traffic, thus limiting their ability to make multiple deliveries in quick succession and drastically reducing earnings by no longer paying for 'idle' time spent waiting between jobs. The ensuing demonstrations and negative publicity forced the company to back down—in part, at least, and for the time being.[67]

Deliveroo's turnaround was a rare exception, however. Rosenblat and Stark highlight the cynicism with which some platforms promote these constant changes:

> To promote rate cuts, Uber typically shows drivers graphs demonstrating that lower fare rates lead to a 'huge boost in demand, and partner earnings per hour increased by 25%—that's a lot of extra money!' Uber's logic is that drivers will earn more through increased trips, and greater optimization of their time online, from the 'boost in demand.' In reactions that echo other driver responses to rate decreases in other cities, including Austin, drivers in forums respond with incredulity, calling it 'Uber math,' 'propaganda,' and Orwellian double-speak. Drivers contend that they have to work longer hours and accrue additional expenses to earn what they made prior to rate cuts.[68]

For many, the image of flexibility and self-determination in on-demand work is thus nothing more than a mirage: one-sided flexibility on part of the platforms exposes workers to constant changes, often without much time to adapt, and nearly always to their immediate financial disadvantage.

Freedom?

The promise of freedom, finally, rings equally hollow, with platforms' business models making it difficult for workers to assert their fundamental rights, including the freedom to form a union and bargain collectively. Most operators are unsurprisingly hostile to any efforts at organizing genuinely independent worker representation. When unionization was on the cards in Seattle, Uber's call-centre representatives were instructed to ring up drivers and 'share some thoughts' about how 'collective bargaining and unionization do not fit the characteristics of how most partners use the Uber platform'.[69]

As former *New York Times* correspondent Steven Greenhouse notes:

In many ways, digital on-demand workers face far more obstacles to organizing and being heard than workers in the traditional economy. Isolated as so
many of them are, on-demand workers rarely meet face to face, and online
forums are a second-best substitute for building trust and solidarity. Sometimes
when these workers communicate online, companies spy on them—and even
kick potential troublemakers off their platforms. Moreover, since on-demand
workers are frequently considered independent contractors, they aren't protected by federal labor laws that prohibit companies from retaliating against
employees who join together to improve conditions.[70]

More and more platforms also use their superior bargaining power to
force workers into signing away some of the most basic freedoms that a
genuine entrepreneur might enjoy—from sending in substitutes and soliciting new customers to bringing disputes before a court. As part of the
sign-up process, workers usually have to agree that they are under a duty
personally to perform any work offered. TaskRabbit's manual notes that
'TaskPosters want to see your smiling face, not anyone else's', thus explicitly
prohibiting budding entrepreneurs from sending 'someone that hasn't gone
through our vetting process'.[71]

Nearly every platform also has clear contractual prohibitions on direct
contracts between workers and consumers. Some websites even invite their
users to report other customers or workers striking private bargains: 'If
someone you know is participating in fee avoidance,' TaskRabbit exhorts its
workers, 'please contact our Customer Support so that we can act accordingly.'[72] It appears that the disrupters don't care much for being disrupted
themselves.

Should any dispute arise, more and more on-demand workers will not
even be able to exercise their basic freedom of appealing to a court of law.
Take this clause from Deliveroo's London scooter contract as an example:

2.2 You further warrant that neither you nor anyone acting on your behalf
    will present any claim in the Employment Tribunal or any civil court in
    which it is contended that you are either an employee or a worker.
2.3 If, despite clause 2.2 above, either you or anyone acting on your behalf (or
    your substitute or anyone acting on your substitute's behalf) presents
    any claim in the Employment Tribunal or any civil court which would
    not be able to proceed unless it was successfully contended that you (or
    your substitute) are an employee or a worker within the meaning of any
    employment rights legislation, you undertake to indemnify and keep indem-
    nified Deliveroo against costs (including legal costs) and expenses that it

incurs in connection with those proceedings, and you agree that Deliveroo may set off any sum owed to you against any damages, compensation, costs or other sum that may be awarded to you in those proceedings.

You agree not to sue the platform, in other words—and even if you do, it will hold you responsible for any resulting cost. In reality, such clauses may often be unenforceable—and, following public uproar when a parliamentary committee criticized these provisions, Deliveroo's contracts have now been rewritten. The original inclusion of the term nonetheless sent a strong message to individuals contemplating a challenge to their legal status.[73]

Individual arbitration clauses are another major concern. In jurisdictions including the United States, platforms have generally sought to ban jury trials and class-action law suits (which might be easier to bring for low-income workers), and are insisting that any suit must not be brought before a public court and should be diverted into private arbitration instead. Professor Katherine Stone of the University of California Los Angeles spells out the far-reaching consequences of this 'lethal combination':

> [A] company can not only get an exemption from specific employment laws, it can avoid the entire issue of whether its workers are covered by the laws in the first place... Individual workers can raise this argument in their individual arbitration proceedings, but even if they win, it will not apply to others and the outcomes will be hidden behind arbitration's veil of secrecy. Thus not only do workers lose their employment rights—we as a society potentially lose our entire framework of employment protection that we spent a century constructing.[74]

Worst of all, workers increasingly find themselves tied into particular platforms. We have already seen the powerful ways through which rating mechanisms can lock individuals in: most algorithms weight scores by the number of tasks completed and award 'elite worker' status on the same basis. The high ratings that frequent work brings mean access to more attractive tasks, at (slightly) better pay, and at least some buffer against the occasional negative rating. Fees structures can be designed to similar effect. With UpWork's 'lifetime billing' strategy, commission decreases over time to keep workers locked in: the platform charges 20 per cent commission for the first US$500 a freelancer bills a client across all contracts with that client, then 10 per cent for total billings with a client to a value between $500.01 and $10,000, and 5 per cent for total billings with a client that exceed $10,000.[75] Rather than diversifying their activity—and thus the risk of deactivation or other sanctions across different platforms—the system motivates workers to put all of their eggs into one basket.[76]

Despite these powerful incentive structures, however, the reality of work in the on-demand economy can be so disheartening that workers move on to different platforms. According to Uber's own data, only a little over 50 per cent of registered drivers are still active a year after they first signed up.[77] This 'churn', or turnover, is a serious threat to the expansion of businesses premised on the constant availability of a large workforce. In their quest to lock workers into a particular ecosystem, platforms have thus begun to go yet farther—including the most draconian of all commitment devices: debt.

Some companies have arranged loan facilities to enable workers to access the necessary tools. When Uber's original collaboration with Santander ended in 2015, the platform's wholly owned subsidiary Xchange Leasing, LLC, stepped in to pick up the slack with a US$1 billion credit facility arranged by Goldman Sachs. A detailed Bloomberg investigation revealed a scheme with all of the hallmarks of what some of the financial experts interviewed classed as 'predatory' lending—offering loans to workers with poor credit scores, overvaluing cars, charging high rates—and a twist: Uber can tap straight into the workers' income stream (after commission, of course) to repay itself. As fares spiral downwards and the platform's cut goes up, workers find themselves trapped: 'It got to the point that I would drive just to meet my payment', one driver told Bloomberg News. 'If you were short on your payment for a week it would roll onto the payment for next week. It starts adding up.'[78] Yet new financial products keep emerging. In April 2016, Uber teamed up with financial services start-up Clearbanc to offer its drivers 'Advance Pay'—the euphemistic label for start-up loans costing up to 125 per cent of the borrowed principal.[79]

Entrepreneurship...or an On-Demand Trap?

In exploring the reality behind entrepreneurship, one of the sharing economy's most pervasive narratives, we have seen how it is all too easy for many workers to get lost—and even trapped—in the crowd. Instead of economic empowerment for all, we found workers tightly controlled by their platforms, with low pay, long hours, and questionable working standards far more commonplace than we are led to believe. Indeed, the picture that has emerged shows that these are increasingly the norm, rather than an exception.

For many on-demand economy workers, the dream of 'turnkey entrepreneurship' delivered by 'powerful technology platforms' to workers 'across the country and around the world' has quickly turned out to be a nightmare as they find themselves locked into a life of subordination, dependence, and economic precarity driven by intense, multidimensional control over all aspects of their work—all whilst being denied the freedom, autonomy, and self-determination of genuine enterprise.

Rather than worrying about the harsh working conditions we have encountered, however, some platforms publicly advertise them as a desirable feature. At its most extreme, the entrepreneurship narrative actively celebrates (self-)exploitation. *New Yorker* journalist Jia Tolentino has highlighted a series of instances of 'the gig economy celebrat[ing] working yourself to death':

> It does require a fairly dystopian strain of doublethink for a company to celebrate how hard and how constantly its employees must work to make a living, given that these companies are themselves setting the terms... Fiverr, an online freelance marketplace that promotes itself as being for 'the lean entrepreneur'... recently attracted ire for an ad campaign called 'In Doers We Trust'. One ad, prominently displayed on some New York City subway cars, features a woman staring at the camera with a look of blank determination. 'You eat a coffee for lunch,' the ad proclaims. 'You follow through on your follow through. Sleep deprivation is your drug of choice. You might be a doer.'[80]

Public discourse is slowly beginning to wake up to many of these problems. There doesn't appear to be a serious broadsheet newspaper or weekly magazine that hasn't featured an exposé of sharing-economy working conditions, or dispatched one of its journalists to share their (usually depressing) experiences of spending a week or two attempting to make a living in the on-demand world. Remember that this doesn't mean that the gig economy is universally problematic: we have already encountered plenty of positive examples. The evidence we have seen nonetheless poses a serious challenge to entrepreneurial narratives: for many, sharing-economy work has come to symbolize the exact opposite.

What, then, about our second core narrative—that is, gig-economy work as the result of digital innovation? Even critical reports are often prone to fall into the trap of seeing the consequences of a revolution or a brand new model at work. In reality, however, we need to be similarly careful before concluding that much is new about the precarious work in highly fragmented employment relationships that the on-demand economy embodies. In the next chapter, we take a look at some of the historical precedent for today's on-demand labour markets in an effort to understand whether the sharing economy is genuinely innovative—or whether the problematic elements we have encountered are but the latest (and most extreme) instantiation of business models designed to shift economic and legal risk away from corporations, and concentrate it on workers and consumers instead.

4

The Innovation Paradox

Hans Christian Andersen tells the story of an emperor in ancient times, exceedingly fond of the latest trends in fashion. One day, two weavers arrive to offer him a very special garment indeed: woven of incredible colours and patterns, and invisible to all but the worthy and intelligent. New robes are soon commissioned and the emperor sends a series of courtiers to inspect progress—and although they can see nothing but empty looms, gushing reports are made to the emperor, lest the courtiers be deemed unworthy. One day, finally, the emperor himself arrives to be dressed in the mythical garbs and, after much admiration from his ministers, sets off on a celebratory procession. A bewildered public feels duty-bound to celebrate the emperor's new clothes as the finest in the land—until a child pipes up: 'But he hasn't got anything on!'[1]

Breathless tales of a digital revolution and radical innovation in the on-demand economy often remind me of Andersen's cautionary tale: are we being spun a tale that we don't dare challenge, lest we appear ignorant, Luddite, or worse? In the previous chapter, we explored the reality behind on-demand work on different apps and platforms, discovering how their claims that everyone can become a mini-entrepreneur are far from the reality of many workers' daily lives. In this chapter, we turn to the second claim at the heart of sharing-economy doublespeak: innovation. This, we saw, centred on two ideas: first, that technology has reshaped work in unprecedented ways; and second, that the new patterns of business organization emerging as a result are unlike anything we have seen before—that is, that '[d]igital innovation is creating entirely new ways to do business'.[2]

The innovation claim is central to sharing-economy doublespeak. It is designed to keep regulators in general, and employment law in particular, at bay. Regulation is said to stifle innovation. If work organization and business models are genuinely novel, why should we squeeze them into the straitjacket

Humans as a Service: The Promise and Perils of Work in the Gig Economy. First Edition.
Jeremias Prassl. © Jeremias Prassl 2018. Published 2018 by Oxford University Press.

of existing regulatory frameworks? And if the on-demand economy is a radically new way of doing business, what justification is there to treat platforms like other market operators?

Much like entrepreneurship, it is hard to disagree with innovation. Which politician, journalist, or citizen wants to be cast as a Luddite, out to smash the machines in an attempt to hold back progress? (And why should they?) Before jumping to any regulatory conclusions, however, we must ask ourselves to what extent gig-economy work is genuinely novel.

In so doing, we encounter a fundamental paradox: it *is* undoubtedly true that key elements behind the rise of the sharing economy are completely new—first and foremost, their reliance on the Internet, smartphone apps, and digital platforms for communication, intermediation, and control. Intense competition between different start-ups and the ongoing evolution of on-demand economy platforms has been the source of much innovation, at least as far as technology is concerned.

When it comes to *work* in the on-demand economy, on the other hand, the story is a very different one. In the last chapter, I hinted at a first parallel with historical developments when exploring how Taylorist control led to low wages and harsh working conditions for gig-economy workers. But it is not only gig-economy working conditions for which there is ample historical precedent; the parallels are much starker than that. The very business model of the gig economy—matching a large supply of on-demand workers with ever waxing and waning demand for work—can be traced back for centuries, cropping up in economies as diverse as Japan and Continental Europe, rural England and major urban areas from New York to Marseille.

Despite Jeff Bezos' claims to the contrary, the idea of 'humans as a service' is nearly as old as work itself. And it is an idea that had already begun to take hold once more before the advent of the Internet, as the fragmentation of work—from outsourcing and subcontracting to labour agencies—became a feature of labour markets in the late twentieth century.

This is the central claim of this chapter: as far as work is concerned, gig-economy innovation is a myth. The software and hardware on which apps and platforms draw are often the direct result of truly revolutionary innovation and breakthroughs, from GPS locators and the Internet, to powerful processors that fit into the palm of your hand. Contrary to the industry's claims, however, the underlying business model is anything but novel. Low-skill tasks instead of complex jobs; powerful intermediaries controlling large workforces;

hybrid arrangements between open market and closed hierarchies: the gig economy is but the latest (and perhaps the most extreme) example of labour-market practices that have been around for centuries.

Nothing New under the Sun

This assertion sits at odds with the seamless integration of the Internet into every element of our everyday lives. AOL co-founder Steve Case suggests that we are faced with a revolutionary 'Third Wave' of the Internet[3]—which will have a particular impact on labour markets: 'We need to recognize that the nature of work itself has changed', he argued in an interview with news outlet CNBC. 'I think that will accelerate in the third wave and that will put more pressure on policymakers to keep up with the innovations.'[4]

This is not simply technological hype: the claim to innovation seems firmly steeped in economic theory. Arun Sundararajan of New York University Stern Business School draws on a wide range of literature to suggest that platforms 'represent a new structure for organizing economic activity, one that is an interesting hybrid of a market and a hierarchy, and that could signal the evolution of 20th century *managerial capitalism* into 21st-century *crowd-based capitalism*'.[5] The starting point for this assertion is a juxtaposition between two models for organizing modern economies: 'Markets... where Adam Smith's famed "invisible hand" determines the prices that balance supply and demand. And then there is the "visible hand"—the "hierarchies" that we typically think of as firms or organizations (or government entities).'[6]

Drawing on the work of Massachusetts Institute of Technology (MIT) economists Tom Malone, Joanne Yates, and Robert Benjamin, Sundararajan suggests that gig-economy innovation will fundamentally reshape our economy by incentivizing entrepreneurs to move away from the hierarchical organization of business in large corporations towards open markets: '[A]s digital technologies progress, the coordination costs associated with handling complex product descriptions through markets decrease, thus making market-based activity feasible for a larger set of activities.'[7] The result? Instead of seeing the rise of the on-demand economy as 'a natural culmination' of digital trends, of outsourcing, and of 'the permeable boundaries of the firm', Sundararajan identifies platforms as 'new institutions' with a radical feature, 'as a hybrid between a pure market and a hierarchy'.[8]

And it is not only the organization of businesses that has been fundamentally reinvented. '[E]verything about work [will] need to change' too.[9] Spanning 'job design, organizational structures, management systems, anything associated work processes', the impact of digital innovation seems to know no bounds:

> [W]e are seeing the dismantling of centralized workplaces as more and more businesses operate without a headquarters and without a pool of permanent workers, opting instead to build enterprises by drawing on workers who are brought in to complete specific projects or tasks.[10]

Digital innovation is presented as the key to this revolution:

> [I]n the past, hiring thousands of workers to carry out small tasks wasn't feasible because of the high administrative costs of such a structure. Today, smaller and smaller tasks can increasingly be outsourced with minimal transaction costs to crowds of workers connected to digital platforms.[11]

How, then, is it possible to assert that there is nothing fundamentally new, let alone innovative, about work in the on-demand economy?

To sustain this counter-intuitive claim, we need to look beyond platforms' digital infrastructure and scrutinize two central elements of the claim to innovation: first, that the future of work is characterized by generalist workforces, providing businesses with an immediate labour supply to tackle a series of discrete tasks; and second, that the underlying business model is a new hybrid form of enterprise organization in its unique blend of hierarchy and market.

Sundararajan and others are absolutely correct to highlight these features as central elements in the organization of on-demand economy work. Neither, however, is a novel aspect of platform work—nor are they features specific to digitally mediated labour markets.

Back to the Future

Professor Matt Finkin of the University of Illinois was amongst the first to point out the close parallels between the gig economy and historical forms of organizing work, focusing in particular on the so-called putting-out system of home production.[12] This involved a central entrepreneur organizing the production of a wide variety of goods—the leading work on the subject covers everything from textiles (wool, cotton, and silk), clothing and lace making, to boots, shoes, nails, and chains—by breaking down the manufacturing process into individual steps: spinning wool, weaving cloth, cutting fabric, stitching buttons, and so on. Each of these tasks would be completed by workers in their own home or a small workshop; a series of intermediaries delivered materials and instructions to each homeworker, and, upon completion of the task, returned the goods to a central warehouse or passed them on to the next worker.[13]

Known under labels ranging from 'outwork' and 'sweated trades', to 'homework' or 'domestic production' (although the work was by no means necessarily limited to the home), this business model was prevalent in most industrialized countries well into the twentieth century. Its earliest origins can be traced back to Ancient India in the middle of the first millennium BC.[14] And it wasn't limited to manufacturing, either: early service industries, such as dockworkers unloading ships in ports across the world, were often organized along similar lines.

A foray through the history books soon reveals a vast number of closely related business models across continents and centuries. Powerful intermediaries were key to organizing work in ancient Babylon and medieval Florence; we find close similarities in the Japanese *Tonya* organization and the German *Verlagssystem*.[15] Just as with work in the on-demand economy, there are many differences and variations across countries and over time, of course— but the similarities are even more striking. As a British parliamentary report noted in 1908: 'More or less similar conditions prevail, not only in all the great countries of the Continent of Europe, but also in the United States of America, and even in Australasia.'[16]

It is against this background that we can challenge the claims of Sundararajan and others to innovation driven by technological advances. Drawing on accounts of outwork and dockyard labour in the nineteenth century, we will revisit each of the supposedly novel features of work in the on-demand economy to show how, despite all technological innovation, the underlying business model is anything but new—be it the breaking down of jobs into small tasks, to be completed by large crowds of workers, the role of powerful intermediaries, or the impact on wages and working conditions.

From Workforce to Taskforce

Let's begin with changes to work itself. Two elements are said to be of particular importance to gig-economy innovation here: first, the reversal of 'progressively greater specialisation' observed 'for most of the past 500 years, and specifically since the advent of industrialization' through the re-emergence of a low-skilled workforce; and second, a new 'immediacy of labor supply' in 'task economies', in which jobs are broken down into small constituent units and 'labor efficiency is increased not by extracting more out of existing employees but rather by foraging for lost moments of time that can be turned into work'.[17]

Both the existence of a large pool of workers competing for routine and often low-skilled jobs and the resulting competition for work have a long historical pedigree. The transformation of a workforce into a taskforce, in other words, was one of the hallmarks of nineteenth-century labour markets in the UK and beyond.

At their most fundamental, both the gig economy and nineteenth-century outwork break jobs down into small units that can easily be standardized, controlled, and measured. This seems straightforward in the case of low-skilled work, be it the delivery of goods from a vessel to a warehouse or a taxi ride from A to B. Highly skilled jobs, which require years of training and apprenticeship, intuitively appear to be relatively safe from this commodification: think of a tailor's craft, or a lawyer's judgement in preparing commercial contracts. Even those jobs, however, are threatened by the rise of 'task economies', because complicated workflows can be broken down into individual steps.[18] Each task is then parcelled out to an ever-increasing number of outworkers—in much the same way as Amazon's Mechanical Turk (MTurk) today permits scientists to break down a large data sample into small snippets, each of which can then be posted online so that individual Turkers can spot particular features or patterns.

The consequences of this commodification of work were far-reaching, as a contemporary report noted:

> It is a remarkable thing how these people are unacquainted with the whole of the trade...the labour is so much divided that the worker in the coat trade does not know the actual price given for the whole garment.[19]

And it wasn't only a lack of knowledge that resulted from the rise of the task economy; the costs of production were also increasingly shifted to individual workers.

Consider down-time as an example. When a Lyft driver is idly roaming the streets of Manhattan waiting for her next ride or an Upwork designer is scrolling through lists of task descriptions, neither is paid. The exact same was true for outworkers, who sometimes had to invest significant amounts of unpaid time in between tasks. Stories abound of outworkers in London travelling at their own expense across different boroughs to collect and deliver work:

> [I]t was not uncommon in many parts of London...to pass outworkers and children of outworkers on the streets and trams, hurrying to employers with baskets of sewn uppers, stacks of finished trousers, or bundles of newly buttonholed shirts.[20]

The same was true for capital expenditure. Outworkers were usually expected to provide all of the tools and incidental materials required to complete each task at their own expense in precisely the same way as Lyft drivers are responsible for their own cars and petrol, and Turkers work from their own personal computers. Most also had to provide their own premises, which, more often than not, meant a bedroom or living room at home.[21]

Drawing in the Crowds

A task economy doesn't require much by way of job-specific skills or training: most of us can engage in low-skilled work. The pool of potential labourers available for any one job was thus increased dramatically, as previous segmentation within the labour market broke down: a tailor could now assemble shoe soles and a bootmaker, sew on shirt buttons. The commodification of work meant that employers no longer had to stop there, either: *everyone* could be drawn into the labour market to ensure a steady supply of potential workers—and undercut existing structures.

Recruitment was targeted at groups traditionally excluded from urban labour markets: former servicemen, women, children, and rural workers— some London middlemen reportedly hiring from as far afield as Ireland, Eastern Europe, and Asia. Workers were not infrequently lured in by misleading descriptions of working conditions and earnings. In 1849–50, *Morning Chronicles* metropolitan correspondent Henry Mayhew reported an increasing incidence of 'kidnapped men', usually rural or Irish workers, who had been enticed by the sweaters ('or, more commonly,...sweaters' wives') with false promises of high income and were subsequently detained with promises of future earning opportunities—or threats of lawsuits against them and their families.[22]

The gig economy has similarly unlocked new ways of tapping into otherwise idle time through increased labour-market participation for traditionally excluded groups, from immigrant workers to homebound carers. This can make a real and markedly positive difference. Uber, for example, has long been hailed for its creation of new job opportunities in France's *banlieues*, the Paris suburbs suffering from persistent structural unemployment.[23]

Task-app Fiverr similarly boast stories such as 'How a mom found professional success while staying at home with a newborn' on its company blog.[24] That 'mom', Jenn Apgar, first came across the platform whilst browsing a magazine at her doctor's office: 'Inside was a tip for teenagers to make extra money over the summer; selling on Fiverr.com.' She was intrigued—and soon signed up herself: 'I've got nothing but time.'[25]

At first glance, what's not to like about this aspect of on-demand work? Governments across the world have long struggled to develop policies that increase labour-market participation and bring traditionally excluded groups into work. Gig-economy innovation, it appears, has finally delivered a tool towards that elusive goal.

History, however, warns us of a darker consequence: as entrepreneurs pass the risks of fluctuating demand on to the crowd, individuals are pitched into aggressive competition against one another for every scrap of work. Mayhew graphically describes the daily scramble:

> He who wishes to behold one of the most extraordinary and least-known scenes of this metropolis, should wend his way to the London Dock gates [at] half-past seven in the morning. There he will see congregated within the principal entrance masses of men of all grades, looks, and kinds...[26]

The crowds have arrived to compete for work—and as supply outstrips demand, competition amongst them is fierce. Matters might not get quite as physical in today's on-demand economy, as apps remotely assign tasks— but the underlying structural problem is precisely the same:

> Then begins the scuffling and scrambling, and stretching forth of countless hands high in the air, to catch the eye of him whose voice may give them work...some men jump upon the backs of others...all are shouting... [I]t is a sight to sadden the most callous, to see *thousands* of men struggling for only one day's hire, the scuffle being made the fiercer by the knowledge that hundreds out of the number there assembled must be left to idle the day out in want.[27]

Any work obtained in the docks was physically demanding and pay was low. And yet, Mayhew reports with some astonishment, most of those turned away in the morning would continue to hang around in the dockyard: 'Rain or sunshine, there can always be found plenty ready to catch the stray shilling or eight pennyworth of work.'[28]

The Intermediaries

Task economies feature a particular logistical challenge: how can work be assigned and labourers monitored without permanent structures? Today, this is easily achieved through fast communication technology, algorithmic monitoring, geolocation, and a host of other innovative tech solutions. Technology is said to be at the heart of blurring the lines between hierarchy and market.[29]

Once more, however, there is little that's genuinely innovative here. Whether in outwork and dock labour or the gig economy today, the creation of hybrid structures between fully open markets and internal company hierarchies requires a set of powerful intermediaries to identify consumers and workers, to allocate tasks and pay, and to ensure quality control:

> Large-scale outwork...enhanced the importance of the third 'partner'—the agent, putter-out, 'fogger', 'bagman'...To the distant urban merchant, he became a manager-figure who took care of labour recruitment and discipline, who did a good deal of the basic book-keeping, and who solved many of the irksome problems of transport and carriage: to the worker, he was the essential source of employment and income...Ubiquitous but elusive...the ambiguous role of the middleman demonstrates the flexibility of the outwork system.[30]

Technology apart, the essential features of most intermediaries' business model were identical to platforms' and apps' digital work intermediation in the on-demand economy: they acted as a broker for a set of tasks, exercised tight control, and took a cut of workers' earnings.

As regards intermediation, first, the middlemen were usually in charge of worker selection and termination, as well as setting prices. Mayhew's description of how work was allocated in the London ports was mirrored in harbours all over the world. In the port of New York, for example, the hiring practice was known as the 'shapeup': a flag was run up on the pier where a vessel was about to land and a large mass of workers quickly assembled in a semi-circle at the docks, waiting to be selected by hiring agents.[31] The dockyard foremen would then come out to distribute the days' work— sometimes literally on a 'first come, first served' basis, or on the basis of bribes and personal preferences, but more frequently through experience of workers' reputation for regular attendance, hard work, and obedience.[32]

The middlemen were also in charge of keeping the workforce constantly tailored to business demands: no one was necessarily guaranteed a full day's work. In the port of Liverpool, for example, men were often laid off at noon if most of the work had been done. This, the middlemen suggested, ensured their particular efficiency, 'because men had to produce or they would be dispensed with'.[33] It also meant that workers had to accept any price offered to them by the middlemen—which frequently varied as different middlemen tried to undercut each other in turn.[34]

The middlemen were also responsible to their superiors for quality control—which proved challenging, as they could not be in multiple locations at once. As a result, control had to be exercised indirectly, through economic pressures: at its simplest, through fines levied for inadequate workmanship.[35] More important, however, was the constant threat of not assigning future work. Job insecurity thus became a powerful tool of control at all times, as a report of the English Poor Law Commission found in 1909: 'The [middlemen] responsible for getting the work done are afraid to give [workers] security of tenure for fear it should weaken their power over them.'[36]

Having a large workforce available was not only to the employer's (and middleman's) advantage during times of peak demand; it arguably played an even more important role in times of unemployment or underemployment. Workers were 'encouraged under penalty of being ignored in the future to sit about all day near the office ready to be called, [yet] paid nothing except for the time they [were] actually occupied'.[37] As Beatrice and Sidney Webb noted as early as 1897, the profits of this system are one-sided: a large group of workers standing at the ready had no cost for the entrepreneur *and* it meant that each individual worker was 'more completely at this mercy... Where this "reserve army" exists... the employer can practically dictate terms.'[38]

A final, historically much-criticized, element of the intermediaries' business model was the cut, or 'stoppage', which they took from workers' wages. Framework knitters in the outwork industry, for example, were often charged rent for their frames, as well as a host of ancillary charges—from payment for wear and tear, materials, and tools, to fines for (allegedly) bad workmanship.[39] This made income unpredictable—and meant that a significant amount of working time (up to two days per week) had to be spent paying various costs before any income was earned. In the ports, similar problems arose, albeit less openly: 'The abuse might have been mere acceptance of an occasional drink or a cigar, or it might have gone as far as an actual "cut" from the earnings of the longshoremen.'[40]

Struggling in the Crowd

It is not only the gig-economy business model for which we can find ample historical precedent; some of the working conditions explored in the last chapter closely mirror those of outworkers in the nineteenth century. Indeed, an already familiar narrative was not unheard of: outwork was sometimes promoted as entrepreneurship, promising workers that they 'had a better opportunity of doing a little business on [their] own account and hence a better prospect of becoming their own employer',[41] thus avoiding the long hours and 'inferior moral habits' of factory work.[42] The reality was rather different, marked by low and unpredictable wages, highly irregular work patterns, and a complete lack of bargaining power.

Competition between workers had a dramatic impact on wages: '[T]he greater the subdivision of labour the lower the grade of the work, and the lower the grade of the work the lower the earnings of the worker.'[43] It was 'almost common knowledge' that:

[T]he earnings of a large number of people—mainly women who work in their homes—are so small as alone to be insufficient to sustain life in the most meagre manner, even when they toil hard for extremely long hours.[44]

The availability of a large workforce furthermore led to highly irregular work for individuals. Given employers' lack of investment in machinery or training, and the safe knowledge that additional workers could be found whenever demand spiked, they and their middlemen had 'little incentive to keep...workers in times of depressed trade or in the off season'.[45] As none other than Friedrich Engels noted of Lancashire cotton weavers in the 1840s: 'These poor wretches are the first to be thrown out of work when there is a commercial crisis, and last to be taken on again when trade improves.'[46]

Women and children were particularly exploited:

Accustomed to low pay, anxious for work which they could combine with domestic duties, lacking other ways of adding their mite to total family income, and generally incapable of collective self-defence, [they] became the key element in that persistent cheapness of labour which was one of the prime requirements of a viable outwork system.[47]

In response to increasing public concerns, middlemen and other defenders of the outwork systems insisted that much of this work was to be character-ized as additional income—and thus not subject to the same standards as 'regular' work. 'With a labour force so heavily made up of women, children, and old people', it was easy to characterize the work 'as something essentially part-time, casual, and supplementary to income coming into the household from other quarters'.[48]

This tale of 'additional income' that shouldn't therefore attract the same legal scrutiny continues to crop up across the centuries. It was used again to great effect in the early years of the temporary work industry, for example to justify low and insecure wages for a mostly female workforce. Professor Erin Hatton of Buffalo University, New York, has documented these arguments, citing one of the industry's earliest US players:

> Instead of seeking to replace 'breadwinning' union jobs with low-wage temp work, temp agencies went the culturally safer route: selling temp work for housewives who were (allegedly) only working for pin money. As a Kelly executive told *The New York Times* in 1958, 'The typical Kelly Girl...doesn't want full-time work, but she's bored with strictly keeping house. Or maybe she just wants to take a job until she pays for a davenport or a new fur coat.'[49]

None of this is to suggest, of course, that in centuries past—as today—there wasn't the same heterogeneity of motivations behind casual work, including instances of work to earn genuine supplementary income and while away the idle hours, or even those who genuinely preferred to stay away from work directly supervised by a boss, or from the often coarse environments of the factory and workshop floor.[50]

The overall impact of the 'hybrid' market–hierarchy model on labour markets is nonetheless clear: a large, low-skilled taskforce fundamentally undermines workers' individual and collective bargaining power. The isolation and irregularity of the work made it hard to organize collectively,[51] leaving some employers to brag in 1876 that the system allowed them to enjoy:

> a kind of auction reversed. On a Monday morning the contractors or mastermen assemble at the master's warehouse...he calls them in one by one, and test them as to what prices they will make certain chains for, invariably giving the work to those who offer the lowest tender.[52]

History Repeats Itself

Even a brief historical survey can thus debunk the on-demand economy's claim to innovation, at least as far as work is concerned. Employers have long experimented with each of the elements we saw, from putting out work through powerful intermediaries to recourse to casual labour. Digital innovation has joined together the individual pieces, potentiating many of the underlying problems—without fundamentally changing the nature of work.

At the same time as showing up a series of historical parallels, however, it is important not to fall for claims that on-demand economy work is simply a return to historical labour markets or a new 'digital feudalism'.[53] Powerful intermediaries coordinating large, generalist workforces and the resulting low-wage, precarious work once more became a feature of modern labour markets long before the rise of the Internet. As a recent report by the United Nations' International Labour Organization (ILO) notes:

> [O]ver the past few decades, in both industrialized and developing countries, there has been a marked shift away from standard employment to non-standard employment... [including] temporary employment, part-time work, temporary agency work and other multi-party employment relationships, disguised employment relationships and dependent self-employment.[54]

The innovation myth is just as, if not even more, important in creating a sense of discontinuity and difference between the on-demand economy and outsourcing, temp agencies, zero-hours contracts, and similar work arrangements, which have come under increasing criticism and scrutiny in the United States, Europe, and beyond.

The literature on the fragmentation of work in modern labour markets and its negative impact on the economy is vast. One of the most accessible accounts is *The Fissured Workplace* by Professor David Weil of Boston College, who also served as Head of the Wage and Hour Division in the US Department of Labor under the Obama Administration. Weil describes how financial performance pressures led more and more firms to outsource peripheral activities—from cleaning and security, to accounting and human resources. This breaking down of work into smaller tasks spread across multiple layers of agencies and outsourcing companies, 'right into employment activities that could be regarded as core to the company', from 'housekeeping in hotels' to 'basic legal research in law firms'.[55]

As each intermediary takes its cuts, problems begin to appear:

> [T]he further down one goes, the slimmer are the remaining profit margins. At the same time,... labor typically represents a larger share of overall costs... That means the incentives to cut corners rise—leading to violations of... fundamental labor standards.[56]

As we saw in Chapter 2, portraying gig work as a radically new and innovative economic model to bring entrepreneurship to all is a crucial step in shielding the gig economy against increasing regulatory efforts to hold both intermediaries and those ultimately benefiting from the work responsible for compliance with tax laws and employment regulation.

Not everyone agrees with these futurist claims. Valerio De Stefano, formerly of the ILO and now Professor of Labour Law at KU Leuven, has long maintained that on-demand work shares many dimensions with other non-standard forms of work. The gig economy, he suggests, is simply a combination and rebranding of long-established models.[57] Indeed, there is a clear continuum between existing forms of non-standard work and the on-demand economy, with modern technology replacing earlier modes of control.[58] As Matthew Finkin has demonstrated, this sense of continuity extends right back to outworkers and dock labourers in centuries past: '[T]here was nothing transitional in the deployment of home-based contract work in the twentieth century and beyond... The cold calculus of capitalism has remained ever constant.'[59]

In the nineteenth century, two factors were often blamed for sub-standard working practices: first, 'the "unhealthy craze" for cheap goods'; and second, decentralized production, 'aggravated by uneven... regulation and ineffective labor organization'.[60] Finkin builds a more sophisticated account of the 'economic logic' of fragmented labour markets. He takes us to the earlier work of two Cambridge economists, Jill Rubery and Frank Wilkinson, who identified a number of factors that drove the fragmentation or segmentation of work. These include capital investment and technology (can the work be fragmented?), work organization (can control over workers be exercised remotely, for example through financial incentives?), market flexibility (how fluctuating is demand for the product or services?), and incentives to avoid collective action and legal regulation.[61]

Technology has, in many ways, made each of these factors more salient. Because of the Internet, jobs can now be fragmented into tasks that are no longer geographically bound—competition between workers in different London boroughs has become global. Technological innovation, from geolocators to screenshot software, lets platforms exercise a hitherto unknown degree of control over each worker, at all times and with next to no cost. Algorithms dispatching workers to meet demand for a service in a particular area can be trained to anticipate, rather than merely respond to, consumers' needs.

The underlying structures, however, have remained surprisingly constant. Innovation, at least as far as work is concerned, is mostly a myth. Much like

Andersen's swindlers exploiting the emperor's weakness for the latest fashion, platforms have latched onto our deserved support for innovation—and
sold us a century-old model as a radically new way of organizing work.

Why Should We Care?

The claim to innovation thus rings as hollow as did that to entrepreneurship
in the previous chapter. Upwork CEO Stephane Kasriel agrees quite happily: 'The freelance economy is really just going back to what [work] was
prior to a set of constraints that no longer exist.'[62]

But even if it is true that there is nothing novel about platform-based
work, why should we care? Marketing departments all over the world constantly sell products and services as brand new and novel, after all, and we
happily acquiesce even though we know their claims not to be true.

The on-demand economy's claims to innovation, however, might be
more pernicious than that. They are not merely corporate doublespeak,
designed to keep customers and workers interested, and regulators at bay.
The language of innovation conceals two deeper, and much more problematic, aspects of the gig economy's business model: first, a radical shift of business risk away from platforms and onto individual workers; and second, the
real danger that this recourse to cheap labour incentivizes the very opposite
of genuine innovation.

Shifting Risk—without the Rewards

Sharing-economy doublespeak of new (hybrid) marketplaces and an economic revolution suggests a world in which traditional employers and large
corporations lose their entrenched power over consumers and workers.
Gig-economy platforms step in to restore choice and control for each of us.
To some extent, that is true, of course: independent contractors enjoy much
more flexibility than regular employees, who have traded some of their
freedoms for stability and protection, and consumers might gain access to
hitherto unaffordable products and services.

But be careful what you wish for: markets allocate not only the spoils of
economic activity; they also distribute risk. This is the fundamental trade-off
which every entrepreneur has had to grapple with for centuries: in return
for taking on the risk that her service or product might not find any buyers

and that investments of time, money, and resources may thus be lost, she gets the chance to enjoy a near-unlimited upside when things work out.

When we look beyond the 'innovative' arrangements discussed in this chapter—from historic outwork and more recent temp agencies, to gig-economy platforms—and focus once more on the underlying economics, a different problem emerges. The gig-economy business model is designed to divorce the fundamental entrepreneurial trade-off inherent in fully functioning markets: cost and risk are shifted onto workers, whilst the intermediaries get to enjoy the profits. The workers' supposed freedom means little more than the 'liberty to go home with nothing', as British statesman Ernest Bevin put it.[63] Put differently, fragmentation, intermediaries, and other 'hybrid' arrangements serve as an arbitrage tool that allows platform operators to extract profits without having to put much of their own capital at risk.

Seen thus, the rise of the gig economy is but the latest instalment in a more fundamental economic trend—described by Jacob Hacker of Yale University as the 'Great Risk Shift'.[64] Professor Hacker argues that an increasing emphasis on 'personal responsibility' in an 'ownership society' of free choice has cloaked the brutal erosion of security and protection for workers.[65]

Platforms' emphasis on entrepreneurship and innovation plays perfectly into this narrative. When a driver complained to Uber's then CEO that recent pricing changes had bankrupted him, Travis Kalanick's response was revealing: 'You know what, some people don't like to take responsibility for their own shit. They blame everything in their life on somebody else. Good luck.'[66]

We will return to the mechanisms behind this risk shift, as well as its broader implications for us all, in the final chapter. For now, suffice it to say that the language of innovation serves as convenient cover against challenges of this kind: when things don't work out as promised, workers are at fault for not taking responsibility for their business, and critical commentators can easily be painted as hopeless Luddites.

Innovation Incentives

Innovation, finally, also plays a huge role in developing our economies at large—but something funny is going on. As Christine Lagarde, President of the International Monetary Fund (IMF), highlighted in the spring of 2017, economists and politicians are increasingly concerned about the ways in which innovation is reshaping markets—or rather, the ways in which it is not:

> Let me start with the good news. Technological innovation seems to be moving faster than ever, from driverless cars to robot lawyers to 3D-printed human organs. The not-so-good news is that we can see technological breakthroughs everywhere except in the productivity statistics.[67]

Much ink has been spilt by commentators trying to grapple with this paradox. One school of thought, for example, argues that recent decades haven't seen anywhere as much innovation as we commonly think. We might have adapted and reconfigured existing technologies, the argument goes, but we have failed to achieve any genuine breakthroughs.[68] Another idea is that falling investment in capital is to blame: *Financial Times* journalist Martin Sandbu has highlighted economic reports that consistently show weak capital investment in advanced countries over the past decade.[69] Put differently, even if new technologies exist, employers do not seem to be adopting them.

This productivity puzzle has been the subject of extensive and heated debate.[70] It is by no means confined to the gig economy alone—yet there is an important link that we should not ignore. In certain respects, work in the on-demand economy isn't merely the digital reincarnation of old employment models; it might be the very opposite of what we have been promised.

There are two closely related challenges to the on-demand economy's claim to have fostered a revolutionary culture of innovation: first, that many of its supposedly innovative elements are, in fact, simply aimed at entrenching existing operators against future competitors; and second, that platforms' business models might in fact disincentivize the investment in research, development, and working conditions that spurs innovation.

Pernicious Innovation

Take rating algorithms as an example. The dramatic increase in information available about workers and consumers alike has gone a long way towards alleviating the information asymmetries that traditionally plague two-sided markets. The case for productivity-enhancing innovation looks straightforward: extensive information allows for easy matching of supply and demand, increasing service provision for platform users, and income for workers. Upon closer inspection, however, not all is quite as it seems. As we saw in the previous chapter, two of the most important functions of algorithmic ratings are to control workers—and to lock them into a particular app's 'eco-system': ratings need to be built up over time and cannot be taken from one platform to another.

The gig economy is a network business. Platforms will thrive only if they can quickly corner, and then hold on to, a significant share of the market—both in terms of workers and consumers. Given the lack of infrastructure or similar capital-heavy investments, this isn't easy: any competitor seeking to challenge Amazon would first need to establish a formidable network of warehouses, aeroplanes, and delivery centres. Entry into most gig-economy markets, on the other hand, remains a tempting and easy possibility for other providers, requiring not much more than an app (and the willingness to lose some venture capital money whilst gaining market share) to take on even the largest of operators.

Algorithmic ratings (as well as other lock-in mechanisms we explored earlier) are an attempt to make life difficult for competitors, who cannot gain the necessary momentum when workers and, to a lesser extent, consumers would have to start from scratch after defecting. Other examples of questionable innovation with similar goals are increasingly discussed in the media. In the spring of 2017, a series of reports alleged that Uber had modified its software to nefarious ends: a tool by the name of 'Greyball' was designed to defeat law enforcement operatives by rejecting their ride requests; another project, with the cheerful name 'Hell', is alleged to have targeted rival operator Lyft by 'building up profiles of individuals and figuring out who was driving for Uber and Lyft. Uber then prioritized sending rides to drivers who used both apps, hoping to persuade drivers to abandon Lyft.'[71]

The company has suggested that Greyball was used as an important tool in combatting fraudulent ride requests and investigations into Hell are ongoing. If the underlying allegations turn out to be true, however, both programs would be further instances of pernicious innovation. Rather than improving overall welfare by increasing market efficiency, this is innovation with a much more dubious goal: the construction of barriers against new entrants in a platform's market.[72]

Hampering Innovation

Perhaps even more worrying is the fact that the gig economy doesn't just fail to live up to its innovative claims; it might be hardwired to achieve the exact opposite. The three elements of the business model on which we have focused in this chapter—recourse to cheap labour, the fragmentation of workers into an individualized taskforce, and an insistence on operating outside the scope of employment law—have all been identified as factors that disincentivize and discourage innovation.

Let us look at cheap labour first. The basic idea here is that as long as humans can complete a certain task at very low cost, there is no need to invest in the development, installation, and maintenance of innovative machines. As *The Economist's* Ryan Avent puts it:

[T]he abundance of labour, and downward pressure on wages, reduces the incentive to invest in new labour-saving technologies. Until pressed, firms don't overhaul and automate their warehouse or swap out some wait staff for touchscreens. So productivity within sectors grows more slowly than it otherwise might. There are dynamic effects as well: when you don't deploy new technologies because labour is cheap, you don't get all the tweaks and knock-on innovations and accumulation of intangible capital that contributes to still more productivity growth down the road.[73]

There is plenty of evidence to support this claim, both historically and more recently. A UK parliamentary committee investigating the outwork industry in 1855, for example, expressed its concern that historical precursors of the on-demand business model had a detrimental impact not only on workers, but also on the economy at large. Entrepreneurs' reliance on cheap out-workers was said to 'perpetuate the use of imperfect and inferior machinery…and thus prevent the adoption of improved and more economical models of production'.[74]

Two immediate counter-arguments come to mind. First, what about Uber's well-publicized efforts to develop self-driving cars? And, in any event, might a delay in innovative automation not be to the benefit of workers whose jobs would otherwise be threatened by a rise of the robots? As regards the first of these arguments, Uber's emphasis on autonomous vehicles has increasingly been questioned by experts from both technological and economic perspectives: the company's efforts seem to lag significantly behind competitors' technological advances.[75] In any event, why would Uber replace its current asset-light model, under which drivers bear the full cost of providing cars, petrol, and their time, with a massive investment in an expensive fleet of self-driving cars? As the *Financial Times* concludes, 'this sort of thinking fundamentally mis-assesses the economics of the car market'.[76]

Workers, too, suffer from the gig economy's threat to innovation. Economic historian Duncan Bythell makes a strong case that innovation, and even automation, do not necessarily harm workers' interests; any such direct conflict between workers and technological innovation, he suggests, is observed only 'in the final death throes' of an industry.[77] In the meantime, innovation tends to make work easier, safer, and, most importantly, more productive: '[T]he problems of intermittent employment and low wages which faced the typical outworker arose, not because machines were replacing him, but because they were *not* replacing him.'[78] The central element of the on-demand business model, instant recourse to a large pool of cheap workers, is thus not only not innovative; it may well help to sustain firms, services, and products that fail to invest in genuine innovation and compete on cheap labour cost instead.

Employment structures in the gig economy, finally, might also hamper innovation in less direct ways. There is a growing body of evidence that suggests that employment law norms that guarantee workers stability in a single job—including, notably, unfair dismissal protection—'enhance employees' innovative efforts and encourage firms to invest in risky, but potentially mould-breaking, projects'.[79] Creativity and innovation furthermore seem to be linked to working in coordinated group environments: 'Organisation and institutions enable creativity and bring us the prosperity that goes with it. Disorganisation and fragmentation don't. [A] fragmented and disconnected workforce will find it much more difficult to harness their group genius.'[80] In other words, the gig economy's highly individualistic, task-by-task model of independent contracting fundamentally undermines many of the proven (if serendipitous) conditions required for innovation to prosper.

The Unicorn's New Clothes

In her challenge to the 'taxi unicorn's new clothes', *Financial Times* journalist Izabella Kaminska argues that the 'only innovation in hand is the fact that the old "You rang m'Lord" system has been transformed into a "you hailed me on your app m'Lord" one instead'.[81] This claim might be a bit too stark—but only just. Our exploration of the innovation myth in this chapter has shown that none of the fundamental elements lying behind the gig economy's business model are novel: large taskforces, powerful intermediaries, and the resulting poor working conditions have been around for centuries—and had already reappeared in modern-day labour markets long before the advent of the Internet.

Much of the technology behind gig-economy apps and platforms is genuinely novel, of course—but as far as labour is concerned, we must make sure not to fall for the industry's claims to have reinvented work as we know it. Just as the emperor eventually got called out, so we should focus on the reality of the situation—and ensure that the truly innovative elements of the gig economy can flourish, whilst its more pernicious aspects are kept at bay.

How can this be achieved? Let's turn to the next chapter to explore the options.

5

Disrupting the Disruptors

Major policy problems, Machiavelli warns, are easy to diagnose, but difficult to cure.[1] Is this true of regulating the gig-economy? Not necessarily—as long as the cure is driven by a proper diagnosis. Gig-economy work provides entrepreneurship opportunities for some and tightly controlled precarious work for others; the technology is innovative and exciting, whereas the underlying business model has long historic roots.

Any proposed solution must be sensitive to the heterogeneity of on-demand work. We need to maintain flexibility in the labour market—whilst tackling the insecurity to which it can give rise. The key lies in recognizing that on-demand gigs, tasks, rides, and 'Human Intelligence Tasks' (HITs) are work—and should be regulated as such. Employment law facilitates a crucial trade-off: workers agree to be subordinated to their employer's orders, in return for which they enjoy a series of protective standards. Technology apart, the control exerted by on-demand platforms is not fundamentally different from the control exerted by other businesses—nor should the baseline protection for workers be.

How would this work in practice? There are two steps to consider in turn. First, we need to tackle what employment lawyers refer to as the 'personal scope question': are gig workers employees or independent contractors? And who is their employer? At least as regards this first question, there is little need to reinvent the wheel: we have to focus on levelling the playing field by ensuring that all actors play by the same, long-established rules. We will explore how different legal systems across the world have learned to respond to employers' attempts to mischaracterize work as independent entrepreneurship—and how responsibility can be assigned accurately even if traditional lines between employees and customers have become blurred. The implications of these comparatively straightforward steps are wide-reaching: employment law protects workers against many of the difficulties

Humans as a Service: The Promise and Perils of Work in the Gig Economy. First Edition. Jeremias Prassl. © Jeremias Prassl 2018. Published 2018 by Oxford University Press.

we encountered thus far—without threatening the flexibility that made gig work so attractive in the first place.

Once within the scope of employment law, workers enjoy access to a basic floor of rights, from minimum wage entitlements to discrimination protection. When it comes to the specific rules of employment law, however, there might be a need to develop existing standards in response to specific elements of gig work—from portable ratings and higher wage levels for flexible hours, to renewed social partner involvement. In concluding, finally, we need to tackle the myth that employment rights and flexibility are inherently incompatible—one of the most misleading, and harmful, misperceptions holding back equal protection for all workers.

Regulating Work in the On-Demand Economy

Legal regulation of the labour market hinges on a fundamental trade-off between security and control: employees working under a contract of employment are protected; independent contractors are not. Most countries' employment laws have adopted a version of this 'binary divide' model to structure their employment law, tax, and social security systems. If in doubt, workers and their employers can turn to the courts. Through a series of legal tests (often including elements such as control, subordination, and/or economic dependence), experienced labour judges determine who is a worker—and who is a genuine entrepreneur.

Nobel-Prize-winning economist Ronald Coase was amongst the first to develop a theory underpinning this approach. He famously identified the bilateral contract of employment as the secret behind entrepreneurs' tight control over their workforce: in return for regular wages, employees submitted themselves to the employer's orders.[2] Employment and social security law responded to ensure that these powers were exercised responsibly. A contract of employment gives employers the right to control everything from how work is done and paid to hiring and firing employees. It also regulates how these powers might be exercised. An employer cannot force its workers to labour all day long, must pay them a minimum wage, and may not illegally discriminate against particular groups in hiring and firing.[3] Employers deduct payroll taxes, and contribute to pensions and insurance payments; independent contractors can set higher rates in return for being responsible for their own tax returns and long-term economic security.

Some strands of gig-economy doublespeak suggest that platform compliance with employment law is impossible. How can ancient red tape keep up
with cutting-edge innovation? Isn't regulation designed for the workforce
of the twentieth century ill-suited to today's entrepreneurial world? And
isn't it all far too complicated, in any event? Well, not quite. As we will see
over the coming pages, legal systems around the world continue to evolve
and have increasingly addressed many of the challenges arising from work
in the on-demand economy. Regulating platforms' business models might
require some careful updating or development of specific rules, but the
overall message is clear: genuine entrepreneurship is beyond the scope of
employment law; tightly controlled, dependent work is not.

To the extent that 'disruption' has become Silicon Valley shorthand for
breaking the law, it's time to 'disrupt the disruptors' and ensure that the
sharing economy competes on a level playing field. In the first instance,
what's required is as simple as bringing on-demand work back into the
scope of existing employment law rules: ignoring platforms' attempts to
misclassify workers as entrepreneurs and accurately ascribing employer
responsibility.

Playing by the Rules

Tight control over a workforce is crucial in delivering a consistent and carefully curated customer experience—but it also triggers a series of worker-
protective regulations. At the sharp edge of the gig economy, on-demand
platforms try to have the best of both worlds, combining the full control
and financial rewards enjoyed by employers with the lack of responsibility
inherent in contracting with independent service providers. This is why
many on-demand economy operators insist that they are mere intermediaries rather than employers and that they should therefore not be regulated
like their competitors.

Ignoring employment law is a crucial factor in this equation—and an
especially problematic one when workers are left with little room for genuine entrepreneurship. The mechanisms used by platforms to shirk their
responsibilities are surprisingly simple and far from innovative. This 'disruption' is based on contractual misclassification (the simple assertion in platforms' terms and conditions that workers are independent contractors rather
than employees) and the increasing use of multilateral work arrangements,

through the sharing and blurring of employer control between customers and platforms.[4]

Let's look at how the law can grapple with each of these challenges.

(Mis)Classifying Workers

When we explored the reality of work in the on-demand economy, we saw how tight control over all aspects of service delivery was the very hallmark of algorithmic management. Employment classification should be quite straightforward, then: when a platform controls everything from which tasks are assigned to how they are performed and paid, surely we can't speak of 'grey areas'? Creating such uncertainty, however, is the very point of the carefully drafted and strongly worded terms and conditions that prospective workers and customers must accept before joining a platform:

> TASKERS ARE INDEPENDENT CONTRACTORS AND NOT EMPLOYEES OF COMPANY. COMPANY DOES NOT PERFORM TASKS AND DOES NOT EMPLOY INDIVIDUALS TO PERFORM TASKS. USERS HEREBY ACKNOWLEDGE THAT COMPANY DOES NOT SUPERVISE, DIRECT, CONTROL OR MONITOR A TASKER'S WORK AND IS NOT RESPONSIBLE FOR THE WORK PERFORMED OR THE TASKS IN ANY MANNER.[5]

Everyone has agreed, it appears, that on-demand platforms are but neutral intermediaries, facilitating transactions between independent contractors and their clients—and thus most certainly outside the scope of local, national, or international employment regulation.

But the law isn't quite so easily defeated. Contractual parties' freedom to 'agree' any particular label for their legal relationship is strictly controlled by the law. As the UK's highest court famously held in 1985:

> The consequences in law of [an] agreement, once concluded, can only be determined by consideration of the effect of the agreement...The manufacture of a five-pronged implement for manual digging results in a fork even if the manufacturer, unfamiliar with the English language, insists that he intended to make and has made a spade.[6]

In response to employers' attempts to misclassify their workforce as independent entrepreneurs, legal systems all over the world have developed a variety of doctrines to ensure that the law classifies a relationship according to the realities of the situation, rather than the labels that one party might have foisted on the other.

In the UK, this is often referred to as 'sham self-employment'. In the leading decision of *Autoclenz*, the Supreme Court recognized the economic reality behind the conclusion of most workers' contracts and emphasized that a set of written terms dictated by the employer could not be conclusive proof of entrepreneurship beyond the scope of employment law:

> [T]he relative bargaining power of the parties must be taken into account in deciding whether the terms of any written agreement in truth represent what was agreed and the true agreement will often have to be gleaned from all the circumstances of the case, of which the written agreement is only a part.[7]

Different versions of this 'purposive approach', whereby courts take into account a contract's broader context in determining the legal effects of parties' agreements, have been adopted all over the world. In the United States, for example, parcel delivery and logistics provider FedEx has long been embroiled in misclassification lawsuits. Like many on-demand platforms today, the company exercised tight control over its delivery drivers, whilst maintaining that they were independent contractors. In one of the leading decisions against FedEx, the Court of Appeals for the Ninth Circuit in 2014 upheld drivers' claims that they were employees under Californian law, with Circuit Judge Trott adding the following observations:

> Abraham Lincoln reportedly asked, 'If you call a dog's tail a leg, how many legs does a dog have?' His answer was, 'Four. Calling a dog's tail a leg does not make it a leg.' Justice Cardozo made the same point... counselling us, when called upon to characterize a written enactment, to look to the 'underlying reality rather than the form or label'... Bottom line? Labeling the drivers 'independent contractors' in FedEx's Operating Agreement does not conclusively make them so.[8]

Most European jurisdictions know similar approaches as the 'principle of the primacy of facts', which has also been recognized in Recommendation 198 of the International Labour Organization (ILO) on the employment relationship, under which worker classification:

> should be guided primarily by the facts relating to the performance of work and the remuneration of the worker, notwithstanding how the relationship is characterized in any contrary arrangement, contractual or otherwise, that may have been agreed between the parties.[9]

Professor Miriam Cherry of St. Louis University is a leading expert on worker misclassification in the on-demand economy. Whilst doublespeak of entrepreneurship and innovation initially held back workers' claims, she argues, litigation is now in full swing, with platforms offering everything from handyperson services to food and groceries delivery faced with worker classification suits.[10] California's courts have been at the centre of many disputes, both because of the state's relatively generous employment and labour laws, and because most Silicon Valley companies are legally domiciled there, but litigation is increasingly global: in the summer of 2016, a Central London employment tribunal heard a first set of claims brought by Uber drivers alleging that they had been employed as the platform's workers.[11]

In the ensuing decision, which caught the attention of journalists and regulators across the world, Judge Snelson was unequivocal in finding that claimant drivers were workers, rather than independent contractors. The language in *Aslam, Farrar v Uber* was unusually pointed:

> [87] …we have been struck by the remarkable lengths to which Uber has gone in order to compel agreement with its (perhaps we should say its lawyers') description of itself and with its analysis of the legal relationships between the two companies, the drivers and the passengers. Any organisation (a) running an enterprise at the heart of which is the function of carrying people in motor cars… (c) requiring drivers and passengers to agree, *as a matter of contract*, that it does not provide transportation services… and (d) resorting in its documentation to fictions, twisted language and even brand new terminology, merits, we think, a degree of scepticism. Reflecting on [the platform's] general case, and on the grimly loyal evidence of [Uber manager] Ms Bertram in particular, we cannot help being reminded of Queen Gertrude's most celebrated line:
>
> The lady doth protest too much, methinks.
>
> [88] Second, our scepticism is not diminished when we are reminded of the many things said and written in the in the name of Uber in unguarded moments, which reinforce the [drivers'] simple case that the organisation runs a transportation business and employs the drivers to that end…
>
> [89] Third, it is, in our opinion, unreal to deny that Uber is in business as a supplier of transportation services. Simple common sense argues to the contrary.[12]

Uber appealed against this decision—without success. In dismissing the appeal, Her Honour Judge Eady QC held that 'the [tribunal] was entitled to conclude there was a contract between [Uber] and the drivers whereby the drivers personally undertook work for [Uber] as part of its business of providing transportation services to passengers'.[13]

The employment tribunal's clear words have triggered a wave of similar cases in the UK—with judges consistently willing to look behind contractual terminology. In deciding a cycle courier's claim for unpaid holiday pay, for example, Employment Judge J. L. Wade rejected the notion that the claimant gig worker could freely choose when and how to work—not least because 'she feared not being given more work if she refused'. This, the tribunal concluded, was 'inequality of bargaining power at work'.[14]

It is not only workers who are suing over employee misclassification; when employers fail to pay National Insurance and pension contributions, taxpayers lose out too. In France, social security administrators URSSAF and ACOSS are pursuing Uber for several million euros' worth of contributions that the platform has refused to pay, insisting that its drivers are but independent contractors.[15] Regulators around the world are starting to take notice. A set of interpretative guidelines under the US Fair Labor Standards Act of 1938, released by the US Department of Labor's Wage and Hour Division in the spring of 2015, was widely seen as a warning against independent contractor misclassification in the on-demand industry.[16] The UK government's Department for Business, Energy and Industrial Strategy (BEIS) explicitly reminded delivery service Deliveroo that its drivers had to be paid the legal national minimum wage unless a court or tribunal ruled to the contrary.[17]

At the time of writing, many cases are still pending or are working their way through the appellate system. The results of claims resolved thus far vary dramatically, for several reasons: courts and administrative bodies across the world have developed competing tests and interpretations (US law even applies different tests depending on the statute under which a claim is brought), and constant changes in on-demand platforms' business models—and litigation strategies—makes it difficult to paint a consistent picture.

Cherry's detailed analysis suggests that whilst some platforms have successfully defended their cases, others decided to reclassify their workers as employees.[18] Uber's initial stance in the United States—which saw it lose a high-profile (but ultimately non-binding) wage and expenses claim brought by driver Barbara Ann Berwick before California's Labor Commission in 2015[19]—was considerably softened in April 2016, when the platform offered to settle, for a lump-sum payment of US$84 million and several changes to its business model, two class-action lawsuits brought by its 'Driver-Partners' seeking employee status in California and Massachusetts.[20] The Californian deal was short-lived, however, with US District Judge Edward Chen rejecting it over concerns that the settlement terms short-changed drivers, as well as letting the platform off the hook for substantial penalties in excess of $1 billion.[21]

The underlying message is clear: however strongly worded, platforms' denial of employment status will not automatically succeed in classifying workers as independent contractors. Depending on each jurisdiction and claim, the ordinary tests of employment and labour law apply to work in the on-demand economy—and, given platforms' tight control over many aspects of service delivery, they will often point towards employment status, leaving only the genuine entrepreneurs outside the scope of protective laws and regulations.[22]

The facts of individual cases will continue to create difficult borderline questions. In that regard, however, work in the on-demand economy is little different from the circumstances faced by claimants in many other workplaces today. Factual complexity is an irrelevant argument in suggesting that on-demand platforms should not be subject to employment laws: resolving difficult claims is precisely what first-instance labour judges and administrators have long been trained to do.

Identifying the Employer

One further complication might arise in some legal systems, however. Employment law has long been premised on contracts between a worker and a single employer—so-called bilateral relationships. We have already seen how platforms' business models can go a long way towards blurring the lines between customers, employers, and workers. Whilst some operators exercise full control over all aspects of their product, others grant their users considerable leeway. Taskers can set a price for their services on TaskRabbit, Requesters on Amazon's Mechanical Turk (MTurk) specify the working time available for each task, and clients on platforms such as Upwork often stipulate precisely how work is to be completed. In other words, both workers and customers may sometimes exercise control over areas that were traditionally in the employer's prerogative.

Business models within which control is dispersed amongst platforms and users can cause problems for legal systems, including, notably, the English one, which thinks of employment as a bilateral relationship—that is, as a contract between two individual parties: the worker and her employer.[23] How can we recognize the fact that there might be more than one employer? The solution lies in adopting a more flexible approach to determining who should be responsible.

A Functional Concept of the Employer

In legal terms, we can analyse employers' powers—and the law's control over them—as 'functions of the employer'. In a previous book exploring *The Concept of the Employer*, I identified five such functions, from hiring and firing to control over work and pay.[24]

Traditionally, a single party—Coase's famous 'entrepreneur-coordinator'— would have exercised all of these functions, controlling her employees through the contract of employment. Independent entrepreneurs, on the other hand, set their own wages, determine which work they are willing to do, and take the risks (and reap the rewards) of engaging in market competition.

This is no longer the case in the on-demand economy's world of apps, portable technology, and algorithms. Platforms don't require a contract of employment to coordinate and control their workforce, and different parties can use their digital infrastructure to exercise specific employer functions. The resulting variations are potentially endless: some platforms, including most ride-share apps, exercise nearly all of the five traditional employer functions; others parcel out certain functions to consumers (think of MTurk customers specifying what is to be done, for how long, and at which price); operators following the TaskRabbit business model might share key functions, such as determining wages, directly with individual workers.

Once the exercise of employer functions is shared or parcelled out amongst different parties, the search for a responsible employer becomes a bit more difficult: we can no longer identify a single party as *the* employer. One potential response is to conclude that the worker is therefore not an employee and must be an independent entrepreneur instead. But that can't be right: work controlled by several parties via a platform is far from genuine entrepreneurship. Another solution could be to decree that the platform is responsible as the employer under all circumstances, as is the case with labour-outsourcing agencies in some jurisdictions. In certain scenarios, however, that might again be problematic, albeit for opposite reasons: what if a genuinely independent tradesperson wants to advertise her services through TaskRabbit?

Instead of falling into the trap of this 'all or nothing' approach, we should be more flexible and adopt a functional concept of the employer. Those responsible for controlling one or more employer functions will have to comply with the regulations applicable to their actions: if a platform sets its workers' pay rates, for example, it must ensure compliance with minimum wage conditions. We no longer limit our enquiry to the elusive search for 'the' contract of employment, asking a much more intuitive question instead: *who is in charge?*

The Easy Cases: Platforms as Employers; Genuine Entrepreneurs

In many cases, the buck stops with the platform—either because it exercises full control or because it shares control (and thus responsibility) with its customers. Even if the latter become involved in setting prices or specifying tasks, ongoing control and remuneration remain in the platform's hands. It is only in situations of genuine entrepreneurship—when a worker determines which work to accept, sets her own rates, and has full control over how and by whom a task is completed—that she herself exercises employer functions, thus falling outside the scope of employment law's protection. Together with Professor Martin Risak of Vienna University, I have illustrated how this would work in practice by looking at a relatively straightforward example: the payment of workers' expenses and wages.[25]

At one end of the spectrum, a single platform exercises all employer functions. As a result, things are relatively straightforward: if the platform sets rates of pay, for example by determining fare levels or offering a fixed price per task, it clearly exercises full control over the worker's opportunity to make a profit—or loss—and must therefore ensure that workers earn the minimum wage after all costs of providing the service have been taken into account.

Ride-sharing platforms are a good example of on-demand business models where the functional concept of the employer clearly identifies the platform as the employer. The company's algorithms determine which driver is offered a particular ride, control drivers' routes and acceptance rate, set the fare and thus the wages, and 'terminate' drivers according to internal policies. Courts should be happy to ignore any 'sham' contract terms asserting entrepreneurship and pin responsibility for everything, from minimum wages and expenses to health insurance, on the platform instead. They should also be unimpressed by arguments that drivers have full control over their earnings—that is, that they could simply drive longer hours to make more money. During the Obama Administration, the US Department of Labor made it clear that:

> [In] considering whether a worker has an opportunity for profit or loss, the focus is whether the worker's managerial skill can affect his or her profit and

loss... the worker's ability to work more hours and the amount of work available from the employer have nothing to do with the worker's managerial skill and do little to separate employees from independent contractors—both of whom are likely to earn more if they work more and if there is more work available.[26]

Because the platform clearly exercises a relevant employer function—determining pay—it will be responsible for the concomitant legal obligations, ranging from providing the worker's tools and ensuring compliance with minimum wage standards, to deducting payroll taxes and paying social security contributions.

The functional concept of the employer also works at the other end of the spectrum, where genuinely independent entrepreneurs use on-demand economy platforms to advertise their services. Imagine a local plumber who turns to a platform to find new customers in addition to her regular trade. She is able to set her own wage levels depending on what she judges the difficulty of the task to be. The platform will take a cut of her earnings as a fee for the introduction, but the plumber is able to operate freely as an entrepreneur, determining how work is to be completed, for example by hiring assistants, and is thus in control of her own profits and losses. A platform that simply offers workers the opportunity to bid for work in this way does not exercise employer functions; it is the entrepreneur herself who does so—and therefore it is she who will have to comply with tax and insurance provisions.

The Harder Cases: Multiple Employers

As variations amongst on-demand business models can be endless, many cases will fall in between the two extremes just described, especially when the exercise of one or more employer functions is shared between consumers and the platform. How can the functional concept of the employer deal with these situations? We have already encountered a number of platforms that share their wage-setting functions with individual customers. On Amazon's MTurk, for example, Requesters indicate both the time and remuneration available for any one HIT. The platform provides the infrastructure communicating these offers to potential workers, charging a predetermined commission and paying Turkers in regular intervals. Does that mean that *both* the platform and the Requester should be seen as exercising employer functions, and thus be burdened with a legal duty to ensure minimum wage payments? In principle: yes.

In practice, this approach could lead to some difficulties. How can an individual know where a worker is based or what the minimum wage is? And how can we avoid both platforms and customers turning around and blaming each other when an underpaid worker tries to assert her rights? As regards minimum wage compliance, platforms easily have all relevant information to hand: remember how Requesters on MTurk can already specify the geographic origin of eligible Turkers. Under a functional concept of the employer, the platform would be responsible for setting up its systems such that, for any given amount of working time, no value below the relevant proportion of an hourly minimum wage can be entered by the customer.[27] The answer to potential enforcement problems similarly lies in recognizing that platforms often stay involved in the exercise of employer functions, their contractual assertions to the contrary notwithstanding. Under a legal doctrine known as 'joint and several liability', a worker could therefore choose to pursue either of her employers for the full sum owed, leaving the joint defendants to settle proportions between themselves afterwards.

We will return to the broader economic and political case for ascribing employer responsibilities to platforms, users, and even workers themselves in the next chapter. For the time being, it is important to note that many elements of the functional approach to identifying the employer, or even multiple employers, have already been recognized in jurisdictions across the world. The French courts, for example, have held 'co-employers' responsible when several parties become closely involved in the exercise of key employer functions,[28] and the Court of Justice of the European Union has similarly indicated its willingness to interpret the concept of the employer widely.[29] In the United States, joint employer status has been part of the US Fair Labor Standards Act since 1938;[30] in the UK, the common law has similarly evolved to hold multiple employers responsible.[31]

The question of employer responsibility in the on-demand economy is thus considerably less intractable than it first appears. Mere contractual assertions are never enough to deny workers' proper classification as employees; a functional concept of the employer can accurately and consistently assign responsibility even where multiple parties exercise traditional employer functions. By including on-demand workers who cannot enjoy the benefits of genuine entrepreneurship within the scope of employment law, a level playing field is restored: platforms that provide services, rather than mere introductions between independent contractors and their clients, are recognized as employers, with a duty to pay and protect their on-demand workforce accordingly.

A Floor of Rights

Classifying on-demand platforms as employers and gig workers as their employees will not solve all of the problems identified in previous chapters—but it's a crucial first step towards tackling some of the most pressing problems facing gig workers, from dangerously long hours to discriminatory algorithms.[32]

Consider the unpredictability of work and income as an example. We saw how platforms continuously vary all elements of work and pay, from task assignment and prices to commission structures, which makes it very difficult for workers to plan ahead. Many employment law systems limit employers' powers to vary contracts and balance managerial prerogatives against worker interests by means of 'employment protection rules and rules regarding information, consultation and co-determination when they aim for such variation'.[33] Or think back to Amazon's practice of paying some MTurk workers in gift vouchers redeemable only on the Amazon website itself. Similar models have existed since medieval times—but so-called Truck arrangements were soon recognized as extremely abusive and declared illegal in England as early as 1464.[34]

From a financial perspective, the primary consequence of employee classification would be the right to minimum wages and expense reimbursement.[35] Many platforms have long resisted compliance with local minimum wage legislation, arguing that even if workers were classified as employees, it would be impossible to determine how much time any one individual has actually spent on their particular service. A driver might have both Uber's and Lyft's apps open on different phones when looking for rides, for example, or may attempt to complete micro-tasks on her phone for Fiverr whilst waiting to pick up passengers in an airport queue.

Measuring Working Time

Harris and Krueger are strong proponents of the view that gig-economy working time is hard to measure.[36] Indeed, 'the immeasurability of work hours' sits at the heart of their arguments that existing employment laws cannot apply to on-demand workers:

> The boundary between work and nonwork for independent workers is largely indeterminable. A worker in the online gig economy could be primarily engaged in personal tasks while one or more intermediaries' apps are turned on. It would stretch any reasonable definition of 'work' to count this time as work hours... Conceptually, workers' hours spent waiting to be engaged in work cannot be apportioned to a specific employer.[37]

Upon closer inspection, however, their argument quickly unravels.

As regards 'immeasurability', first, it was none other than Professor Krueger who co-authored Uber's 2015 paper on its driver labour market—including detailed statistics of working hours and average hourly wages. The notion that a worker can use multiple platforms simultaneously might sometimes rest on similarly shaky ground: remember the sanctions that some operators' algorithms have in store for those who don't accept particular tasks (such as short-term deactivation when too many work requests have been declined) or those who share their work across too many platforms (because frequency and quality of work form part of rating algorithms).

What about time spent looking for work? Drivers need to roam the streets in search of the next ride, just as Turkers scroll through Amazon's forums looking for available HITs, often spending as much time between individual tasks as they do when working for a particular client—without being paid. At the very least, as long as sanctions for non-acceptance of work are in place, this time should be counted as working time for minimum wage purposes. On-demand workers aren't furthering a platform's economic interests only when they are actually at work; it's the very availability of a large workforce that underpins the business model.[38]

The literary-minded employment judge in *Aslam v Uber* turned to Milton to express his agreement:

> [100] . . . It is essential to Uber's business to maintain a pool of drivers who can be called upon as and when a demand for driving services arises. The excellent 'rider experience' which the organisation seeks to provide depends on its ability to get drivers to passengers as quickly as possible. To be confident of satisfying demand, it must, at any one time, have some of its drivers carrying passengers and some waiting for the opportunity to do so. Being available is an essential part of the service which the driver renders to Uber. If we may borrow another well-known literary line:
> They also serve who only stand and wait.[39]

Employment law can thus counteract many of the problems that face on-demand workers. Employee classification is important for individual workers trapped in the gig economy—but it is no panacea. Even where platforms are found to be employers of their workforce, work remains highly fragmented and precarious. As I have argued in previous work co-authored with Rachel Hunter, basic employment law standards will overcome some of the worst problems faced by gig-economy workers—but, in the longer run, we still have to tackle the underlying labour-market problems, from low income to unpredictable shifts, that result from a lack of guaranteed work.[40]

Rebalancing the Scales

What makes the difference between flexibility and insecurity? Inequality of bargaining power. Gig workers are a vastly heterogeneous group. Flexible work ranges from the barrister taking her clients' cases to different courts each day to the zero-hours agency worker employed to clean lawyers' offices. In all but the very top end of this spectrum (and certain pockets, such as students looking for flexible work to fit around their courses), a lack of promised future work will often lead to a high degree of insecurity—and thus even more subordination, with workers required to tend to their employers' every (algorithmic) whim for fear of losing the next shift. It's a problem facing more and more workers—whether employed through digital platforms or labouring under 'traditional' zero-hours contracts.

Employment law tackles this problem by rebalancing the scales. The basic labour standards that apply to all workers, however, are just that: basic standards. Developed in a world of long-term stable employment, they are not always suited to tackling the problems of intermittent work.[41] In the longer run, more than merely restoring the scope of employment law is needed to ensure that crowdwork delivers on its promises of empowering individual workers; we need to think about specific standards to address unequal bargaining power in a world of flexible work.

This should not be mistaken as a call for new, free-standing approaches along the lines criticized earlier; rather, my proposals focus on developing existing standards and are explicitly designed to operate in conjunction with them. Employment law in the European Union provides us with an interesting blueprint: over the years, the Union has responded to labour-market problems faced by workers in particular situations (such as employer insolvency) or those employed in emerging work arrangements (such as temporary agency staff, or those employed under fixed-term and part-time contracts) by developing standards aimed at the particular problems faced by each group. The resulting directives, however, were not designed to replace national laws, but to provide additional protection to complement existing domestic norms.

In this spirit, three aspects of platform-based work should be at the fore-
front of policymakers' concerns: the unpredictability of on-demand working hours; the lock-in effect resulting from rating algorithms' central role in
allocating work and determining pay; and the difficulties facing workers
trying to organize the collective representation of their interests.

The freedom to choose when to work is one of the major attractions of
the on-demand economy. In reality, however, we have seen how flexibility
can quickly become one-sided as platforms shift the risk of troughs in customer demand directly onto workers. The result is insecurity, rather than
flexibility. Bill Clinton's Secretary of Labor and now Berkeley Professor
Robert Reich has called this the 'share the scraps economy':

> Defenders of on-demand work emphasize its flexibility. Workers can put in
> whatever time they want, work around their schedules, fill in the downtime in
> their calendars...But how many of them would be happier with a good-
> paying job offering regular hours? An opportunity to make some extra bucks
> can seem mighty attractive in an economy whose median wage has been
> stagnant for thirty years and almost all of whose economic gains have been
> going to the top.[42]

That, however, 'doesn't make the opportunity a great deal. It only shows
how bad a deal most working people have otherwise been getting.'[43]

One solution to the problem of unpredictability, adopted by several jurisdictions in Continental Europe, is for legislation to stipulate minimum
working-hour guarantees: employers have to promise (and pay for) a set
number of hours each week or month. Another variant of this approach
gives workers a right to ask for a set number of hours after a certain period.
It's a promising start—although with some fairly significant drawbacks. The
promised number of hours can be very low, for example, and rights to
request fixed usual hours tend to come with a qualifying period—which
can easily be evaded by terminating an employment relationship just before
that threshold is crossed.

A Surge Price for Gig Work

A market-based mechanism might be more promising in shaping employers' incentives (rather than creating avoidance incentives). Employment
standards must maintain worker freedom, whilst also ensuring that flexibility is a genuine choice. To achieve this, the risk of unpredictable future work
should be priced into pay rates through a system of tiered minimum wages:

think of it as a 'surge price for gig work'. If an employer does not guarantee her workers certain shifts with reasonable advance notice, she will be obliged to pay a percentage multiple of prevailing wage rates.

Australia has long had a version of such a 'casual loading' system in place.[44] As the government's Fair Work Ombudsman explains: 'Casual employees are entitled to a higher hourly pay rate than equivalent full-time or part-time employees.'[45] A sample provision relating to casual loading in the retail industry reads: 'A casual employee will be paid both the hourly rate payable to a full-time employee and an additional 25% of the ordinary hourly rate for a full-time employee.'[46]

There is some debate in the Australian literature over why casual loading was first introduced. Some argue that the key purpose was 'to compensate [casuals] for the absence of the various benefits they must forgo', whereas others suggest a broader range of motivations—from providing 'a wage supplement for the worker, who by virtue of the nature of the industry and work was unable to be a "breadwinner" ',[47] to acting 'as a deterrent lest that normative conception of the employee was challenged'.[48] In reality, of course, these purposes will often overlap. Indeed, if set at the right level, a flexible work uplift would ideally serve *both* to reward the employee for taking on riskier work *and* to guide employers away from guaranteed hours unless there is a genuine business case for flexible work.

A 'surge price for gig work' can also be explained in economic theory. Part-time workers receive fewer fringe benefits and need to be compensated for that loss; they are also more productive per hour worked than permanent staff, given their deployment during peak demand periods.[49] The proposed uplift would therefore reflect some of the cost-saving advantages that flexible work brings for employers, who can shift the risk of idle demand onto workers and compensate workers for the corresponding insecurity. In the longer run, it would also motivate employers to move workers into stable employment relationships, because predictable core demand can be met more cheaply by a permanent workforce.[50]

The implementation of a differentiated (minimum) wage for casual work would raise a number of technical challenges, of course: how do we define 'casual work'? How can a worker know her entitlements in a world of proliferating differential rates? And wouldn't it be unfair, or even discriminatory, to regular workers who engage in the same work to be paid less? In the larger scheme of employment law, however, none of these challenges would be impossible to overcome.

Casual work, for example, could be set up as a residual category for anyone not guaranteed fixed hours from month to month, to ensure wide coverage. In terms of multiple wage rates, remember that loading wouldn't apply only to minimum wage jobs (although it is in the lowest-paid sectors that the initial impact would likely be most noticeable). In any event, many countries already use multiple (minimum) wage rates, for example when differentiating by age band. A statutory duty on employers to print hours worked and basic wage rates on each payslip would also make it easy for employees to work out whether they have been paid appropriately. And, as regards equal treatment, it's important to think of income as more than just a spot price for work: how much someone gets paid is often as important as their having a sense of stability—of knowing that they will also be able to pay the bills next month. Casual workers don't have this income stability—which justifies a higher hourly income. Risk, in every sense, would be priced back into the wage rate.[51]

At the same time, it is important to highlight other, more serious, concerns that would have to be carefully thought through before adopting differential wage rates for casual work. As economists never fail to remind us, incentives matter: we would need to get the rate right so that employers are deterred from excessive reliance on casual work, whilst at the same time making sure that regular employees aren't tempted into (sham) reclassification as casuals.

Even more importantly, a differential wage rate must not become a way of buying out workers' rights. Labour is not a commodity—and nor are the basic entitlements of statutory employment law. A 2012 attempt by the UK government to introduce a mechanism for employers to buy out workers' unfair dismissal rights with shares provides a stark warning. As Lord Pannick noted in that context, employment rights must not become tradable, precisely 'because the inequality of bargaining power between employee and employer means that freedom of contract is quite insufficient to protect the employee'.[52] None other than Lord King, Margaret Thatcher's employment minister, agreed that any such commodification could easily be exploited 'by some very dubious employers indeed'.[53]

The Australian experience in particular shows the dangers of casual loading becoming a way of 'cashing out' of workers' rights. Critics have highlighted the risk that:

> [T]he concept of a casual loading recognises that fundamental rights can be traded off... This in turn reinforces the concept of a commodification of casual

labour. The loading itself is not sufficient to fully compensate for what is lost. Casual workers are unlikely to progress up classification scales regardless of experience. They are less likely to have access to training and career or skills development etc.[54]

If a higher wage rate for flexible work is to meet its underlying goal of rebalancing bargaining power between employees and employers, it needs to be designed as a compensatory mechanism for the insecurity flexibility can bring—not as a buyout mechanism for basic rights.

Tiered wage payments, finally, aren't the only incentive-driven mechanism to consider. Another approach, perhaps less dramatic but still fundamentally incentives-based, can be found in a recent Polish change to minimum wage laws. As of 2016, nearly all work is subject to the same minimum wage (or price)—regardless of whether the underlying contract is structured as an employment relationship or a contract for services.[55] This move, designed to deter employers' 'abuse' of independent contracting, levels the playing field between different legal categories.

Indeed, it is important in this context to remember that casualization is often driven not only by differential wage levels, but also by financial incentives created by the tax and social security system. This is neither the time nor place to delve into arcane public finance design questions—but, as I have argued elsewhere with my Oxford colleagues Professors Abi Adams and Judith Freedman, any solution focused on employment law alone will not gain traction unless the underlying fiscal incentives are equally balanced.[56]

Portable Ratings

Another problem that current labour standards fail to address is the power that algorithmic ratings have in tying workers into particular platforms: as long as better work and higher pay are limited to workers with high ratings, individuals will struggle to diversify their crowdwork portfolio and end up tied into one company's ecosystem. A system of portable ratings would empower workers to follow up grievances and negotiate for better conditions—or to move on to a different platform. European Union law provides some interesting pointers as to how such a system could be designed.

In a famous 1988 paper, Andrei Shleifer and Lawrence Summers argued that hostile takeovers expropriated value by breaching trust between incumbent management and their employees—that is, by allowing the new shareholders to seize workers' long-term investment in firm-specific human capital on the implicit understanding that they would receive a fair share in the resulting economic gains.[57] Platforms' rating mechanisms expose workers to similar dangers: carefully built-up scores can become worthless overnight when a platform's business model changes or the user is deactivated. Responding to concerns about worker expropriation in corporate takeovers, in the 1970s the European Union introduced legislation to protect workers during corporate takeovers. Terms and conditions of employment were not to be changed as a result of a business transfer, and workers' acquired rights transferred from one employer to the next.[58]

In terms of system design, a helpful starting point here could be the General Data Protection Regulation (GDPR), adopted in April 2016. One of the key consumer-protective elements of the legislation is so-called data portability: an individual's 'right to receive the personal data concerning him or her...in a structured, commonly used and machine-readable format', including 'the right to transmit those data to another controller without hindrance from the controller to which the personal data have been provided'.[59] Portable ratings could operate along similar lines, with standardized metrics accounting for experience, customer friendliness, and work quality, and additional task-specific ratings taking account of task-specific skills, from driving to assembling flatpack furniture. Different start-ups would soon spring up to offer 'rating passports' and similar products to workers and platforms alike.

Once ratings have become each individual worker's personal property, freely transferable across different platforms, work in the on-demand economy will become much closer to platforms' promises of self-determination, independence, and free choice. When conditions change or negotiations with a platform for better terms break down, crowdworkers would be free to move on to another provider. The resulting mobility across different platforms would not only benefit the workers themselves: Cambridge's Simon Deakin has pointed towards overwhelming empirical evidence that employees' freedom to compete is strongly linked to innovation and economic development.[60]

Once more, it is important to consider potential drawbacks as well as advantages. What, for example, if a worker seeks to start with a clean slate on a new platform: could she decide to abandon her previous rating? We would also need to create a mechanism to ensure that workers can have recourse against ratings that they perceive to be unfair—as well as to ensure that robust mechanisms are in place to tackle problems of algorithmic discrimination, lest portable ratings entrench it. It is also important to highlight, finally, that because portable ratings improve workers' bargaining power vis-à-vis different platforms, any resulting entrepreneurial freedom to move across different operators may end up pointing in the direction of independent contractor status.

Collective Action

The third, and perhaps most salient, development required to rebalance the scales is effective collective representation of worker interests. At the moment, unionization efforts can be logistically difficult and legally fraught: the fragmentation of work in the gig economy is a serious challenge for union organizers. Gone are the regular shifts before and after which groups of workers would congregate to voice their grievances, the geographic proximity of workers with shared interests, and the sense of being a united workforce. Whereas London cab drivers can congregate in their famous little tea huts dotted across the streets of the city, ride-sharing drivers are forced to hide out in increasingly rare open parking lots, often struggling to find a place to rest or even to go to the toilet.[61]

Most countries grant union organizers paid time off for their work and protect them against employer reprisals, as employers and legislators recognize the value of having a clear voice to represent workers' concerns. On-demand economy workers, however, must attempt to organize colleagues using their own time and resources, and can easily be deactivated from their platform in retaliation.[62] Even when they are successful, on-demand unions might fall foul of anti-trust or competition law: groups of genuinely independent entrepreneurs are not generally allowed to come together and use their dominant position to set prices and negotiate conditions.[63]

Local initiatives have already begun to overcome some of these obstacles, with new unions such as the Independent Workers Union of Great Britain (IWGB) actively engaged in organizing gig-economy workers.[64] Given that gig-economy workers heavily rely on their smartphones and computers, organizing is increasingly taking place over the Internet and communication apps. The results are sometimes reasonably akin to historical union actions: when Deliveroo drivers wanted to protest against the radical changes in guaranteed pay we saw in Chapter 3, for example, they relied on social media, including Facebook and WhatsApp, to rally their colleagues and organize protests outside the company's London headquarters.

Political activism has also led to localized legal protection. In Australia, a concerted campaign by Unions New South Wales (UNSW) led to a detailed agreement with gig-economy platform Airtasker, including above-minimum-wage pay rates and recourse to independent dispute resolution mechanisms.[65] In December 2015, Seattle City Council unanimously enacted an ordinance granting the city's drivers 'a voice on the job and the opportunity to negotiate for improved working conditions at their companies'.[66] As Council Member Mike O'Brien explained:

> We've heard from Seattle drivers making sub-minimum wage, and companies like Uber have turned a deaf ear to their concerns. This bill was only intro-duced out of necessity after witnessing how little power drivers themselves had in working for a living wage.[67]

In 2016, the French Labour Code (*Code du Travail*) was similarly modified to ensure the protection of basic collective labour rights vis-à-vis gig-economy platforms.[68]

Other efforts have led to ingenious solutions for problems faced by workers on particular platforms. When Lilly Irani and Six Silberman realized that workers on Amazon's MTurk had no easy way of providing feed-back about dishonest and abusive customers, they developed feedback software to be installed in workers' browsers. TurkOpticon, as the plugin is called, allows Turkers to rate Requesters on factors from accuracy of task description to promptness of payment, thus warning future users off unre-liable clients.[69]

Traditional trade unions should also do much more to embrace technol-ogy. Germany's IG Metall, for example, has been closely involved in the creation of FairCrowdWork, a website that allows workers to rate and com-pare different platforms' working conditions, payment rates, and access to basic legal advice.[70] In future, unions or workers' collectives might even set up their own platforms—or develop international certification standards for gig-economy operators who agree to design their business models in line with appropriate employment standards.[71]

The success of individual initiatives notwithstanding, the overall problems for organized labour remain acute. Once work in the on-demand economy is properly classified as employment, workers will be able to organize them-selves and form trade unions to bargain directly with platforms over their terms and conditions—backed up, if necessary, by the power to mandate negotiations and threaten industrial action.

Rights vs Flexibility?

In making the case for employment protection, there is one final argument we need to tackle: the myth that many gig-economy workers might not actually want employment law rights, because they enjoy the flexibility that independent contracting brings. Employment law, this narrative suggests, is downright harmful to workers' interests, as it will return us to the days of the overbearing bosses and 9-to-5 shifts.

In response to the employment tribunals ruling in favour of London Uber drivers, for example, the company's then regional general manager, Jo Bertram, noted that:

> Tens of thousands of people in London drive with Uber precisely because they want to be self-employed and their own boss. The overwhelming majority of drivers who use the Uber app want to keep the freedom and flexibility of being able to drive when and where they want.[72]

This claim is corroborated by an Uber-commissioned survey of its drivers, in which 76 per cent said that 'flexibility in choosing own hours is more important than holiday pay and guaranteed minimum wage'.[73] Dan Warne, managing director of Deliveroo UK, similarly told a House of Commons enquiry that if the company's delivery drivers:

> were not self-employed, we could not offer them the same degree of flexibility that we do, even working 30 to 40 hours in a week. If we were to make them employees, we would have to restrict that flexibility, which we know that they value. If we were to make them employees, then we are restricted from providing some of the benefits that we would, as a business, like to provide.[74]

A recent study by the Chartered Institute of Personnel and Development (CIPD) reveals how these supposed contradictions weigh on gig workers' attitudes to regulation. On the one hand, more than half of those surveyed agree that 'gig economy firms are exploiting a lack of regulation for immediate growth' and nearly two-thirds think that 'the Government should regulate the gig economy so that all those working in it are entitled to receive a basic level of rights and benefits'.[75] On the other, only 50 per cent agree that '[p]eople working in the gig economy make a decision to sacrifice job security and workers' benefits for greater flexibility and independence'.[76]

Similar results have cropped up in studies across the world. As the CIPD report notes:

> This tension between independence and security was also apparent in a large-scale survey of 3,000 American workers by Penn Schoen Berland, published in January 2016. This showed that US gig economy workers were split about whether they preferred the security and benefits of working for a traditional company (41%) or the independence/flexibility of the on-demand economy (43%).[77]

The assertion that employment law somehow leads to rigid, inflexible work, however, is simply untrue. There may well be a *business case* for shift patterns and predictable working hours—but, legally, there is nothing at all to stop employers from giving workers full employment rights, as well as unlimited flexibility, from flexible shift arrangements to unmeasured working time. Any suggestion that employment rights are inherently incompatible with flexibility is a myth—and a harmful one at that.

Responsibility Restored

Sharing platforms, Vanessa Katz has argued, 'often operate in legal gray areas, and the regulatory vacuum surrounding these services has raised complex legal questions'.[78] This may be true in so far as some traditional regulatory areas, such as transport or local zoning, are concerned—but when it comes to questions of employment law, the issues are clearer than some would have us think.

The argument developed throughout this chapter is central to understanding the sharing economy: whatever labels different platforms might use, work in the gig economy is just that—and must be treated as such by the law. The moment we are ready to see through platforms' contractual attempts to misclassify their employees as independent entrepreneurs and to assign responsibility in line with the exercise of traditional employer functions, many of the most pressing problems resulting from on-demand economy work can be addressed. The inequality of bargaining power inherent in different platforms' business models might require further targeted intervention—but it is important to tread carefully, to watch out for unintended consequences, and to design new mechanisms to operate in line with, and complementary to, existing norms.

Restoring employment law responsibility will bring huge benefits to workers—and is key to ensuring the gig economy's long-term sustainability. Consumers, taxpayers, and even platforms themselves will ultimately benefit from a marketplace in which everybody plays by the rules.

Let's turn to examine these broader perspectives.

6

Levelling the Playing Field

The focus of our discussion so far has been work: we have looked at the centrality of on-demand crowds for the gig-economy business model, explored the competing narratives of entrepreneurship and innovation, and charted solutions to restore gig workers' employment rights. In the final chapter, we take a step back and look beyond the working crowds: what are the implications of the on-demand economy for consumers and markets?

You might think it unlikely that you will spend a lot of time driving for Uber, cleaning for TaskRabbit, or earning a side income by completing 'Human Intelligence Tasks' (HITs) on Amazon's Mechanical Turk (MTurk)— or even use their services. Yet an increasing body of empirical evidence suggests that, both as consumers and as taxpayers, we are all potentially liable for the real cost of on-demand services. This doesn't mean that we should ban the platforms: the gig economy has great potential to make everyone better off. In order to achieve that goal, however, we need to redress structural imbalances and create a level playing field—with employment law at its foundation.

Consume Now . . . Pay Later?

In January 2013, *New Yorker* staff writer Patricia Marx had had enough of the hassles of organizing her next book-club meeting. She decided to out-source the lot—from buying flowers and baking little cakes, to actually reading the book and preparing discussion points—to a host of on-demand platforms, which had enticed her with promises of quick, excellent work, at low prices.

Humans as a Service: The Promise and Perils of Work in the Gig Economy. First Edition.
Jeremias Prassl. © Jeremias Prassl 2018. Published 2018 by Oxford University Press.

She even spent US$98 commissioning the following paragraph to explain the history of outsourcing for her eventual magazine article:

> The 22 Carat genuine outsourcing however happened only with the advent of the Internet. Much like the all powerful, all purveying multitasking cult Hollywood super heroes Superman and He-man, Internet as the omnipresent and omniscient tool of the king as well as the commoner spawned an era of seamless outsourcing from the late 1990s till date.[1]

I'm not quite sure I understand that paragraph—and that's the point: the bargains we make as consumers in the on-demand economy might be nowhere near as good as those we are promised. Low prices and the labour conditions that make them possible come—well, at a price. And it's not only the immediate bargain that may turn out to be less enticing than promised: when things go wrong, platforms will often treat customers no differently from their workers, and refuse to step in and take responsibility.

Unravelling the Bargain

The on-demand promise is crystal-clear: great products and services, delivered to you at market-beating prices. Upon closer inspection, however, this bargain quickly unravels, as problems with the quality of gig services and the actual price charged to consumers become apparent.[2]

Patricia Marx's experience with outsourcing her research is by no means an isolated incident. Media reports and online forums are awash with concerns about the quality of most platform services—and even though some complaints can probably be ignored as spoiled kids' problems ('the chips are usually a bit lukewarm'),[3] the overall tenor is clear: despite platforms' tight control over all elements of their product, the quality of sharing-economy services can lag far behind expectations.

Researchers on Amazon's MTurk, for example, are increasingly struggling with the low quality of survey responses. As a result, more and more questionnaires include specific quality-control questions, such as asking participants 'to show that you are paying attention, please select the third option below', even though that option might be nonsensical. A more sophisticated quality study by researchers at Carnegie Mellon University suggested that nearly 40 per cent of those surveyed did not answer surveys conscientiously. Their results didn't come as a surprise to experienced MTurker spamgirl:

> [S]ure, if you pay $1 the work will get done, but it will be completed by scammers using 'bots' (automated answering systems), people who don't

necessarily understand the instructions (as English is not their strongest language), or those who don't care about the quality of the work they complete.[4]

Concerns are not limited to quibbles about product quality. On occasion, consumers are faced with much more serious problems. Ride-sharing passengers have reported maltreatment because of their sexual orientation and research in the United States has indicated that passengers with African-American-sounding names experience discrimination on transportation platforms. In Australia, former Disability Discrimination Commissioner Graeme Innes saw his ride cancelled when he turned up with his guide dog—and was charged a cancellation penalty fee to boot. When the National Federation of the Blind sued Uber in the United States for illegal discrimination against blind passengers and their guide dogs, the platform blamed its drivers and swiftly settled the claim for nearly a quarter of a million US dollars—without admitting any liability.[5]

Ride services in particular might also expose their customers to physical dangers. The Taxicab, Limousine & Paratransit Association (TLPA)—a US taxi industry lobby group, whose website provides a long list of alleged ride-sharing incidents, including 'deaths, assaults, sexual assaults, kidnappings, felons, imposters, Drive DUI [drink driving] & other'[6]—has repeatedly criticized platforms' vetting procedures (for which passengers are sometimes charged in addition to their fare) as inappropriately lax.

The Real Cost of On-Demand Services

Even the vast majority of consumers whose interaction with on-demand platforms finishes without major incidents, as well as those who see the cheaper price as a worthwhile trade-off for the occasional customer service problem, might not receive what they bargained for. Platforms' conscious styling as affordably priced choices may well turn out to be untrue.

Some platforms initially display a low 'price estimate' in the hope that customers won't notice any subsequent fees and price hikes added during the fully automated payment process. Delivery service Postmates has repeatedly been criticized for this tactic, with some invoices coming in significantly higher than original quotes.[7] Prices will continue to rise. In Chapter 1, we saw how platforms often use vouchers, discounts, and other loss-making pricing tactics to gain market share. This is an unsustainable tactic—and an unnecessary one once a platform has cornered a large section of its market.

Another common tactic is the use of variable rates, such as Uber's surge-pricing model. When a gunman took 18 hostages in downtown Sydney in late 2014, anyone hoping to use an Uber car to flee the area was initially met with the cheerful in-app message that 'Demand is off the charts!'—and charged a minimum fare of AU$100 for the ride to safety. In less extreme situations, algorithms designed to respond to increased demand with higher prices will still hike the cost of on-demand services far beyond advertised levels. And you might not even be told about it: Uber has recently begun to experiment with 'upfront' price quotes instead of surge surcharges, much in the same way as previously touted fare cuts are often discreetly rolled back once media attention has subsided. More worryingly, Keith Chen, Uber's then head of economic research, revealed in an NPR interview that the company could monitor its users' phone battery levels—and that those with low batteries were more willing to accept surge pricing.[8]

Prices might even rise long after a consumer's interaction with an on-demand platform. Under TaskRabbit's terms and conditions, for example:

> [Every c]lient agrees to indemnify TaskRabbit and its affiliates from any and all claims, liabilities and reasonable costs arising from or in connection with...any other relevant third-party claims under any employment-related laws, such as those relating to employment termination, employment discrimination, harassment or retaliation, as well as any claims for overtime pay, sick leave, holiday or vacation pay, retirement benefits, worker's compensation benefits, unemployment benefits or any other employee benefits.[9]

In other words: if it turns out that our taskers are employees after all, we'll come back to you and collect your share of any fine imposed on us—as well as our lawyers' costs! Whether these terms could actually be enforced in practice is questionable, both legally and in terms of the ensuing public relations fallout. The underlying message, however, is clear: on-demand services might come at a dearer price than expected.

Platform Responsibility

If something goes wrong for a customer or even an innocent bystander, platforms are often quick to disavow the responsibilities that every normal business faces. In perhaps the most tragic on-demand-economy accident to date, 4-year-old Sofia Liu was run over and killed by a San Francisco Uber driver in January 2014. In response to a wrongful death suit brought by her parents, Uber noted that the driver was in between rides and that, as a mere online platform, it simply 'allow[ed] riders to connect with, and request transportation services from, a range of independent transportation providers'.[10] After a media storm, the company eventually backed down and settled the claim for an undisclosed amount—but there is no guarantee that future victims will be similarly compensated.

Platforms might even refuse to identify which of their workers caused an accident. When Richard Vaux was run over by a Deliveroo cyclist in London, breaking both his wrists, 'the company refused to accept liability because its riders are self-employed, and would not pass on the rider's details so he could make an insurance claim'.[11] When asked for comment by the *Sunday Times*, Deliveroo insisted that the platform did 'an enormous amount to ensure safety. All couriers are screened and trained. Data-protection laws prevent us from revealing individual couriers' identities.'[12]

Could insurance be the solution? In response to increasing public concerns about safety and liability, more and more platforms are now offering guarantee packages for individual tasks—or requiring workers to buy their own liability insurance. In reality, however, these guarantees can be worth little in practice when things go wrong: many insurance policies are not valid for commercial use; local regulations and requirements vary widely; and the multiplicity of parties involved in an incident can make it extremely difficult to identify those responsible.[13]

Consumers can benefit from the gig economy—or end up paying a much steeper price than promised. Ryan Calo and Alex Rosenblat have highlighted the risks of digital market manipulation: '[S]haring economy firms, which observe in detail the activities of all participants under the scaffolding of an app, have both the means and the incentive to engage in complex techniques of self-dealing.'[14] They rely on several aspects of Uber's business model—including, notably, surge pricing—to suggest that the platform might exploit its superior knowledge to the detriment of passengers and drivers alike: '[A]ccess to information coupled with control of design permits sharing economy firms, such as the subject of our case study [Uber] to manipulate their users.'[15]

Taxing Questions

For both consumers and workers, then, the on-demand bargain can unravel rather quickly: users potentially end up paying a much higher price and receive worse-quality services than promised. But what about everyone else? If you have never worked through an app or platform or enjoyed its services, is there anything to worry about? Yes, there is: we are all potentially on the hook—in a variety of ways. Not only does the gig-economy business model lead to significant tax-income losses; as taxpayers, we might even be left to make up the shortfall and subsidize the industry in myriad ways.

Most multinational corporations are engaged in various 'tax-efficient' schemes to squirrel away their earnings to low-tax jurisdictions. There is nothing novel or different about the gig economy in this regard. At the very least, however, traditional companies tend to have little choice in terms of avoiding basic local taxation wherever they operate: think sales taxes and social security contributions. The gig economy is different. Many platforms' business models open up a number of avenues for tax avoidance—and worse.

The most comprehensive study of gig-economy taxation to date is focused on the US context—but its central conclusions match experiences in other jurisdictions and can easily be writ large. Professors Shu-Yi Oei and Diane Ring argue 'that the application of substantive and doctrinal tax laws to sharing is generally (though not completely) clear and not particularly novel'[16]— a claim well aligned with what we discovered as regards employment law in the previous chapter. More importantly, however, they go on to note that the gig-economy business model presents two inherent compliance and enforcement problems. The first is that platforms 'have displayed the propensity (and distinct capacity)' to engage in 'tax opportunism'[17]—that is, they rely on their supposedly novel business models to exploit any ambiguity in existing rules with a view to minimizing tax obligations. The second arises from the fact that gig-economy earnings are shared by a large number of individual workers (or 'micro-businesses'), meaning that the low amounts and large numbers at stake 'may make compliance challenging for taxpayers and enforcement difficult for [tax officials]'.[18]

A Big VAT Problem

A good illustration of the first of these problems can be found in platforms' compliance with value added or sales taxes, which are levied on goods and services in most jurisdictions. In the UK, for example, transportation services are generally subject to the standard rate of value added tax (VAT) at

20 per cent. Once a business's turnover exceeds a set threshold (£85,000 as of 1 April 2017), it needs to register with the tax authorities, charge its customers the additional 20 per cent tax, and pay that money over to the Exchequer in quarterly arrears.[19]

Despite the company's turnover exceeding the VAT threshold by a significant margin, however, Uber's passengers in the UK are not generally charged the tax. The platform's argument is predictable: as a mere matchmaker, it does not supply transportation services. 'If drivers earn above the VAT threshold,' Uber informed *The Guardian* newspaper, 'then the tax is their responsibility.'[20] The platform, in other words, is a mere intermediary between workers and customers; if complications arise, recourse should be had directly against each individual worker.

Jolyon Maugham QC, a senior tax barrister and campaigner in London, has set out to challenge this account. He argues that Uber, rather than its drivers, provides the 'taxable service' in question and that the company should therefore be responsible for paying VAT. In the spring of 2017, he took an Uber to visit a client—and demanded a VAT receipt, which was not forthcoming.[21] At the time of writing, Maugham has initiated legal proceedings before the UK High Court, with potentially far-reaching implications: if Uber is ordered to produce the receipt, the resulting tax bill would be significant. According to Maugham's own calculations, Uber's tax liability would be £20 million in London alone—for one year, that is. Add in the distinct possibility that regulators might seek to claw back previous years' tax debts and that tax authorities in other countries could soon follow suit, and the sums at stake are daunting.[22]

Employment Taxes and Social Security Contributions

Even bigger amounts crop up in employment-related taxes and contributions. We have already charted platforms' attempts to argue that existing rules are outdated and do not adequately capture their business model. Tax experts Oei and Ring disagree: '[E]ven here, the tax rules are not inadequate. The ambiguity lies in the question of whether the existing regime applies to sharing.'[23] The operating model adopted by most platforms leads to significant tax losses—both directly, through unpaid taxes, and indirectly, through taxpayer-funded subsidies for platform workers.

Let's begin with direct tax losses, driven by the gig economy's insistence that workers be self-employed. This harms the tax base in two ways: first, by exempting platforms from payroll taxes; and second, by hampering the cheapest and most efficient way of collecting tax from individuals. The precise arrangements for payroll taxes vary across jurisdictions, but the basic principles hold true in most industrialized countries: when an employer pays her staff, she needs to pay additional taxes directly to the state, and to deduct ('withhold') a certain percentage of income tax and employment-related insurances. As mere intermediaries for independent contractors, gig-economy platforms argue, they should not be subject to either of these obligations.

This leads to a direct tax loss: by engaging independent contractors, platforms are not responsible for any of the payroll taxes levied on other companies. In many countries, this loss is further compounded by the fact that governments have historically sought to incentivize entrepreneurship through lower rates of social security contributions for the self-employed. Gig-economy work can thus be offered at significantly cheaper prices. The sums at stake are large: according to UK Chancellor Philip Hammond's 2017 Budget speech, '[t]he lower National Insurance paid by the self-employed [alone was] forecast to cost [UK] public finances over £5 billion' per year.[24]

Tax authorities are increasingly challenging platforms' insistence that workers operate as independent contractors. French social security administrators URSSAF brought a claim for nearly €5 million in unpaid contributions during a period of 18 months in 2012–13. The case was dismissed at first instance, primarily for procedural reasons; litigation continues.[25] Other countries might follow suit: soon after a UK employment tribunal's ruling that Uber drivers were workers for the purposes of employment law in the autumn of 2016, calls mounted for Her Majesty's Revenue and Customs (HMRC) to scrutinize the company's approach to National Insurance contributions.[26]

Tax authorities do not only lose out on the employer's share of revenue; devolution of tax responsibility to individual contractors also makes collection cumbersome and patchy. In the United States, independent contractors have to report their earnings on Income Revenue Service (IRS) Form 1099 (hence the name '1099 economy', which sometimes crops up as a synonym for the gig economy). The technical details are confused and confusing,[27] but the upshot is clear: gig-economy workers are struggling to comply with the law and the sums at stake for each individual are so small that enforcement actions are hardly worth the effort.

The result is a significant cost for individual workers and tax losses for states. A recent study by Caroline Bruckner of the American University's Tax Policy Center reports IRS estimates that a tax gap of US$194 billion 'is attributable to the misreporting of individual business income and related self-employment taxes'.[28] Not all of this is due to the on-demand economy, of course—but we should not underestimate its importance as a growing business model. No wonder, then, that US Senator Elizabeth Warren has listed gig-economy taxation as one of the top three priorities for 'strengthening the basic bargain for workers in the modern economy', asserting that 'electronic, automatic, and mandatory withholding of payroll taxes must apply to everyone—gig workers, 1099 workers, and hourly employees'.[29] From a technical perspective, few solutions would be easier to implement. Indeed, in Estonia, Uber has already begun to cooperate with local tax authorities.[30]

In addition to these direct losses, taxpayers are also subsidizing gig-economy platforms indirectly. Traditional employers have a number of legal obligations towards their workers even when they are not economically active. In addition to paying an employee's salary, companies usually have to provide a host of benefits, such as sick pay or parental leave. In the gig economy, these costs are born by the workers themselves—which, in reality, often means that they have to fall back on the welfare state. Insuring a pool of workers is much more efficient, and thus cheaper, than providing for one individual at a time, which makes private health insurance a lot less affordable than employer-provided plans. No wonder, then, that some of the most vocal support for President Obama's healthcare scheme in the United States came from Silicon Valley, with gig-economy work platforms Uber, Lyft, Fiverr, Handy, TaskRabbit, and others all working with the US government to enrol their workers.[31]

These indirect subsidies are not limited to periods out of work. In some jurisdictions, taxpayers might end up subsidizing gig-economy platforms through the social security system even when someone is working full-time. A recent enquiry by the UK Parliament's Work and Pensions Committee, for example, heard that, after working long hours, some Uber drivers were still unable to earn enough to survive in London without recourse to benefits such as housing support.[32]

Levelling the Playing Field

When we add these problems for consumers, workers, and taxpayers to the questionable economics behind many platforms' business models, as discussed in Chapter 1, it's not difficult to see why some argue that we should ban the platforms. To fall for that temptation, however, would be a terrible idea: we would destroy all benefits and innovation, and leave at least some consumers and workers worse off.

Once we look beyond narratives of technological exceptionalism and Luddism, there is a surprisingly straightforward middle way in between banning the gig economy and giving it free unlimited rein. Regulators should focus on the industry's key ingredient—work—and regulate it as such. By treating gig workers as employees and (most) platforms as employers, we can throw out the bathwater—and save the baby.

The promise of employment law in bettering the workers' lot in the gig economy was at the core of the last chapter—but it is by no means limited thus. Once gig-economy workers are treated as employees and platforms as their employers, many of the problems facing consumers, tax authorities, and indeed the market at large are quickly solved.[33]

Consumer Protection

Take consumers as a first example. We saw how the on-demand economy sometimes delivers sub-par services and how, in some (fortunately relatively rare) circumstances, consumers and even bystanders might be harmed outright: think of a collision involving a delivery cyclist or ride-sharing car. The vast majority of platforms respond in these circumstances by denying responsibility: as mere intermediaries, they suggest, there is little they can (or should) do.

Platforms' contractual denial of employer status has an important consequence for their so-called vicarious liability—a legal doctrine that holds employers responsible for wrongs committed by their employees.[34] Detailed rules vary across jurisdictions, but independent contractor status is nearly always the easiest way of wriggling out of responsibility. This will usually leave the injured consumer or bystander without meaningful recourse, as it is unlikely that every on-demand worker will have deep enough pockets or sufficient insurance to settle claims or pay damages. Employers, on the other hand, are responsible for their employees' actions in the course of business: if you are hit and injured by a London bus, the best avenue in most cases will be to proceed directly against the operating company. Once platforms are brought within the scope of employment law, gig-economy customers will enjoy the same protection.

In addition to this direct benefit to consumers, employment law will also provide a host of indirect benefits by improving overall service quality. Consider working time and minimum wage protection (or wage and hours laws, as they are known in some countries) as an example. An independent contractor who has been on the road for most of a day and decides to put in another few hours to pay her expenses will be considerably less alert a driver than one who has enjoyed a series of statutory rest breaks, safe in the knowledge that she is covered by a minimum income threshold.

Tax

The benefits of recognizing platforms as employers would be even starker in the tax context: just about every one of the problems we have identified could be solved by holding intermediaries directly responsible. As regards VAT, first, assertions that individual workers, rather than the platform, are selling a service to the consumer could no longer be sustained, bringing the on-demand economy in line with other businesses.[35] Second, tax authorities would see a large increase in employment-related income—both in the form of employment-income taxation and through social security contributions collected directly from the platforms.

A central collection mechanism would also bring a host of indirect benefits. We saw how losses accrue when each individual worker is responsible for filing her own income taxes, given the multiplication of paperwork and enforcement difficulties. This is why tax law has traditionally devolved collection of employees' income taxes to employers, who can simply withhold the relevant percentage at source and remit it in a single payment to the authorities. Gig-economy taxation in a world of employed workers would be both easier and significantly cheaper. Given the detailed data streams available in the on-demand economy, treating platforms as employers would also become a promising way of bringing large parts of the informal, or 'cash-only', economy back into formalized legality.

As a final benefit, employment status for gig-economy workers would furthermore dramatically reduce indirect state subsidies for the industry—reducing the number of individual workers who have to draw on benefits to supplement their low and unpredictable earnings. Once platforms are employers, they would be obliged to pay all workers a minimum wage, alongside baseline standards such as sick pay, holidays, or parental leave, thus reducing recourse to public funds.

Revisiting the Business Model

Perhaps the most important consequence, however, would be a fundamental change to the gig-economy business model itself. In Chapter 1, we encountered a series of competing explanations of the industry's economics. Some argued that platforms create value by means of faster matching of consumer demand and worker supply, relying on clever algorithms and sophisticated rating systems to grasp business opportunities that would otherwise be wasted. Another school of thought was more critical, suggesting that regulatory arbitrage and negative externalities are at the core of most platforms' valuations.

On a deeper level, the problems we have identified—for workers, consumers, taxpayers, and markets—are all driven by a single, closely related issue. By presenting themselves as mere matchmakers, rather than powerful service providers and digital work intermediaries, platforms can shift much of their business risk and cost onto their stakeholders. Regulatory arbitrage, externalities, and asset misallocation: all skew the playing field in favour of platforms and impose cost on everyone else.

Employment law has a unique potential to level the playing field. If we want platforms to bear the cost of their operations, we have to ensure that they obey the rules like any other business. Given the centrality of a large, on-demand workforce to the gig business model, employment law has a key role to play: it is the prime 'vehicle for channelling and redistributing social and economic risks, through the imposition on employers of obligations of revenue collection, and compensation for interruption to earnings'.[36]

Cambridge Professors Simon Deakin and Frank Wilkinson refer to this as the 'risk function' of employment law: in return for the employer's control over her workers, the risks and cost of economic insecurity are channelled so as to impose obligations on the party with superior resources.[37] Put differently, a properly regulated labour market in which platforms exercising a high degree of control over every aspect of service delivery are held responsible as employers will ensure that gig-economy operators not only reap the benefits of the economic activity, but also have to 'assume responsibility for social and economic risks arising from the employment relationship'.[38]

Viewed thus, the importance of employment law goes beyond regulating the immediate relationship between workers and their employers. As Professor Alain Supiot of the Collège de France explains:

Under the model of the welfare state, the work relationship became the site on which a fundamental trade-off between economic dependence and social protection took place. While it was of course the case that the employee was subjected to the power of another, it was understood that, in return, there was a guarantee of the basic conditions for participation in society.[39]

Deakin and Wilkinson go as far as to characterize the state as an 'implicit third party' in employment relationships.[40] Individual workers are rarely in a good position to hedge against economic risk: investors can easily minimize their exposure to risk by diversifying their bets and splitting their money across different assets; it is rather hard to do the same with jobs. Workers are unable to protect themselves through portfolio diversification because their entire (human capital) stake will usually be concentrated in a single job.[41] Employment law steps into the breach, 'channelling the risks of economic insecurity throughout the workforce as a whole through the social insurance system, and using social security contributions and income taxation to support the public provision of welfare services'.[42]

Some might object, at this point, that employment law is too complicated a mechanism for (risk) redistribution: wouldn't it be easier to let platforms operate freely and then tax their profits to provide workers with state benefits instead? From this perspective, platforms would still be forced to bear the cost of their business activities, but could continue with independent contractor classification. Even if we ignore the practical problems with this approach (remember the difficulties with tax collection chronicled earlier), however, it turns out that employment law appears to be much the most efficient way of ensuring that employers internalize the cost of their business activities.

Harvard University's Larry Summers was amongst the first to explore this question, weighing up direct government provision (tax and redistribute) and mandated employer benefits. His conclusion? Placing responsibility for worker protection, from social security to unfair dismissal law, on employers offered 'substantial efficiency gains to accomplishing social objectives in ways other than government taxation'.[43] Making firms bear these burdens, he noted, was not only the best way of combating externalities, but also afforded workers more choice and was 'likely to involve fewer distortions of economic activity'.[44]

This focus on employment should not be taken as a suggestion that other areas—such as, notably, consumer law and tax law—don't have an important subsidiary role to play in regulating the on-demand economy. Calo and Rosenblat, for example, suggest that consumer protection law's 'long emphasis on information and power asymmetry' might be well suited to tackling many of the challenges facing both consumers and workers in the gig economy,[45] whilst Oei and Ring have developed promising short- and long-term models for tax enforcement.[46] It is furthermore not the role of employment law to stop investors from investing as they see fit: equal competition in which each business bears its cost also ensures that financial markets do not misallocate assets away from genuinely productive and innovative entrepreneurs. The first and fundamental step, however, must be the recognition that where platforms sell work, they should be treated as employers.

Towards a Sustainable Platform Economy

One final objection should be addressed in concluding: who will pay the price of this rebalancing? The answer: first and foremost, the investors and shareholders behind platforms designed and valued on the basis of existing regulatory arbitrage. Restoring platforms' responsibility will undoubtedly cause disruption in the short term: platform employers will have to face the full cost of their activities, from equipment and consumables, to wages and insurance premiums. The price of certain services will rise and some business models might turn out to be unsustainable altogether.

To the extent that avoidance of basic labour standards has been key to many platforms' business models, compliance will affect their profitability—and thus valuations. Investors lured by promises of multibillion-dollar opportunities might see the value of their shares plummet. That said, the negative consequences of proper employment classification are often deliberately overstated. Consider US platform HomeJoy, which ceased operations in 2015, supposedly as result of a worker misclassification suit brought under the US Fair Labor Standards Act of 1938. Professor Miriam Cherry is rightly suspicious:

> The rhetoric that Homejoy failed because its workers sued for minimum wage and overtime protections failed to establish a key element: causality. While labor unrest is certainly not good for business, it is not clear that paying workers minimum wage was the cause of Homejoy's bankruptcy filings. In fact, Homejoy's business model was in financial trouble before the company's legal troubles began . . . As such, it would be overblown to conclude from only this one isolated example that paying workers minimum wage would mean the immediate bankruptcy of the on demand economy.[47]

Some operators would strongly disagree with this conclusion, pointing towards the many positive externalities of their services. Uber has repeatedly argued, for example, that its service significantly decreases the number of drink-driving arrests.[48] These claims, however, are heavily contested: when Professors Noli Brazil and David Kirk scrutinized the platform's drink-driving claims, they found that 'deployment of Uber services in a given metropolitan county had no association with the number of subsequent traffic fatalities, whether measured in aggregate or specific to drunk-driving fatalities or fatalities during weekends and holidays'.[49]

As President Franklin D. Roosevelt once noted, it seems 'plain that no business which depends for existence on paying less than living wages to its workers has any right to continue'.[50] Despite much doublespeak to the contrary, the application and enforcement of employment law in the gig economy is not a question of enforcing burdensome rules to thwart innovation.

Businesses can compete on a level playing field only if existing employment laws are equally applied and consistently enforced. If anything, the insolvency of platforms that cannot sustain their activities once they have to bear the true cost of their services will benefit others in the long run, as resources are reallocated to more efficient businesses. The demise of rogue operators opens up space and consumer demand for new start-ups—Schumpeter's creative destruction at work.

Following the steps outlined in the previous chapter to bring gig-economy work back into the scope of employment law will turn out to benefit everyone: workers, consumers, taxpayers—and even markets at large. Employment classification cuts off rogue operators' regulatory arbitrage opportunities, and will force platforms to enter into genuine competition on matching and product quality. This is the key to a level economic and social playing field: '[T]he argument for [employment law protection] is, in the final analysis, an argument in favour of an integrative mechanism... which makes it possible for a market economy and a social state to co-exist.'[51]

Ensuring the full application of employment law is crucial if we want to make the gig economy work for all. Nothing in this analysis suggests that we should shut platforms down: improved matching and its associated algorithms have the definite potential to add value to our economy, to create job opportunities, and to give us all access to better products and services. For the industry to operate to everyone's benefit, however, we need to ensure that platforms can no longer arbitrage around existing rules and have to bear the cost of their operations. Employment law is the key to equitable conditions for all workers, and equal competition amongst businesses new and old.

Epilogue

Amidst the economic depression of the 1930s, Cambridge economist John Maynard Keynes penned a note about the *Economic Possibilities for our Grandchildren*. Where others saw stagnation and decline, he predicted prosperity and development. Unprecedented technological improvements in manufacture and transport were key to this vision. In the long term, the resulting productivity gains would bring manifold improvements in living standards for all. In the short term, however, 'the very rapidity of these changes is hurting us and bringing difficult problems to solve':[1]

> We are being afflicted with a new disease of which some readers may not yet have heard the name, but of which they will hear a great deal in the years to come—namely, *technological unemployment*. This means unemployment due to our discovery of means of economising the use of labour outrunning the pace at which we can find new uses for labour.[2]

Similar fears have been voiced throughout the past century. President Kennedy, for example, regarded maintaining full employment 'as the major domestic challenge, really, of the '60s... when automation, of course, is replacing men'.[3]

Reality, however, couldn't be further from vision of 'three-hour shifts or a fifteen-hour week'.[4] What happened? Why are we still at work? Today's economists point to a number of factors, income or capitalization effects central amongst them. Technology makes us more productive, reducing prices and raising real income. As we become better off, our appetite for more products and services creates new job opportunities in emerging industries: think of the miner retrained as a computer engineer.

Over the past few years, the spectre of technological unemployment has nonetheless returned to haunt us: whether it's the rise of artificial intelligence or the advent of self-driving cars, the robots are said to be coming for

Humans as a Service: The Promise and Perils of Work in the Gig Economy. First Edition. Jeremias Prassl. © Jeremias Prassl 2018. Published 2018 by Oxford University Press.

our jobs once more. What does this mean for the gig economy? Why should policymakers worry about ride-sharing drivers' working conditions today, when the real challenge is a complete absence of work just around the corner? If anything, might foisting expensive employment protection on platforms not increase their incentives to automate?

Not quite. The rapid emergence of new technologies will confront regulators with a panoply of difficult questions—but this must not distract us from the problems at hand. As far as the future of work is concerned, the immediate challenge lies not in the rise of the robots, but in the realization that the gig economy is but the tip of a much larger iceberg of insecure, precarious work.

The End of Work?

Automation's impact on the labour market should not be underestimated: technology continuously reshapes the workplace. At the same time, however, it is unlikely to spell the end of work—at least for those toiling in the gig economy. Indeed, automation might further spur platform growth, as more and more complex jobs can be broken down into discrete microtasks, ready for outsourcing to the crowd.

The Rise of the Robots

In a 2013 paper looking at the US labour market, Oxford colleagues Carl Frey and Michael Osborne made a startling prediction: as a result of advances in machine learning, just under half of total US employment was at a 'high risk' of being automated in the near future.[5] Their model suggested that workers employed in management, business, and finance had little to worry about. Job losses would be concentrated at the bottom end of the labour market: '[C]omputerisation will mainly substitute for low-skill and low-wage jobs...most workers in transportation and logistics occupations, together with the bulk of administrative and support workers, and labour in production occupations, are at risk.'[6]

We have seen how the spread of the gig economy has affected a wide range of industries—but it's clear that most platform-based work, from Uber drivers and Deliveroo cyclists to Turkers entering data and Taskers coming to clean your flat, is concentrated right in Frey and Osborne's risk zone. Erik Brynjolfsson and Andrew McAfee of Massachusetts Institute of Technology (MIT) agree that technological progress will have a starkly polarizing impact on the labour market:

> There's never been a better time to be a worker with special skills or the right education, because these people can use technology to create and capture value. However, there's never been a worse time to be a worker with only 'ordinary' skills and abilities to offer, because computers, robots, and other digital technologies are acquiring these skills and abilities at an extraordinary rate.[7]

The predictions, then, seem clear: given the exponential growth of machine learning and artificial intelligence, the gig economy is but a transitional phenomenon, with the majority of low-skill platform-based work soon to be handed over to algorithms and robots. With the advent of self-driving cars and laundry robots, the business model will shift away from digital work intermediation, leaving large swathes of the workforce unemployed.

The consistent application of employment law standards, as advocated in previous chapters, might even create additional pressures to hasten this transition: the cost imposed on platforms will incentivize innovation—not least in the low-wage sector. As Professor Cynthia Estlund puts it: 'Automation is an entirely lawful—indeed, almost unassailable—way to avoid the costs of employing people.'[8] The cost of employment protection, she argues, will be felt particularly harshly by low-income workers: 'Especially at the bottom of the labor market, raising the floor on wages, benefits, and working conditions strengthens the business case for automation of technically automatable jobs.'[9]

This is correct as a matter of labour economics—as long as jobs *are* automatable. The extent to which machine learning can grapple with platform-based work, however, is much more contested than some authors would have us think. Upon closer inspection, it is not at all clear to what extent the latest wave of technological unemployment will affect the gig economy.

The Limits of Automation

Automation does have huge impacts on the labour market—not least in terms of accentuating income inequality. But is it really a looming threat to the low-skill, low-wage work characteristic of many gig-economy platforms? There are good reasons to doubt claims that the rise of the robots will spell the end of the gig economy. Given the nature of most platform-based tasks, automation's disparate impact on the labour market will have little effect on gig-economy workers. If anything, it seems likely that the medium-term impact of automation will be to increase the number of jobs that become susceptible to digital work intermediation.

Polanyi's Paradox

MIT economist David Autor is one of the leading sceptics when it comes to grand claims of automation and job destruction. With computers everywhere, he argues, it is tempting to assume that they can take over most jobs: 'But that leap of logic is unfounded.'[10] Modern algorithms are vastly superiors to workers when it comes to routine tasks that can be distilled into a clear set of instructions, such as crunching the numbers in a complex financial model—but many aspects of the modern labour market are much harder to automate than we assume, if they can be automated at all.

This is 'Polanyi's paradox', named after Michael Polanyi's observation that 'We know more than we can tell.' Human intuition, it turns out, is crucial across the labour market—including at the bottom end. Whether it's a chef breaking eggs into a mixing bowl or a professor writing a persuasive new lecture, Autor explains that:

> the tasks that have proved most vexing to automate are those demanding flexibility, judgment and common sense—skills that we understand only tacitly. At a practical level, Polanyi's paradox means that many familiar tasks, ranging from the quotidian to the sublime, cannot currently be computerized because we don't know 'the rules.'[11]

Turning to the range of tasks currently completed by gig-economy workers, it quickly becomes apparent that many will demand just those skills. Think of the cleaner, who has to reach behind a desk to dust an ever-changing array of tangled cables, the delivery cyclist weaving between cars and dodging jaywalking pedestrians on a rainy London evening, or the crowdworker sorting through hundreds of online images. These jobs might count as low-skilled labour—but their ever-changing, unpredictable nature makes them near impossible to translate into a simple algorithm.

McAfee and Brynjofsson disagree: because 'humanity has recently become much better at building machines that can figure things out on their own,' they suggest, ' "Polanyi's paradox" is not the barrier it once was; machines can learn even when humans can't teach them.'[12] It is true that engineers have been working hard to develop cleaning robots, self-driving cars, and image-recognition software. Even after years of work and billions of investments, however, the algorithms continue to struggle—from a robotic cleaner getting tangled in its owner's hair until she could be freed by paramedics, to self-driving cars confused by ice, snow, faded road markings, and stray plastic bags.[13]

Artificial Artificial Intelligence
In the long run, the gig economy will not remain beyond the reach of algorithms. As long as the routine nature of the task is central to its automation, however, technology is likely to advance much more rapidly in other sectors of the economy.[14] Consider legal discovery and due diligence as an example: once the preserve of well-paid junior lawyers, locked away for weeks on end to wade through crates of documents, it has quickly become dominated by language- and pattern-recognition software.[15]

For now, it seems more likely that automation will drive further gig-economy growth. Technology increasingly allows traditional jobs to be broken down into discrete tasks. Think of a commercial lawyer advising on a merger transaction: traditionally, she would have had to begin with due diligence before sitting down to draft a series of contracts, meeting with the other side to negotiate terms, and continuously communicating updates to the client. Today, some of these tasks will be easily automated—with many of the remaining non-routine elements increasingly available for outsourcing to the crowd.[16]

Automation will almost certainly destroy some jobs—but we should be careful about assuming that it will have significant short-term consequences for the gig economy. Remember the goal behind Amazon's Mechanical Turk (MTurk)? To provide *artificial* artificial intelligence, by getting humans to do what computers cannot.

Rethinking Employment Law for the Future of Work

Regardless of how automation unfolds, it is crucial that the promise of self-driving cars and robot servants does not detract from the urgency of ensuring decent working conditions in the gig economy—and across the entire labour market. As long as we are working, we need labour law—first and foremost, to ensure fundamental protection for workers themselves. As we saw in the previous chapter, labour law also plays a crucial role in protecting consumers and markets, encouraging innovation and competition on a level playing field.

Just as with technological unemployment, the threat of labour law to jobs themselves is often overstated. The central claim of this book is that most gig-economy work falls within the scope of employment law—to the potential benefit of all involved: employment regulation is key to a sustainable future for on-demand services. Instead of provoking mass unemployment, treating gig workers as employees and platforms as their employers will create a framework for productivity and growth.

Ensuring the consistent application of employment law in the gig economy, however, is but the first step towards tackling the challenge of rethinking employment law for the future of work. Technological developments and the rise of the gig economy are but two of many factors driving work away from the stable, bilateral work relationships between employees and employers around which employment law developed in the last century. In their place, we see a rise of intermittent work, often for multiple employers, and perhaps interspersed with periods of genuine entrepreneurship. Indeed, whilst some aspects of the gig economy, from algorithmic control to platforms' business models, are industry-specific phenomena, many of the underlying problems are by no means limited to platform work and have long been the subject of intensive academic scrutiny.

As we move towards a labour market in which growing numbers of workers share the challenges faced by their gig-economy colleagues, there is a real need for creative approaches to new models of worker protection. It's a daunting task—but one we cannot afford to ignore.

Notes

INTRODUCTION

1. Tom Standage, *The Mechanical Turk: The True Story of the Chess-playing Machine that Fooled the World* (Allen Lane 2002). For entertaining reviews, see Simon Singh, 'Turk's gambit', *The Guardian* (20 April 2002), http://www.theguardian.com/books/2002/apr/20/scienceandnature.highereducation, archived at https://perma.cc/T9XK-W7N4; Dick Teresi, 'Turkish gambit', *The New York Times* (2 June 2002), http://www.nytimes.com/2002/06/02/books/turkish-gambit.html, archived at https://perma.cc/77YA-9U5K. If you are interested in watching the Turk in action, a replica can be seen here: 'Meet the Mechanical Turk, an 18th century chess machine', *BBC News* (22 March 2013), http://www.bbc.co.uk/news/av/magazine-21882456/meet-the-mechanical-turk-an-18th-century-chess-machine, archived at https://perma.cc/77JK-G8JC

2. Ursula Huws, 'New forms of platform employment or crowd work', in Werner Wobbe, Elva Bova, and Catalin Dragomirescu-Gaina (eds), *The Digital Economy and the Single Market* (FEPS 2016), 73, sets out the breadth of gig-economy services:

   > At the high end can be found companies like Axiom, which provides legal services, Heal and Medicast providing medical services, the Business Talent Group providing senior executives and Eden McCallum providing management consultancy. Lower down the scale can be found companies such as Handy, Taskrabbit, Helpling and Hassle which provide simple services such as cleaning, running errands or basic house-hold maintenance tasks. In between can be found a vast array of occupational categories including teachers, cooks, tree surgeons, hairdressers, translators and film editors.

3. Steven Hill, *Raw Deal: How the 'Uber Economy' and Runaway Capitalism Are Screwing American Workers* (St Martin's Press 2015).

4. Rachel Botsman and Roo Rogers, *What's Mine Is Yours: The Rise of Collaborative Consumption* (Collins 2011).

5. Arun Sundararajan, *The Sharing Economy: The End of Employment and the Rise of Crowd-Based Capitalism* (MIT Press 2016), 19.

6. Sangeet Paul Choudary, Geoffrey G. Parker, and Marshall W. Van Alstyne, *Platform Revolution: How Networked Markets Are Transforming the Economy and How to Make Them Work for You* (Norton & Co. 2016), 5.

7. Tom Slee, *What's Yours Is Mine* (O/R Books 2015), 10:

> Rather than bringing a new openness and personal trust to our interactions, it is bringing a new form of surveillance where service workers must live in fear of being snitched on, and while the company CEOs talk benevolently of their communities of users, the reality has a harder edge of centralized control.

8. Steven Hill, *Raw Deal* (St Martin's Press 2015), 13.
9. Lilly Irani, 'The cultural work of microwork' (2013) 17(5) New Media & Society 720, 720. As far as I can tell, at 11:37 in http://techtv.mit.edu/videos/ 16180-opening-keynote-and-keynote-interview-with-jeff-bezos, archived at https://perma.cc/D39A-MSPD, Bezos actually offers 'people' rather than 'humans' as a service, before going on to demonstrate how code can 'put the human in the loop' on the next slide—but the underlying point is the same, and 'humans as a service' stuck.
10. Moshe Marvit, 'How crowdworkers became the ghosts in the digital machine', *The Nation* (5 February 2014), http://www.thenation.com/article/how-crowdworkers-became-ghosts-digital-machine/, archived at https://perma.cc/544Q-BL4S
11. Treaty of Versailles (1919), Art. 427 (establishing the predecessor institution to today's ILO). This commitment was emphatically restated in the Declaration of Philadelphia in 1944.
12. Lilly Irani, 'The cultural work of microwork' (2013) 17(5) New Media & Society 720, 729.
13. Ibid., 732.
14. Ibid., 738.
15. Jeff Howe, *Crowdsourcing: How the Power of the Crowd Is Driving the Future of Business* (Random House 2009), 15.
16. Frank Pasquale, 'Two narratives of platform capitalism' (2016) 35(1) Yale Law & Policy Review 309, 312.

CHAPTER I

1. Jeff Howe, 'The rise of crowdsourcing', *Wired* (1 June 2006), http://www. wired.com/2006/06/crowds/, archived at https://perma.cc/44XE-MLDR
2. Ibid. See also Jeff Howe, *Crowdsourcing: How the Power of the Crowd Is Driving the Future of Business* (Random House 2009). Crowdsourcing is by no means limited to labour markets: consumers, governments, and businesses have turned to the Internet in a wide range of areas—from the US National Aeronautics and Space Administration (NASA) asking citizens for help in its quest to identify exoplanets (http://www.zooniverse.org/projects/marckuchner/backyard-worlds-planet-9, archived at https://perma.cc/LR8S-7QUF), to start-ups raising capital for new business ideas through platforms such as Kickstarter (http://www.kickstarter. com, archived at https://perma.cc/9DNZ-ACZ9).
3. Orly Lobel, 'The law of the platform' (2016) 101(1) Minnesota Law Review 87, 91.
4. European Commission, 'Introduction to Deliveroo' (European Commission 2016), http://ec.europa.eu/information_society/newsroom/image/document/

2016-6/deliveroo_13855.pdf, archived at https://perma.cc/6J2T-8XK9; Foodora, 'About us', http://www.foodora.com/about/, archived at https://perma. cc/4QS9-LB6W

5. David Durward, Ivo Blohm, and Jan Marco Leimeister, 'Principal forms of crowdsourcing and crowd work', in Werner Wobbe, Elva Bova, and Catalin Dragomirescu-Gaina (eds), *The Digital Economy and the Single Market* (FEPS 2016), 46–7, 48.

6. Michael Heiling and Sylvia Kuba, 'Die Ökonomie der Plattform', in Doris Lutz and Martin Risak (eds), *Arbeit in der Gig-Economy: Rechtsfragen neuer Arbeitsformen in Crowd and Cloud* (OGB Verlag 2017), 28, 33–4.

7. No taxonomy of the platform economy today seems complete without mentioning platforms such as airbnb, a California-based company offering room and house rentals across the globe (http://www.airbnb.co.uk, archived at https://perma.cc/TF8R-YUSJ). At first glance, it has much in common with the on-demand economy platforms we are interested in: both match consumers and services through sophisticated rating algorithms, and both offer fully automated payment and feedback systems. They are also subject to similarly polarized debates about their impact on local markets, as well as engaged in high-profile disputes with regulators.

airbnb will nonetheless be excluded from subsequent discussion. The platform's business model is premised on selling short-term access to assets, rather than work. Renting out a house or flat does require a fair amount of labour, of course, from changing sheets to cleaning the bathrooms, but the product offered to the consumer is use of an asset, rather than on-demand labour.

The waters are slightly muddied by the fact that many on-demand work platforms stipulate that workers are to provide the tools of their trade—think of a ride-sharing driver's car or a crowdworker's computer. In reality, however, genuine ownership of the underlying assets is generally not required. A host of third-party providers offering 'Uber-ready' car rentals, for example, have sprung up in cities all over the world (e.g. http://easyuberhire.com, archived at https://perma.cc/Q6QW-FM3N), with the platform itself providing a dedicated Uber Marketplace 'designed to help new and existing partner-drivers rent and purchase vehicles' (https://drive.uber.com/ukmarketplace/location/london/, archived at https://perma.cc/ABB5-DKYN).

8. On occasion, more exotic transport modes, including boats and helicopters, are also offered: Justia Trademarks, 'Everyone's private driver: trademark details', https://trademarks.justia.com/858/16/everyone-s-private-85816634.html, archived at https://perma.cc/9AEQ-SHNV

9. TaskRabbit Support, 'Is TaskRabbit in my city?', https://support.taskrabbit. com/hc/en-us/articles/204411090-Is-TaskRabbit-in-my-city-, archived at https://perma.cc/8RC8-GV5H

10. TaskRabbit Support, 'The TaskRabbit trust & support fee', https://support.task-rabbit.co.uk/hc/en-gb/articles/204943200-The-TaskRabbit-Trust-Safety-Fee, archived at https://perma.cc/2EDG-7MHT

11. TaskRabbit Support, 'Ratings and reviews on the TaskRabbit platform', https://
support.taskrabbit.co.uk/hc/en-gb/articles/204668060-Ratings-and-Reviews-
on-the-TaskRabbit-Platform-, archived at https://perma.cc/FEE8-UN7W

12. Sara Horowith, founder and executive director of Freelancers Union, com-
menting on an Upwork press release about 2014 US freelancing figures:
Upwork, '53 million Americans now freelance, new study finds', http://www.
upwork.com/press/2014/09/03/53-million-americans-now-freelance-new-
study-finds-2/, archived at https://perma.cc/P3Q4-WJH4

13. Frank Kalman, 'Yes, the gig economy is great—but it isn't the future of work',
Talent Economy (18 November 2016), https://medium.com/talent-economy/
yes-the-gig-economy-is-great-but-it-isnt-the-future-of-work-a5629f2b9e2d,
archived at https://perma.cc/Q8MD-4A8C

14. Ibid.

15. For some of the most promising work at the time of writing, see McKinsey
Global Institute (MGI), *Independent Work: Choice, Necessity, and the Gig Economy*
(McKinsey & Co. 2016), 36; Brhmie Balaram, Josie Warden, and Fabian Wallace-
Stephens, *Good Gigs: A Fairer Future for the UK's Gig Economy* (RSA 2017), 18.

16. MGI, *Independent Work: Choice, Necessity, and the Gig Economy* (McKinsey & Co.
2016), 36, citing Lawrence Katz and Alan Krueger, 'The rise and nature of alternative work arrangements in the United States, 1995–2015' (2016) NBER
Working Paper No. 22667; Patrick Gillespie, 'The rapidly growing gig economy is still super small', *CNN Money* (6 May 2016), http://money.cnn.
com/2016/05/06/news/economy/gig-economy-princeton-krueger-tiny/,
archived at https://perma.cc/6ZT9-8EX7

17. Caroline O'Donovan, 'Sen. Mark Warner to San Francisco techies: "the politicians are coming"', *BuzzFeed News* (25 September 2015), http://www.buzzfeed.
com/carolineodonovan/the-politicians-are-coming-sen-mark-warner-has-a-
warning-for?utm_term=.cwyPplxvA#.gxkqvKxOj, archived at https://perma.cc/
UE7Q-6GTK. It is not only the size of the gig economy with which statisticians
struggle; attempts to determine key worker characteristics are also plagued by
similar problems. Consider gender as an important example. Male and female
workforce participation turns out to be very hard to measure, not least given
huge variation across different platforms in recording and displaying worker
demographics. McKinsey, on the one hand, suggests that 'there is gender parity
in independent work, but men are more likely to be free agents and women are
more likely to be supplemental earners' (MGI, *Independent Work: Choice, Necessity,
and the Gig Economy* (McKinsey & Co. 2016), 43), whereas the RSA, a UK think
tank, concludes that 74 per cent of weekly gig workers are men—a figure that
rises to 95 per cent for driving platform Uber (Brhmie Balaram, Josie Warden,
and Fabian Wallace-Stephens, *Good Gigs: A Fairer Future for the UK's Gig Economy*
(RSA 2017), 29).

18. MGI, *Independent Work: Choice, Necessity, and the Gig Economy* (McKinsey & Co.
2016), 30; Diana Farrell and Fiona Greig, *Paychecks, Paydays, and the Online
Platform Economy: Big Data on Income Volatility* (JPMorgan Chase Institute 2016);

Chartered Institute of Personnel and Development (CIPD), *To Gig or Not to Gig? Stories from the Modern Economy* (CIPD 2017), 4.

19. Brhmie Balaram, Josie Warden, and Fabian Wallace-Stephens, *Good Gigs: A Fairer Future for the UK's Gig Economy* (RSA 2017), 13.

20. MGI, *Independent Work: Choice, Necessity, and the Gig Economy* (McKinsey & Co. 2016), 3. Regulators are beginning to take notice. In April 2016, the UK's Office for National Statistics (ONS) released a detailed feasibility study on measuring the sharing economy, presenting several potential options and data sources, as well as a wide range of problems: Michael Hardie, *The Feasibility of Measuring the Sharing Economy* (ONS 2016), http://www.ons.gov.uk/economy/economicoutputandproductivity/output/articles/thefeasibilityofmeasuringthesharingeconomy/2016-04-05, archived at https://perma.cc/8G7C-2LGX. It remains to be seen whether specific measurements will be introduced in due course.

21. Mark Graham, Vili Lehdonvirta, Alex Wood, Helena Barnard, Isis Hjorth, and David P. Simon, *The Risks and Rewards of Online Gig Work at the Global Margins* (Oxford Internet Institute 2017), 1, http://www.oii.ox.ac.uk/publications/gigwork.pdf, archived at https://perma.cc/EZJ4-3AAD

22. Ibid., 2.

23. Brhmie Balaram, Josie Warden, and Fabian Wallace-Stephens, *Good Gigs: A Fairer Future for the UK's Gig Economy* (RSA 2017), 13.

24. Micha Kaufman, 'The gig economy: the force that could save the American worker?', *Wired* (undated), http://www.wired.com/insights/2013/09/the-gig-economy-the-force-that-could-save-the-american-worker/, archived at https://perma.cc/5SSU-RX7Q

25. The following data are cited by MGI, *Independent Work: Choice, Necessity, and the Gig Economy* (McKinsey & Co. 2016), 67. Sources include: CB Insights, 'The on-demand report', http://www.cbinsights.com/research-on-demand-report, archived at https://perma.cc/FG2Q-9CDV; 'Intuit forecast: 7.6 million people in on-demand economy by 2020', *Intuit* (13 August 2015), http://investors.intuit.com/Press-Releases/Press-Release-Details/2015/Intuit-Forecast-76-Million-People-in-On-Demand-Economy-by-2020/default.aspx, archived at https://perma.cc/CZ5H-92FT, citing an 18 per cent growth rate; Diana Farrell and Fiona Greig, *Paychecks, Paydays, and the Online Platform Economy: Big Data on Income Volatility* (JPMorgan Chase Institute 2016), for the multiple of 47.

26. MGI, *Independent Work: Choice, Necessity, and the Gig Economy* (McKinsey & Co. 2016), 76–7. Another factor is the fallout from recent global economic crises, which have reshaped national labour markets. As countries struggle with recessions and high unemployment or underemployment, more and more individuals will turn to platforms in search of work. When comparing Spain, a country marked by recession and struggling with high unemployment, particularly for young workers, with the EU-15 average, MGI found that nearly 42 per cent of workers chose independent work due to economic necessity, as opposed to a 32 per cent average across 15 EU member states: see ibid., 60.

27. Jonathan Shieber, 'Handy hits $1 million a week in bookings as cleaning econ-
omy consolidates', *TechCrunch* (14 October 2014), https://techcrunch.com/
2014/10/14/handy-hits-1-million-a-week-in-bookings-as-cleaning-econo-
my-consolidates/, archived at https://perma.cc/N5SV-ARAM

28. Kaitlin, 'Ringing in 2017 with Uber', *Uber Newsroom* (2 January 2017), https://
newsroom.uber.com/nye2016/, archived at https://perma.cc/CU9E-YGYS;
https://uberestimator.com/cities, archived at https://perma.cc/H4BR-K7YR

    A study commissioned by financial software company Intuit suggested annual
growth rates in excess of 18 per cent, whilst bankers JPMorgan Chase found
that on-demand economy participants grew by a multiple of 47 between 2012
and 2015. The World Bank estimates that the market size of online outsourcing
alone will grow from US$4.4 billion in 2016 to 'gross services revenue in the
range of $15 billion to $25 billion' by 2020: Siou Chew Kuek, Cecilia M.
Paradi-Guilford, Toks Fayomi, Saori Imaizumi, and Panos Ipeirotis, *The Global
Opportunity in Online Outsourcing* (World Bank Group 2015), 3. Large parts of
the market remain untapped: as of 2015, 75 per cent of US consumers are still
unaware of the term 'sharing economy': MGI, *Independent Work: Choice, Necessity,
and the Gig Economy* (McKinsey & Co. 2016), 68, citing Aaron Smith, *Shared,
Collaborative, and on Demand: The New Digital Economy* (Pew Research Centre
2016), based on a national survey conducted in November–December 2015.
McKinsey similarly suggests that 'there is significant room for growth', for a
number of reasons: more workers might be interested in exploring independent
work, not least given the on-demand economy's potential to activate previously
unemployed or underemployed members of the labour force: ibid., 69, 73. The
RSA agrees that 'the workforce of the gig economy could become considerably
larger—there are millions of prospective gig workers': Brhmie Balaram, Josie
Warden, and Fabian Wallace-Stephens, *Good Gigs: A Fairer Future for the UK's
Gig Economy* (RSA 2017), 33. Another study, commissioned by accountants
PricewaterhouseCoopers (PwC), puts familiarity with the sharing economy
amongst the US adult population at 44 per cent: PwC, *The Sharing Economy*
(Consumer Intelligence Series 2015), 5.

29. Jim Edwards, 'Uber's leaked finances show the company might—just might—
be able to turn a profit', *Business Insider UK* (27 February 2017), http://uk
.businessinsider.com/uber-leaked-finances-accounts-revenues-profits-2017-2,
archived at https://perma.cc/V57C-8F57. Tech and finance journalists often put
this number in the context of car manufacturer's valuations to demonstrate how
Uber's valuation has quickly overtaken large and long-established brands such as
General Motors or Ford: Liyan Chen, 'At $68 billion valuation, Uber will be
bigger than GM, Ford, and Honda', *Forbes* (4 December 2015), http://www.
forbes.com/sites/liyanchen/2015/12/04/at-68-billion-valuation-uber-will-be-
bigger-than-gm-ford-and-honda/, archived at https://perma.cc/7P9K-SQYB

    Not everyone sees these numbers as a cause for celebration: see, e.g., Sunil
Rajaraman, 'The on-demand economy is a bubble—and it's about to burst',

Quartz (28 April 2017), https://qz.com/967474/the-on-demand-economy-is-a-bubble-and-its-about-to-burst/, archived at https://perma.cc/MTB8-SQYG

30. For an overview, see Christopher Pissarides, 'Equilibrium in the labor market with search frictions' (2011) 101(4) American Economic Review 1092. His Nobel lecture is also available at http://www.nobelprize.org/nobel_prizes/economic-sciences/laureates/2010/pissarides-lecture.pdf, archived at https://perma.cc/U64H-QRP7

31. Ronald Coase, 'The nature of the firm' (1937) 4(16) Economica 386.

32. Julia Tomassetti, 'Does Uber redefine the firm? The postindustrial corporation and advanced information technology' (2016) 34(1) Hofstra Labor and Employment Law Journal 1, 17.

33. Ibid., pt IV.

34. Ibid., 34.

35. Victor Fleischer, 'Regulatory arbitrage' (2010) 89(2) Texas Law Review 227, 230. Not all commentators agree with the terminology, even though the phenomenon itself is generally accepted. Oei and Ring, for example, characterize platforms' decision to classify themselves as mere intermediaries and their 'affirmative adoption of independent contractor classification' as examples of 'tax opportunism', rather than regulatory arbitrage, whilst acknowledging that the overlap between those categories can be significant—'In some cases, it may be questionable whether the transaction should be viewed as arbitrage (i.e., one that has been deliberately structured, in a manner that incurs some transaction costs, to secure larger regulatory benefits) or opportunism (i.e., taking advantage of an existing gap in the law available due to inherent features of the new sharing model): Shu-Yi Oei and Diane Ring, 'Can sharing be taxed?' (2016) 93(4) Washington University Law Review 1027, 1042, 1051. Other authors suggest the perhaps more problematic term of 'regulatory entrepreneurship' whereby legal dispute lies at the core of the business model: Elizabeth Pollman and Jordan M. Barry, 'Regulatory entrepreneurship' (2017) 90(3) Southern California Law Review 383.

36. Victor Fleischer, 'Regulatory arbitrage' (2010) 89(2) Texas Law Review 227, 230.

37. Questions about the true cost of the gig-economy platform model do not stop there. Individual contractor classification doesn't only shift many business costs to individual workers; it also increases them. Daniel Hemel of Chicago University has highlighted the cost of this 'unpooling'. Whilst employment law bundles risks (from health and longevity, to disability and productivity) from a large group of workers, which makes insurance cheap, as risk is devolved to individual workers the price of individual insurance inevitably rises: Daniel Hemel, 'Pooling and unpooling in the Uber economy' (2017) University of Chicago Legal Forum, forthcoming.

38. Julie Verhage, 'Here's what Morgan Stanley is telling its wealthiest clients about Uber', *Bloomberg* (14 January 2016), http://www.bloomberg.com/news/articles/2016-01-14/here-s-what-morgan-stanley-is-telling-its-wealthiest-clients-about-

uber, archived at https://perma.cc/B3WV-8SSN. The list of currently avoided cost is impressive:

> Among other things, such a determination could entitle certain drivers using the Company's platform to the reimbursement of certain expenses, lead to the potential unionization of drivers, impose tax withholding and reporting obligations on the Company, entitle drivers using the Company's platform to the benefit of wage-and-hour laws, impose applicable leaves of absence requirements, medical insurance, workers compensation insurance, ERISA and similar pension fund obligations and restrictions on the Company.

39. Hubert Horan, 'Will the growth of Uber increase economic welfare?' (2017) 44(1) Transportation Law Journal 1, 8.
40. Eric Newcomer, 'Uber, lifting financial veil, says sales growth outpaces losses', *Bloomberg* (14 April 2017), http://www.bloomberg.com/news/articles/2017-04-14/embattled-uber-reports-strong-sales-growth-as-losses-continue, archived at https://perma.cc/XH63-9ENU; Joshua Brustein, 'TaskRabbit's stalled revolution', *Bloomberg* (22 December 2016), http://www.bloomberg.com/news/articles/2016-12-22/taskrabbit-s-stalled-revolution, archived at https://perma.cc/7ZNJ-T84F
41. Yves Smith, 'Can Uber ever deliver? Part One—Understanding Uber's bleak operating economics', *Naked Capitalism* (30 November 2016), http://www.nakedcapitalism.com/2016/11/can-uber-ever-deliver-part-one-understanding-ubers-bleak-operating-economics.html, archived at https://perma.cc/RN7K-9SSZ. Horan's detailed numbers are now available in a published article: see Hubert Horan, 'Will the growth of Uber increase economic welfare?' (2017) 44(1) Transportation Law Journal 1. Other reports highlight narrowing losses and continuing strong growth. In August 2017, Dan Primack reported that 'Uber's global ride-share business was margin positive last quarter, which is a flip from Q1': Dan Primack, 'Exclusive: inside Uber's financials', *Axios* (23 August 2017), https://www.axios.com/exclusive-uber-financials-2475912645.html, archived at https://perma.cc/7EN9-XUXK
42. Izabella Kaminska, 'Mythbusting Uber's valuation', *Financial Times* (13 September 2016), https://ftalphaville.ft.com/2016/09/13/2173631/mythbusting-ubers-valuation/, archived at https://perma.cc/6EHK-FGUU
43. Joseph Farrell and Paul Klemperer, 'Coordination and lock-in: competition with switching costs and network effects', in Mark Armstrong and Robert Porter (eds), *Handbook of Industrial Organization* (Elsevier 2007), 1967, 1974.
44. Yves Smith, 'Can Uber deliver? Part Four—Understanding that unregulated monopoly was always Uber's central objective', *Naked Capitalism* (5 December 2016), http://www.nakedcapitalism.com/2016/12/can-uber-ever-deliver-part-four-understanding-that-unregulated-monopoly-was-always-ubers-central-objective.html, archived at https://perma.cc/N98A-VLG5. Monopoly concerns have been raised by a number of commentators—see, e.g., Frank Pasquale, 'Two narratives of platform capitalism' (2016) 35 Yale Law & Policy Review 309, 316 (and sources quoted there), for concerns that first-mover

advantages and luck might thus be entrenched—although not everyone agrees—see, e.g., Jared Meyer, 'Uber is not (and will never be) a monopoly', *Forbes* (15 February 2016), http://www.forbes.com/sites/jaredmeyer/2016/02/15/uber-guardian-not-monopoly-ridesharing/#2f4e6c377932, archived at https://perma.cc/3DL6-638C

45. Micha Kaufman, 'The gig economy: the force that could save the American worker?', *Wired* (undated), http://www.wired.com/insights/2013/09/the-gig-economy-the-force-that-could-save-the-american-worker/, archived at https://perma.cc/5SSU-RX7Q

46. Brhmie Balaram, Josie Warden, and Fabian Wallace-Stephens, *Good Gigs: A Fairer Future for the UK's Gig Economy* (RSA 2017), 26.

47. Uber, 'Driver stories', http://www.uber.com/driver-stories/, archived at https://perma.cc/WF2Z-WLKU

48. Uber, 'Driver stories: Yoseph', http://www.uber.com/driver-stories/yoseph/, archived at https://perma.cc/M8WH-DG5E

49. Uber, 'Driver stories: Christine', http://www.uber.com/driver-stories/christine-aston/, archived at https://perma.cc/NE95-QQ5Z

50. Uber, 'Driver stories: Loren', http://www.uber.com/driver-stories/loren/, archived at https://perma.cc/4DE4-F7PL

51. PwC, *The Sharing Economy* (Consumer Intelligence Series 2015), 20.

52. TaskRabbit, 'Task of the week: Venice Beach party help' (14 September 2015), https://blog.taskrabbit.com/2015/09/14/914-task-of-the-week-all-the-kids-party-on-venice-beach/, archived at https://perma.cc/Q3DR-Z335

53. Brhmie Balaram, Josie Warden, and Fabian Wallace-Stephens, *Good Gigs: A Fairer Future for the UK's Gig Economy* (RSA 2017), 45.

54. Jessica L. Peck, 'New York City drunk driving after Uber' (2017) Cuny Graduate Centre PhD Program in Economics Working Paper No. 13.

55. Elliot Martin, Susan Shaheen, and Jeffrey Lidicker, 'The impact of carsharing on household vehicle holdings: results from a North American shared-use vehicle survey' (1 March 2010), http://tsrc.berkeley.edu/vehicleholdings, archived at https://perma.cc/XTX5-6CF2, as cited by Brhmie Balaram, Josie Warden, and Fabian Wallace-Stephens, *Good Gigs: A Fairer Future for the UK's Gig Economy* (RSA 2017), 51.

56. Frank Field and Andrew Forsey, *Sweated Labour: Uber and the 'Gig Economy'* (HMSO 9 December 2016), 3.

57. Ibid., 5.

58. Rebecca Smith and Sarah Leberstein, *Rights on Demand: Ensuring Workplace Standards and Worker Security in the On-Demand Economy* (NELP 2015), 6, citing review at *Glassdoor* (25 July 2013), http://www.glassdoor.com/Reviews/Employee-Review-CrowdSource-RVW2859226.htm, archived at https://perma.cc/Z9GG-C9EJ

59. Rebecca Smith and Sarah Leberstein, *Rights on Demand: Ensuring Workplace Standards and Worker Security in the On-Demand Economy* (NELP 2015), 6.

60. CIPD, *To Gig or not to Gig? Stories from the Modern Economy* (CIPD 2017), 16.

61. Anjana Ahuja, 'Why "gig health" matters', *Financial Times* (25 May 2017), http://www.ft.com/content/bdc90c22-408f-11e7-82b6-896b95f30f58, archived at https://perma.cc/9CVQ-WHZS

62. Ursula Huws, *The Making of a Cybertariat: Virtual Work in a Real World* (Merlin Press 2003); Nick Dyer-Witheford, *Cyber-proletariat: Global Labour in the Digital Vortex* (Pluto Press 2015).

63. Ursula Huws, *The Making of a Cybertariat: Virtual Work in a Real World* (Merlin Press 2003).

64. Brhmie Balaram, Josie Warden, and Fabian Wallace-Stephens, *Good Gigs: A Fairer Future for the UK's Gig Economy* (RSA 2017), 41.

65. Ariel Ezrachi and Maurice Stucke, *Virtual Competition: The Promise and Perils of the Algorithm-Driven Economy* (Harvard University Press 2016); see also Utpal Dholakia, 'Everyone hates Uber's surge pricing', *Harvard Business Review* (21 December 2015), https://hbr.org/2015/12/everyone-hates-ubers-surge-pricing-heres-how-to-fix-it, archived at https://perma.cc/8RST-4G7Q

66. 'There's an app for that', *The Economist* (30 December 2014), http://www.economist.com/news/briefing/21637355-freelance-workers-available-moments-notice-will-reshape-nature-companies-and,archivedathttps://perma.cc/DS63-TKKG, as cited by Brhmie Balaram, Josie Warden, and Fabian Wallace-Stephens, *Good Gigs: A Fairer Future for the UK's Gig Economy* (RSA 2017), 50.

67. Brhmie Balaram, *Fair Share: Reclaiming Power in the Sharing Economy* (RSA 2016), 6.

68. Ursula Huws, 'New forms of platform employment or crowd work', in Werner Wobbe, Elva Bova, and Catalin Dragomirescu-Gaina (eds), *The Digital Economy and the Single Market* (FEPS 2016), 73.

69. Siou Chew Kuek et al., *The Global Opportunity in Online Outsourcing* (World Bank Group 2015), 3.

70. MGI, *Independent Work: Choice, Necessity, and the Gig Economy* (McKinsey & Co. 2016), 8. The study was designed to address 'independent work' overall, a significant and growing proportion of which includes on-demand economy workers. The outcomes on worker choice tally with a subsequent study in the UK context: see, e.g., on worker motivation, Brhmie Balaram, Josie Warden, and Fabian Wallace-Stephens, *Good Gigs: A Fairer Future for the UK's Gig Economy* (RSA 2017), 22.

71. MGI, *Independent Work: Choice, Necessity, and the Gig Economy* (McKinsey & Co. 2016), 7.

72. Ibid., 43:

> About half (48%) of the earners with less than $25,000 in household income participate in independent work, and 37% of them do so out of necessity. This is much higher than the participation rate of earners from households with incomes exceeding $75,000. Among this high-income group, one in three (35%) participate in independent work. Less than a quarter of them do it out of necessity, while the majority participate by choice.

73. Ibid., 53.

74. Cristiano Codagnone and Bertin Martens, 'Scoping the sharing economy: origins, definitions, impact and regulatory issues', Institute for Prospective Technological Studies Digital Economy Working Paper No. 2016/01, 15.

CHAPTER 2

1. George Orwell, *Politics and the English Language* (Penguin 2013), 137.
2. Arun Sundararajan, *The Sharing Economy: The End of Employment and the Rise of Crowd-Based Capitalism* (MIT Press 2016), 138.
3. George Stigler, 'The theory of economic regulation' (1971) 2(1) The Bell Journal of Economics and Management Science 3.
4. Ernesto Dal Bó, 'Regulatory capture: a review' (2006) 22(2) Oxford Review of Economic Policy 203, 203–4; George Stigler, 'The theory of economic regulation' (1971) 2(2) The Bell Journal of Economics and Management Science 3.
5. Tom Slee, *What's Yours Is Mine: Against the Sharing Economy* (O/R Books 2015), 27. The website itself seems to have gone offline at the time of final editing.
6. Anya Kamenetz, 'Is Peers the sharing economy's future or just a great Silicon Valley PR stunt?', *Fast Company* (9 December 2013), http://www.fastcompany.com/3022974/tech-forecast/is-peers-the-sharing-economys-future-or-just-a-great-silicon-valley-pr-stunt, archived at https://perma.cc/6DMG-DGBJ
7. Andrew Leonard, 'The sharing economy gets greedy', *Salon* (1 August 2013), http://www.salon.com/2013/07/31/the_sharing_economy_gets_greedy/, archived at https://perma.cc/M9E6-EVF5. For subsequent details, see Andrew Leonard, 'Who owns the sharing economy?', *Salon* (2 August 2013), http://www.salon.com/2013/08/02/who_owns_the_sharing_economy/, archived at https://perma.cc/AL8X-VZXT
8. Sarah Kessler, 'Peers says its new focus is helping sharing economy workers', *Fast Company* (12 November 2014), http://www.fastcompany.com/3038310/peers-says-its-new-focus-is-helping-sharing-economy-workers, archived at https://perma.cc/D5WR-WXXW
9. Tech:NYC, 'What we are', http://www.technyc.org/what-we-are/, archived at https://perma.cc/Z9ND-3ETH
10. Sharing Economy UK, 'About us', http://www.sharingeconomyuk.com, archived at https://perma.cc/3ENY-TLF3
11. Oxford World's Classics, *The Bible: Authorized King James Version* (Oxford University Press 2008), 1 Samuel 17, 33–5, 40, 42–3, 48–9.
12. Alex Tsotsis, 'TaskRabbit turns grunt work into a game', *Wired* (15 July 2011), http://www.wired.com/2011/07/mf_taskrabbit/, archived at https://perma.cc/JW2L-F23J
13. Matthew Feeney, 'Level the playing field—by deregulating', *Cato Unbound* (10 February 2015), http://www.cato-unbound.org/2015/02/10/matthew-feeney/level-playing-field-deregulating, archived at https://perma.cc/A4J5-ZY88
14. Tim Bradshaw, 'Lunch with the FT: Travis Kalanick', *Financial Times* (9 May 2014), https://next.ft.com/content/9b83cbe8-d5da-11e3-83b2-00144feabdc0, archived at https://perma.cc/98TB-JGZ2
15. Rob Davies, 'Uber loses court case to block English-language written test in London', *The Guardian* (3 March 2017), http://www.theguardian.com/

technology/2017/mar/03/uber-loses-court-case-english-language-test-london, archived at https://perma.cc/W232-G6ZK; Benjamin Parker, 'Bill de Blasio's progressive war on Uber', *The Wall Street Journal* (3 August 2016), http://www. wsj.com/articles/bill-de-blasios-progressive-war-on-uber-1470265626, archived at https://perma.cc/29R5-GUD9; Humphrey Malalo and Drazen Jorgic, 'Uber driver attacked in Kenya, his taxi torched: police', *Reuters* (22 February 2016), http://uk.reuters.com/article/us-kenya-security-idUKKC-N0VV19X, archived at https://perma.cc/4VC7-2Q55; 'Uber managers arrested in France over "illicit" taxi service', *BBC News* (29 June 2015), http://www. bbc.co.uk/news/world-europe-33313145, archived at https://perma.cc/6UZR-6MMJ; The German ban of the UberPOP service was upheld by an appellate court in 2016: Frank Siebelt, 'German court upholds ban of unlicensed Uber taxi service', *Reuters* (9 June 2016), http://www.reuters.com/article/us-uber-germany-ban-idUSKCN0YV1JH, archived at https://perma.cc/YH6G-4FWK; Jon Henley, 'Uber to shut down Denmark operation over new taxi laws', *The Guardian* (28 March 2017), http://www.theguardian.com/technol-ogy/2017/mar/28/uber-to-shut-down-denmark-operation-over-new-taxi-laws, archived at https://perma.cc/WY9U-VPLF

16. Arun Sundararajan, *The Sharing Economy: The End of Employment and the Rise of Crowd-based Capitalism* (MIT Press 2016), 146.

17. Simon Deakin, 'On Uber & Luddism', Centre for Business Research: Cambridge Judge Business School Blog (28 October 2015), http://www.blogs.jbs.cam.ac.uk/cbr/wp-content/uploads/2015/10/uberruling-deakin-article.pdf, archived at https://perma.cc/7CEQ-WE3C

18. Arun Sundararajan, *The Sharing Economy: The End of Employment and the Rise of Crowd-based Capitalism* (MIT Press 2016), 146–7, citing the work of Adam Thierer and Sofia Ranchordàs, respectively.

19. Arun Sundararajan, *The Sharing Economy: The End of Employment and the Rise of Crowd-based Capitalism* (MIT Press 2016), 138.

20. Molly Cohen and Arun Sundararajan, 'Self-regulation and innovation in the peer-to-peer sharing economy' (2015) 82(1) Chicago University Law Review Dialogue 116, 116–17. The authors graciously concede that 'because the interests of digital, third-party platforms are not always perfectly aligned with the broader interests of society, some governmental involvement or oversight is likely to remain useful': ibid.

21. Ibid., 130–1. In their worked example of airbnb (a property rental business), they suggest:

> [delegating] regulatory responsibility relating to information asymmetry to platforms like Airbnb (whose interests are naturally aligned with the global aggregation of information and the mitigation of adverse selection and moral hazard), and let [local housing associations] play a key role in the regulation of local externalities, as the guest-noise and strangers-in-the-building externalities are typically local and primarily affect [the association's] membership.

22. Sharing Economy UK, 'Code of conduct', http://www.sharingeconomyuk. com/code-of-conduct, archived at https://perma.cc/WD6C-TBLK

23. This assumption has clear limitations where regulation serves purposes other than to entrench existing operators. Caps on driver numbers, for example, ensure a stable level of demand; other requirements play an important role in consumer protection. See further Organisation for Economic Co-operation and Development (OECD), 'Taxi services: competition and regulation' (2007) Competition Policy Roundtables, http://www.oecd.org/regreform/sectors/ 41472612.pdf, archived at https://perma.cc/VUA4-XJ4D

24. Orly Lobel, 'The law of the platform' (2016) 101(6) Minnesota Law Review 118, 120.

25. 'Usually', because (as ever!) the heterogeneous nature of the on-demand labour market throws up the occasional example the contrary. Where couriers have to undergo special training and/or rely on particular equipment to deliver medically sensitive products, for example, the existence of specific rosters and/or licences has been noted by the courts: see, e.g., the UK employment tribunal decision in *Dewhurst v Citysprint UK Ltd*, Case No. ET/2202512/2016.

26. Brhmie Balaram, 'RSA calls for new approach to regulating the sharing economy', *RSA* (13 January 2016), http://www.thersa.org/about-us/media/2016/ rsa-calls-for-new-approach-to-regulating-the-sharing-economy, archived at https://perma.cc/NC5L-2ZH7: 'But this isn't the story of David and Goliath in the sharing economy... These companies are networked monopolies that depend on the value created by their users to keep expanding.'

27. Ellen Huet, 'Lyft buys carpooling startup Hitch to grow Lyft line', *Forbes* (22 September 2014), http://www.forbes.com/sites/ellenhuet/2014/09/22/lyft-buys-carpooling-startup-hitch-to-grow-lyft-line/#5bb922452b59, archived at https://perma.cc/5H9D-Q44U; Lora Kolodny, 'Zimride acquires Cherry but won't offer car-washing service', *The Wall Street Journal* (26 March 2013), http:// blogs.wsj.com/venturecapital/2013/03/26/zimride-acquires-cherry-but-wont-offer-car-washing-service/, archived at https://perma.cc/Z52R-B4K8

28. Leslie Hook and Charles Clover, 'Uber abandons car-hailing app battle with China rival Didi Chuxing', *Financial Times* (1 August 2016), http://www.ft. com/content/80125fd4-57a9-11e6-9f70-badea1b336d4, archived at https:// perma.cc/23YY-XG9J. Rather ironically, Didi, in turn, already owns stakes in several of Uber's key competitors, including Lyft in the United States and Ola in India: Leslie Hook, 'Uber makes a U-turn in China as subsidy war ends in Didi deal', *Financial Times* (1 August 2016), http://www.ft.com/content/ 7f6e251a-5801-11e6-9f70-badea1b336d4, archived at https://perma.cc/2MYF-JJ3X; Ma Fangjing and Charles Clover, 'Uber shares soar after Didi deal', *Financial Times* (2 August 2016), http://www.ft.com/content/54217d94-5892-11e6-8d05-4eaa66292c32, archived at https://perma.cc/E4LJ-86NX

29. Clayton Christensen, Michael Raynor, and Rory McDonald, 'What is disruptive innovation?', *Harvard Business Review* (December 2015), https://hbr.

org/2015/12/what-is-disruptive-innovation, archived at https://perma.cc/YUW5-UY2P

30. Ibid.

31. Paul Bradley Carr, 'Travis shrugged: the creepy, dangerous ideology behind Silicon Valley's cult of disruption', *Pando* (24 October 2012), https://pando.com/2012/10/24/travis-shrugged/, archived at https://perma.cc/7FRR-EZ2B. Bradley Carr continues:

> Or perhaps 'evolved' is the wrong word: The underlying ideology—that all government intervention is bad, that the free market is the only protection the public needs, and that if weaker people get trampled underfoot in the process then, well, fuck 'em—increasingly recalls one that has been around for decades. Almost seven decades in fact, since Ayn Rand's 'The Fountainhead' first put her on the radar of every spoiled trust fund brat looking for an excuse to embrace his or her inner asshole.

32. Frank Pasquale and Siva Vaidhyanathan, 'Uber and the lawlessness of "sharing economy" corporates', *The Guardian* (28 July 2015), http://www.theguardian.com/technology/2015/jul/28/uber-lawlessness-sharing-economy-corporates-airbnb-google, archived at https://perma.cc/2ETJ-V3GX

33. House of Commons Business, Innovation and Skills Committee, *Employment Practices at Sports Direct: 3rd Report of Session 2016/17* (HC 2016–17, 219), 3.

34. 'Swalwell, Issa announce the Sharing Economy Caucus', Eric Swalwell press release (12 May 2015), https://swalwell.house.gov/media-center/press-releases/swalwell-issa-announce-sharing-economy-caucus, archived at https://perma.cc/7SN7-M4XG. Ride platform Lyft was 'excited to continue that conversation in Washington, D.C.': 'Lyft joins Sharing Economy Caucus', *Lyft Blog* (13 May 2015),https://blog.lyft.com/posts/2015/5/13/lyft-joins-sharing-economy-caucus, archived at https://perma.cc/875C-N376. It was focused on limiting regulation—not least by ensuring more favourable tax treatment. Other operators similarly called for changes to help 'participants [who] feel the sting of the taxman when filing season comes around': John Kartch, 'Meet the congressional Sharing Economy Caucus', *Forbes* (15 May 2015), http://www.forbes.com/sites/johnkartch/2015/05/15/issa-swalwell-launch-congressional-sharing-economy-caucus/2/, archived at https://perma.cc/2J5Y-EX6D

35. 'Swalwell, Issa announce the Sharing Economy Caucus', Eric Swalwell press release (12 May 2015), https://swalwell.house.gov/media-center/press-releases/swalwell-issa-announce-sharing-economy-caucus, archived at https://perma.cc/7SN7-M4XG

36. The only situation in which platforms might occasionally speak about jobs rather than independent entrepreneurship is in their political lobbying. Through 'partnership with governments and organisations who share [Uber's] vision of opening up economic opportunity in every city', promised David Plouffe, then Uber's Senior Vice President, Policy and Strategy, in late 2015, the platform was 'committed to creating 20,000 new jobs in Australia': 'Uber plans to create 200,000 new jobs in Australia in 2015', *Uber Blog* (11 February 2015), https://

newsroom.uber.com/australia/uber-plans-to-create-20000-new-jobs-in-australia-in-2015/, archived at https://perma.cc/EJV7-4ZD8

37. Brhmie Balaram, *Fair Share: Reclaiming Power in the Sharing Economy* (RSA 2016), 9–10.

38. Lyft, 'Home page', http://www.lyft.com, archived at https://perma.cc/897C-8HFL

39. Favor, 'Frequently asked questions', https://favordelivery.com/faq/, archived at https://perma.cc/642G-SC7D

40. Natasha Singer, 'In the sharing economy, workers find both freedom and uncertainty', *The New York Times* (16 August 2014), http://www.nytimes.com/2014/08/17/technology/in-the-sharing-economy-workers-find-both-freedom-and-uncertainty.html, archived at https://perma.cc/A4A2-Y9CX

41. Share the World's Resources, 'Sharing locally and nationally', http://www.sharing.org/what-is-economic-sharing/sharing-locally-nationally, archived at https://perma.cc/WSR8-3Z3B

42. Natasha Singer, 'Twisting words to make "sharing" apps seem selfless', *The New York Times* (8 August 2015), http://www.nytimes.com/2015/08/09/technology/twisting-words-to-make-sharing-apps-seem-selfless.html?_r=0, archived at https://perma.cc/43BB-4YVL

43. Sarah O'Connor, 'The gig economy is neither "sharing" nor "collaborative" ', *Financial Times* (14 June 2016), http://www.ft.com/content/8273edfe-2c9f-11e6-a18d-a96ab29e3c95, archived at https://perma.cc/7CY8-NCVR. As a recent report for the European Commission noted:

> The public debate and even part of the more scholarly literature is very polarized. There are, on the one hand, passionate normative arguments that promote the sharing economy as a socially and ecologically sustainable alternative to monetized market-based exchange and, on the other hand, equally passionate business-driven promotion campaigns for commercial sharing economy platforms.
>
> (Cristiano Codagnone and Bertin Martens, 'Scoping the sharing economy: origins, definitions, and regulatory issues' (2016) JRC Technological Reports Digital Economy Working Paper No. 2016/01, 23)

44. Bla Bla Car, 'Frequently asked questions', http://www.blablacar.co.uk/faq/question/how-do-i-set-my-price, archived at https://perma.cc/9WA9-RTUF

45. Blancride, 'BlancRiders', https://blancride.com/blancriders, archived at https://perma.cc/AX3C-EDXE

46. Tom Slee, *What's Yours Is Mine: Against the Sharing Economy* (O/R Books 2015), 10.

47. Sarah Butler, 'Deliveroo accused of "creating vocabulary" to avoid calling couriers employees', *The Guardian* (5 April 2017), http://www.theguardian.com/business/2017/apr/05/deliveroo-couriers-employees-managers, archived at https://perma.cc/XW66-CAE5; Sarah O'Connor, 'Deliveroo pedals the new language of the gig economy', *Financial Times* (5 April 2017), http://www.ft.com/content/9ad4f936-1a26-11e7-bcac-6d03d067f81f, archived at https://perma.cc/KY7L-YZ6F

48. TaskRabbit, 'Featured tasks', http://www.taskrabbit.com/m/featured, archived at https://perma.cc/RZY2-BGCP (emphasis added).

49. TaskRabbit, 'Terms of service', http://www.taskrabbit.com/terms, archived at https://perma.cc/S6ZM-VXUS. The UK equivalent (http://www.taskrabbit. co.uk/terms, archived at https://perma.cc/XTH7-Q8V4) attempts to set up functionally equivalent legal structures. We return to a legal analysis of these terms in Chapter 5.

50. Julia Tomassetti, 'Does Uber redefine the firm? The postindustrial corporation and advanced information technology' (2016) 34(1) Hofstra Labor and Employment Law Journal 239, 293:

> Uber and Lyft sublimate their agency in the production of ride services into algorithms, programming, and technology management. The metaphor of the 'platform' transforms Uber and Lyft from subjects into spaces. It evokes a passive space to be inhabited by active agents—drivers and passengers. For example, Lyft argues that drivers' 'low ratings [are] given by passengers, not Lyft. Uber argued that passengers, and not Uber, controlled drivers' work. The companies ventriloquize a disinterested machine.'

We also encounter more localised terminology, such as discussion of the '1099 economy' in the United States, after the tax form independent workers—and those taking payment for fish in cash (!)—use to declare their income.

51. Izabella Kaminska, 'Employers rely on euphemisms to hide gig economy realities', *Financial Times* (6 April 2017), http://www.ft.com/content/a5709f84-1ab3-11e7-bcac-6d03d067f81f, archived at https://perma.cc/RH7S-E6EG

52. *Aslam and Farrar v Uber,* Case No. ET/2202550/2015, 28 October 2015 (London Employment Tribunal), [87]. Uber is appealing the finding.

53. Ibid.

54. 'There's an app for that', *The Economist* (30 December 2014), http://www. economist.com/news/briefing/21637355-freelance-workers-available-moments-notice-will-reshape-nature-companies-and, archived at https://perma.cc/ DS63-TKKG

55. James Silver, 'The sharing economy: a whole new way of living', *The Guardian* (4 August 2013), http://www.theguardian.com/technology/2013/aug/04/ internet-technology-fon-taskrabbit-blablacar, archived at https://perma.cc/ 8KL4-AQJW

56. Natasha Singer, 'In the sharing economy, workers find both freedom and uncertainty', *The New York Times* (16 August 2014), http://www.nytimes.com/2014/ 08/17/technology/in-the-sharing-economy-workers-find-both-freedom-and-uncertainty.html, archived at https://perma.cc/A4A2-Y9CX

57. Ibid.

58. EY, *Global Generations: A Global Study on Work Life Challenges across Generations* (EY 2015),http://www.ey.com/Publication/vwLUAssets/EY-global-generations-a-global-study-on-work-life-challenges-across-generations/$FILE/EY-global-generations-a-global-study-on-work-life-challenges-across-generations.pdf, archived at https://perma.cc/W2NH-2G3T; PricewaterhouseCoopers (PwC),

Workforce of the Future: The Competing Forces Shaping 2030 (PWC 2017), http://www.pwc.com/gx/en/managing-tomorrows-people/future-of-work/assets/reshaping-the-workplace.pdf, archived at https://perma.cc/9JU3-NXFK

59. Debbie Wosskow, *Unlocking the Sharing Economy: An Independent Review* (BIS 2014), 5.

60. RStreet, 'Map of ridesharing laws', http://www.rstreet.org/tnc-map/, archived at https://perma.cc/4QCU-9SNN

61. Heather Somerville and Dan Levine, 'Exclusive: US states pass laws backing Uber's view of drivers as contractors', *Reuters* (10 December 2015), http://www.reuters.com/article/us-uber-statelaws-idUSKBN0TT2MZ20151210, archived at https://perma.cc/PB5L-NM8Y; see also Douglas MacMillan, 'Uber laws: a primer on ridesharing regulations', *The Wall Street Journal* (29 January 2015), http://blogs.wsj.com/digits/2015/01/29/uber-laws-a-primer-on-ride-sharing-regulations/, archived at https://perma.cc/2RUQ-M3QH

62. Ohio 131st General Assembly, Substitute House Bill No. 237, §1, 10–11.

63. Indiana 119th General Assembly, House Enrolled Act No. 1278, §4(1).

64. Texas House Bill No. 1733, §1 (http://www.legis.state.tx.us/tlodocs/84R/bill-text/html/HB01733F.htm, archived at https://perma.cc/DV3P-YZGH).

65. North Carolina, General Assembly Session 2015, Session Law 2015–237, Senate Bill 541, §1, 5.

66. European Commission, *Communication from the Commission to the European Parliament, the Council, the European Economic and Social Committee and the Committee of the Regions: A European Agenda for the Collaborative Economy* (COM (2016) 356 final), 6, 11–13. The Advocate General of the Court of Justice of the European Union (CJEU) disagreed: Case C-434/15 *Asóciacion Profesional Elite Taxi v Uber Systems Spain SL* (Opinion of AG Szpunar, 11 May 2017). My initial analysis can be found at Jeremias Prassl, 'Uber: the future of work . . . or just another taxi company?', *Oxford Business Law Blog* (16 May 2017), http://www.law.ox.ac.uk/business-law-blog/blog/2017/05/uber-future-work...-or-just-another-taxi-company, archived at https://perma.cc/NER8-3CY7

67. Seth Harris and Alan Krueger, 'A proposal for modernizing labor laws for twenty-first century work: the "independent worker"' (2015) Hamilton Project Discussion Paper No. 2015–10.

68. *Cotter et al. v Lyft Inc.*, Case No. 13-cv-04065-VC (ND Cal., March 16, 2017), 19, US District Judge Vince Chhabria denying a cross-motion for summary judgment.

69. Seth Harris and Alan Krueger, 'A proposal for modernizing labor laws for twenty-first century work: the "independent worker"' (2015) Hamilton Project Discussion Paper No. 2015–10, 17. They are not alone in this: Arun Sundararajan, *The Sharing Economy: The End of Employment and the Rise of Crowd-based Capitalism* (MIT Press 2016), 182, similarly posits that 'the specter of future litigation may actually be preventing workers from getting benefits funded by the platforms'.

70. Molly Cohen and Arun Sundararajan, 'Self-regulation and innovation in the peer-to-peer sharing economy' (2015) 82(1) Chicago University Law Review Dialogue 116, 117.

CHAPTER 3

1. Spera, *Freedom Economy Report 2016* (Lehi 2016), 6.
2. James Silver, 'The sharing economy: a whole new way of living', *The Guardian* (4 August 2013), http://www.theguardian.com/technology/2013/aug/04/Internet-technology-fon-taskrabbit-blablacar, archived at https://perma.cc/8KL4-AQJW
3. The original release could be found at https://newsroom.uber.com/an-uber-impact-20000-jobs-created-on-the-uber-platform-every-month-2/. This website is no longer online, but a copy of the press release can still be accessed at http://www.businesswire.com/news/home/20140527005594/en/Uber-Impact-20000-Jobs-Created-Uber-Platform, archived at https://perma.cc/46LG-YJ74
4. Brhmie Balaram, *Fair Share: Reclaiming Power in the Sharing Economy* (RSA 2016), 42.
5. Direct contact between consumers and workers may occur, of course, but the fact that you order your food from a waiter does not make that waiter an independent entrepreneur.
6. Frederick W. Taylor, *The Principles of Scientific Management* (Harper & Brothers 1919).
7. TaskRabbit, 'Summer tasks', http://www.taskrabbit.co.uk/m/summer-tasks, archived at https://perma.cc/49G5-3TPP; 'Digital Taylorism', *The Economist* (10 September 2015), http://www.economist.com/news/business/21664190-modern-version-scientific-management-threatens-dehumanise-workplace-digital, archived at https://perma.cc/97U5-FGBF
8. TaskRabbit, 'Terms of service', Introduction and clause 1, http://www.taskrabbit.co.uk/terms, archived at https://perma.cc/WX39-9PJE
9. Uber, 'US terms of use', clause 2, http://www.uber.com/legal/terms/us/, archived at https://perma.cc/4QCV-CB3R. Following an update in the spring of 2017, the relevant description can now be found in clause 3:

    The Services comprise mobile applications and related services (each, an 'Application'), which enable users to arrange and schedule transportation, logistics and/or delivery services and/or to purchase certain goods, including with third party providers of such services and goods under agreement with Uber or certain of Uber's affiliates ('Third Party Providers').

10. George Akerlof, 'The market for "lemons": qualitative uncertainty and the market mechanism' (1970) 84(3) Quarterly Journal of Economics 488.
11. Tom Slee, *What's Yours Is Mine: Against the Sharing Economy* (O/R Books 2015).
12. Ibid., 100–1.
13. Ibid. This is confirmed by internal Uber documents, which suggest that, in 2014, fewer than 3 per cent of drivers were 'at risk of being deactivated' as a result of a rating below 4.6 stars (out of 5): James Cook, 'Uber's internal charts show how its driver-rating system actually works', *Business Insider UK* (11 February 2015), http://uk.businessinsider.com/leaked-charts-show-how-ubers-driver-rating-system-works-2015–2, archived at https://perma.cc/5UPM-SWFN. It might be argued that this is a result of the pressure of the rating system keeping the worker pool at a high standard, with lower performing bands excluded from the market. As Slee explains, however, this is not the case: 'J-curve rating distributions [where nearly all data points are at the high end of the scale], like

those of the Sharing Economy reputation systems, show up whenever people rate each other' (Tom Slee, *What's Yours Is Mine: Against the Sharing Economy* (O/R Books 2015), 101).

14. The operation of algorithmic control mechanisms tallies closely with 'the most effective and insidious use of power' identified by Oxford and New York University political philosopher Steven Lukes. He argues that control over a situation can be exercised in myriad ways, 'whether through the operation of social forces and institutional practices or through individuals' decisions':

> To put the matter sharply, A may exercise power over B by getting him to do what he does not want to do, but he also exercises power over him by influencing, shaping or determining his very wants. Indeed, is it not the supreme exercise of power to get... others to have the desires you want them to have—that is, to secure their compliance by controlling their thoughts and desires?'
> (Steven Lukes, *Power: A Radical View* (Palgrave 2005), 27)

15. Alex Rosenblat and Luke Stark, 'Algorithmic labor and information asymmetries: a case study of Uber's drivers' (2016) 10 International Journal of Communication 3758, 3775.

16. Ibid.

17. Ibid., 3772 (citations omitted).

18. *Douglas O'Connor v Uber Technologies Inc.*, 82 F.Supp.3d 1133, 1151–2 (ND Cal. 2015).

19. Ibid., citing Michel Foucault, *Discipline and Punish: The Birth of the Prison* (ed. Alan Sheridan, Vintage Books 1979), 201.

20. 'Adventures of a first-time TaskRabbit', *LonePlacebo* (22 July 2014), http:// loneplacebo.com/adventures-of-a-first-time-taskrabbit/, archived at https:// perma.cc/MNG7-QZWR; Tenielle, 'A safe ride from A to B', *Uber Newsroom* (16 July 2015), https://newsroom.uber.com/australia/ubersafeau/, archived at https://perma.cc/CM9X-HXYS. The information required can include financial details and social security numbers, both to ensure extensive screening and to avoid double registration if a worker has been deactivated. Some platforms charge a special vetting fee to users or workers. For a description of Uber's current screening policy, see https://newsroom.uber.com/details-on-safety/, archived at https://perma.cc/94T6-XHTC
    Access can also be denied—with few, if any, reasons given—for seemingly arbitrary decisions. When one of my students tried to sign up to Amazon's MTurk, she was swiftly rejected and told: 'Our account review criteria are proprietary and we cannot disclose the reason why an invitation to complete registration has been denied. If our criteria for invitation changes, you may be invited to complete registration in the future.' A few weeks later, and without any further action on her part, she was mysteriously admitted.

21. Alex Rosenblat and Luke Stark, 'Algorithmic labor and information asymmetries: a case study of Uber's drivers' (2016) 10 International Journal of Communication 3758, 3761, 3762, 3766.

22. Doug H, 'Fired from Uber: why drivers get deactivated, and how to get reacti-
    vated', *Ride Sharing Driver* (21 April 2016), http://www.ridesharingdriver.com/
    fired-uber-drivers-get-deactivated-and-reactivated/, archived at https://
    perma.cc/3MQL-4TWD; Kari Paul, 'The new system Uber is implementing
    at airports has some drivers worried', *Motherboard* (13 April 2015), http://
    motherboard.vice.com/read/the-new-system-uber-is-implementing-at-airports-
    has-some-drivers-worried, archived at https://perma.cc/CV8P-EM7U; '10
    minute timeout', *Uber People* (1 March 2016), http://uberpeople.net/
    threads/10-minute-timeout.64032/, archived at https://perma.cc/AS3C-94EP.
    As part of a recent settlement in the United States, drivers there now enjoy margin-
    ally more clarity, even though temporary deactivation for low acceptance rates is
    still explicitly mentioned: Uber, 'Uber community guidelines', http://www.uber.
    com/legal/deactivation-policy/us/, archived at https://perma.cc/8MR4-GFDL.
    In other cities, temporary deactivation has been replaced by a simple logout.

23. Alex Rosenblat and Luke Stark, 'Algorithmic labor and information asymmetries:
    a case study of Uber's drivers' (2016) 10 International Journal of Communication
    3758, 3768.

24. Upwork, 'How it works', http://www.upwork.com/i/howitworks/client/,
    archived at https://perma.cc/9GM9-MLHF; Upwork, 'A freelancer's guide to
    Upwork', 8, 16, https://content-static.upwork.com/blog/uploads/sites/3/2016/
    06/22094641/Freelancer-Guide.pdf, archived at https://perma.cc/5A4Y-PFE9

25. Uber, 'My driver took a poor route', https://help.uber.com/h/0487f360-dc56–
    4904-b5c9–9d3f04810fa9, archived at https://perma.cc/6QLJ-XC9C; James
    Cook, 'Uber's internal charts show how its driver-rating system actually works',
    Business Insider UK (11 February 2015), http://uk.businessinsider.com/leaked-
    charts-show-how-ubers-driver-rating-system-works-2015–2, archived at https://
    perma.cc/5UPM-SWFN; Uber, 'Uber + Pandora', https://www.uber.com/
    drive/music/, archived at https://perma.cc/3SCK-FRT2; Ryan Lawler, 'Lyft
    sheds some of its quirks as it seeks new users', *TechCrunch* (30 November 2014),
    https://techcrunch.com/2014/11/30/lyft-quirks/, archived at https://perma.
    cc/2QYB-4VZX

26. 'How TaskRabbit works: insights into business & revenue model', *Juggernaut* (10
    August 2015), http://nextjuggernaut.com/blog/how-task-rabbit-works-insights-
    into-business-revenue-model/, archived at https://perma.cc/74ZE-KR4Z

27. Amazon MTurk, 'Amazon Mechanical Turk participation agreement', clause
    3(b), http://www.mturk.com/mturk/conditionsofuse, archived at https://
    perma.cc/6XKA-6QFL

28. Upwork, 'How it works', http://www.upwork.com/i/howitworks/client/,
    archived at https://perma.cc/9GM9-MLHF; Andrew Beinstein and Ted
    Sumers, 'How Uber Engineering increases safe driving with telematics', *Uber
    Engineering* (29 June 2016), https://eng.uber.com/telematics/, archived at
    https://perma.cc/E82S-37NQ

29. TaskRabbit, 'Frequently asked questions', https://support.taskrabbit.com/hc/
    en-us/articles/204409560-Can-I-leave-a-review-for-my-Client-, archived at
    https://perma.cc/K6DR-BV86

30. Andrew Callaway, 'Apploitation in a city of instaserfs: how the "sharing economy" has turned San Francisco into a dystopia for the working class', *The Magazine* (1 January 2016), http://www.policyalternatives.ca/publications/monitor/apploitation-city-instaserfs, archived at https://perma.cc/AP9Z-TZ5J

31. Alyson Shontell, 'My nightmare experience as a TaskRabbit drone', *Business Insider* (7 December 2011), http://www.businessinsider.com/confessions-of-a-task-rabbit-2011-12?IR=T, archived at https://perma.cc/7EYK-86QR

32. Ibid.

33. Crowdflower, 'Crowdsourced content moderation', https://success.crowdflower.com/hc/en-us/article_attachments/201062449/CrowdFlower_Skout_Case_Study.pdf, archived at https://perma.cc/4MY4-AAFX

34. Adrian Chen, 'The labourers who keep dick pics and beheadings out of your Facebook feed', *Wired* (23 October 2014), http://www.wired.com/2014/10/content-moderation/, archived at https://perma.cc/4CJG-UDMT

35. Andrew Callaway, 'Apploitation in a city of instaserfs: how the "sharing economy" has turned San Francisco into a dystopia for the working class', *The Magazine* (1 January 2016), http://www.policyalternatives.ca/publications/monitor/apploitation-city-instaserfs, archived at https://perma.cc/AP9Z-TZ5J

36. Bill Gurley, 'A deeper look at Uber's dynamic pricing model', *Above the Crowd* (11 March 2014), http://abovethecrowd.com/2014/03/11/a-deeper-look-at-ubers-dynamic-pricing-model/, archived at https://perma.cc/9JRL-F96W. More recently, the introduction of so-called route-based pricing in certain locations has drawn considerable media attention: Eric Newcomer, 'Uber starts charging what you're willing to pay', *Bloomberg* (19 May 2017), https://www.bloomberg.com/news/articles/2017-05-19/uber-s-future-may-rely-on-predicting-how-much-you-re-willing-to-pay, archived at https://perma.cc/4J3M-WKXM

37. 'The "X" rejection and feedback on HITs', *Turk Requesters* (30 January 2015), http://turkrequesters.blogspot.co.uk/2015/01/the-x-rejection-and-feedback-on-hits.html, archived at https://perma.cc/A2BK-XT6L; Amazon MTurk, 'Amazon Mechanical Turk participation agreement', clause 3(f), http://www.mturk.com/mturk/conditionsofuse, archived at https://perma.cc/6XKA-6QFL; see also Julian Dobson, 'Mechanical Turk: Amazon's new underclass', *Huffington Post* (21 April 2013), http://www.huffingtonpost.com/julian-dobson/mechanical-turk-amazons-underclass_b_2687431.html, archived at https://perma.cc/9GGZ-5PL5 ('There's no appeal if you think you've been exploited or scammed').

38. Amazon MTurk, 'Worker web site FAQs', http://www.mturk.com/mturk/help?helpPage=worker#how_paid, archived at https://perma.cc/U9TL-MC6K

39. Steven Hill, *Raw Deal* (St Martin's Press 2015), 11.

40. Mariano Mamertino of economics consultancy Indeed, as cited in Recruitment and Employment Confederation (REC), *Gig Economy: The Uberisation of Work* (REC 2016), 52.

41. Elance-Odesk, *Annual Impact Report* (Elance-Odesk 2014), 23, https://blog-static.odesk.com/content/Elance-oDeskAnnualImpactReport2014.pdf, archived at

https://perma.cc/48BE-G7U7; Lilly Irani and M. Six Silberman, 'Turkopticon: interrupting worker invisibility in Amazon Mechanical Turk' (2013) CHI 2013, Changing Perspectives, Paris, France; 'Is digital expert knowledge facing a race to the bottom?', *a-connect* (undated), http://www.a-connect.com/acknowledge/is-digital-expert-knowledge-facing-a-race-to-the-bottom/, archived at https://perma.cc/8ZJ3-P3X4. This tallies with research commissioned by the World Bank, which estimates that a typical online freelancer on Elance-oDesk (now Upwork) or Freelancer.com will work 20–40 hours per week and earn US$200–750 per month, whilst only 'a small subset of highly skilled workers... can earn up to $3000 per month': Siou Chew Kuek, Cecilia Paradi-Guilford, Toks Fayomi, Soari Imaizumi, and Panos Ipeirotis, 'The Global Opportunity in Online Outsourcing' (World Bank 2015), 42, http://www.ipeirotis.com/wp-content/uploads/2015/05/The-World-Bank-The-Global-Opportunity-in-Online-Outsourcing.pdf, archived at https://perma.cc/2AGP-TME6

42. Amazon MTurk, 'Amazon Mechanical Turk pricing', https://requester.mturk.com/pricing, archived at https://perma.cc/58T4-BUE7; Panagiotis Ipeirotis, 'Analyzing the Amazon Mechanical Turk marketplace' (2010) 17(2) XRDS 16, http://dl.acm.org/citation.cfm?id=1869094, archived at https://perma.cc/8C4M-74M8

43. Ibid., 19; Paul Hitlin, *Research in the Crowdsourcing Age: A Case Study* (Pew Research Center 2016), 8, http://assets.pewresearch.org/wp-content/uploads/sites/14/2016/07/PI_2016.07.11_Mechanical-Turk_FINAL.pdf, archived at https://perma.cc/38NZ-97C4

44. Barrie Clement, 'Burger King pays £106,000 to staff forced to "clock off" ', *The Independent* (19 December 1995), http://www.independent.co.uk/news/burger-king-pays-pounds-106000-to-staff-forced-to-clock-off-1526458.html, archived at https://perma.cc/XV3B-2WA5. Today, this practice would no longer be possible under the Minimum Wage Act 1998.

45. Jonathan Hall and Alan Krueger, 'An analysis of the labor market for Uber's Driver-Partners in the United States' (2016) NBER Working Paper No. 22843, 18.

46. Ibid., 23. The cost of these incidentals are also much higher if you have to file your own taxes, pay National Insurance, accountants, negotiate your individual health plan, etc.

47. Johana Bhuiyan, 'What Uber drivers really make (according to their pay stubs)', *BuzzFeed News* (19 November 2014), http://www.buzzfeed.com/johanabhuiyan/what-uber-drivers-really-make-according-to-their-pay-stubs?utm_term=.wwB0BDk1w#.rcMr8qAnb, archived at https://perma.cc/4JSB-M9FD

48. 'New Uber Drivers pay down by £1 per hour', *GMB Newsroom* (24 November 2015). http://www.gmb.org.uk/newsroom/new-uber-drivers-pay-down-by-one-pound, archived at https://perma.cc/55MD-RV3U

49. Jonathan Hall and Alan Krueger, 'An analysis of the labor market for Uber's Driver-Partners in the United States' (2016) NBER Working Paper No. 22843, 11.

50. M. Six Silberman, *Human-Centered Computing and the Future of Work: Lessons from the Mechanical Turk and Turkopticon, 2008–2015* (PhD dissertation, University of California Irvine 2015), 3, http://wtf.tw/text/lessons_from_amt_and_turkopticon_summary.pdf, archived at https://perma.cc/2WN3-D7F5

51. TaskRabbit, *The TaskRabbit Handbook* (on file with author), 9; Task Rabbit, 'Community guidelines', https://support.taskrabbit.com/hc/en-us/articles/204409440-TaskRabbit-Community-Guidelines, archived at https://perma.cc/VX4Q-77CT; Josh Dzieza, 'The rating game: how Uber and its peers turned us into horrible bosses', *The Verge* (28 October 2015), http://www.theverge.com/2015/10/28/9625968/rating-system-on-demand-economy-uber-olive-garden, archived at https://perma.cc/CVU4-GEV7; Benjamin Sachs, 'Uber and Lyft: customer reviews and the right to control', *On Labor* (20 May 2015), http://onlabor.org/2015/05/20/uber-and-lyft-customer-reviews-and-the-right-to-control/, archived at https://perma.cc/9TNM-Y95X

52. Josh Dzieza, 'The rating game: how Uber and its peers turned us into horrible bosses', *The Verge* (28 October 2015), http://www.theverge.com/2015/10/28/9625968/rating-system-on-demand-economy-uber-olive-garden, archived at https://perma.cc/CVU4-GEV7

53. TaskRabbit, 'The TaskRabbit elite', http://www.taskrabbit.co.uk/taskrabbit-elite, archived at https://perma.cc/P2FE-GLM2; Panos Ipeirotis, 'Mechanical Turk changing the defaults: the game has changed', *Behind the Enemy Lines* (5 December 2012), http://www.behind-the-enemy-lines.com/2012/12/mechanical-turk-changing-defaults-game.html, archived at https://perma.cc/8G73-PYWF

54. Alex Rosenblat and Luke Stark, 'Algorithmic labor and information asymmetries: a case study of Uber's drivers' (2016) 10 International Journal of Communication 3758, 3763.

55. Daniel Tomlinson of the UK's Resolution Foundation, as cited in REC, *Gig Economy: The Uberisation of Work* (REC 2016), 53.

56. Greg Harman, 'The sharing economy is not as open as you might think', *The Guardian* (12 November 2014), http://www.theguardian.com/sustainable-business/2014/nov/12/algorithms-race-discrimination-uber-lyft-airbnb-peer, archived at https://perma.cc/DZ8S-D8SL

57. Doug H, 'Fired from Uber: why drivers get deactivated, and how to get reactivated', *Ride Sharing Driver* (21 April 2016), http://www.ridesharingdriver.com/fired-uber-drivers-get-deactivated-and-reactivated/, archived at https://perma.cc/3MQL-4TWD

58. Amazon MTurk, 'Amazon Mechanical Turk participation agreement', clause 11, http://www.mturk.com/mturk/conditionsofuse, archived at https://perma.cc/6XKA-6QFL; Dynamo, 'MTurk suspensions', http://www.wearedynamo.org/suspensions, archived at https://perma.cc/SH8S-VAHW

59. John Arlidge, 'We want it all now—but at what price?', *Sunday Times Magazine* (10 July 2016), 13.

60. Mariano Mamertino of economics consultancy Indeed, as cited in REC, *Gig Economy: The Uberisation of Work* (REC 2016), 52.

61. Caroline O'Donovan, 'Changes to Amazon's Mechanical Turk platform could cost workers', *BuzzFeed News* (23 June 2015), http://www.buzzfeed.com/carolineodonovan/changes-to-amazons-mechanical-turk-platform-could-cost-worke?utm_term=.cvjLONY4qo#.ruxM6v1r5a, archived at https://perma.cc/6HHS-BELG

62. Upwork, 'Freelancer service fees', https://support.upwork.com/hc/en-us/articles/211062538-Freelancer-Service-Fees, archived at https://perma.cc/63CH-LA7F

63. Uber, 'Need help?', https://help.uber.com/h/8ba64dc9-a85b-4923–8277-c0e813395d79, archived at https://perma.cc/A29G-AKDD

64. Noam Scheiber, 'Uber drivers and others in the gig economy take a stand', *The New York Times* (2 February 2016), http://www.nytimes.com/2016/02/03/business/uber-drivers-and-others-in-the-gig-economy-take-a-stand.html?partner=rssnyt&emc=rss&_r=3, archived at https://perma.cc/3VC9-HRG8

65. Ibid.

66. Casey Newton, 'TaskRabbit is blowing up its business and becoming the Uber for everything', *The Verge* (17 June 2014), http://www.theverge.com/2014/6/17/5816254/taskrabbit-blows-up-its-auction-house-to-offer-services-on-demand, archived at https://perma.cc/5E5V-Q8KE; Harrison Weber, 'TaskRabbit users revolt as the company shuts down its bidding system', *Venture Beat* (10 July 2014), http://venturebeat.com/2014/07/10/taskrabbit-users-revolt-as-the-company-shuts-down-its-bidding-system/, archived at https://perma.cc/5E7M-NMZW

67. Sean Farrell and Hilary Osborne, 'Deliveroo boss says sorry for pay dispute', *The Guardian* (15 August 2016), http://www.theguardian.com/business/2016/aug/15/deliveroo-boss-says-sorry-for-pay-dispute, archived at https://perma.cc/5PYH-NCGP

68. Alex Rosenblat and Luke Stark, 'Algorithmic labor and information asymmetries: a case study of Uber's drivers' (2016) 10 International Journal of Communication 3758, 3764.

69. Alison Griswold, 'This is the script Uber is using to make anti-union phone calls to drivers in Seattle', *Quartz* (22 February 2016), http://qz.com/621977/this-is-the-script-uber-is-using-to-make-anti-union-phone-calls-to-drivers-in-seattle/, archived at https://perma.cc/ENZ8-8FHW

70. Steven Greenhouse, 'On demand, and demanding their rights', *The American Prospect Magazine* (28 June 2016), http://prospect.org/article/demand-and-demanding-their-rights, archived at https://perma.cc/CMB2-W8QT

71. TaskRabbit, *The TaskRabbit Handbook* (on file with author), 15.

72. TaskRabbit, https://support.taskrabbit.com/hc/en-us/articles/207814456, archived at https://perma.cc/WS63-FUQN

73. Work and Pensions Committee, *Written Evidence: Self-employment and the Gig Economy* (HC 847 2016–17), extract from Deliveroo contract, http://www.parliament.uk/documents/commons-committees/work-and-pensions/Written_Evidence/Extract-from-Deliveroo-contract.pdf, archived at https://perma.cc/Q3UF-QNXZ; Hilary Osborne, 'Deliveroo workers' contracts ban access to

employment tribunals', *The Guardian* (25 July 2016), http://www.theguardian. com/law/2016/jul/25/deliveroo-workers-contracts-ban-access-to-employ-ment-tribunals?CMP=share_btn_tw, archived at https://perma.cc/9TTH-989J; Shona Ghosh, 'Deliveroo will drop a clause in its contracts that banned couriers from employment tribunals', *Business Insider* (22 February 2017), http://www. businessinsider.com/deliveroo-will-no-longer-forbid-employment-tribunals-in-its-contract-2017-2?r=UK&IR=T&utm_content=bufferd6321&utm_medium=social&utm_source=twitter.com&utm_campaign=buffer, archived at https://perma.cc/R998-SAGS

74. Katherine Stone, 'Uber and arbitration: a lethal combination', *Economic Policy Institute* (24 May 2016), http://www.epi.org/blog/uber-and-arbitration-a-lethal-combination/, archived at https://perma.cc/NM89-AC52. Uber's new terms require workers to:

> agree that any dispute, claim or controversy arising out of or relating to these Terms or the breach, termination, enforcement, interpretation or validity thereof or the use of the Services (collectively, 'Disputes') will be settled by binding arbitration between you and Uber.

They are also required to waive 'the right to a trial by jury or to participate as a plaintiff or class in any purported class action or representative proceeding': Uber, 'US terms of use', clause 2 ('Arbitration Agreement'), http://www.uber. com/legal/terms/us/, archived at https://perma.cc/4QCV-CB3R. Uber's law-yers have described the terms as 'bullet proof' and 'state of the art, plus more': Joel Rosenblat, 'How gig economy is using private arbitration to win on labor classification', *Insurance Journal* (6 June 2016), http://www.insurance-journal.com/news/national/2016/06/06/410983.htm, archived at https://perma. cc/94CR-3ZW7

75. Upwork, 'Freelancer service fees', https://support.upwork.com/hc/en-us/articles/ 211062538-Freelancer-Service-Fees, archived at https://perma.cc/424S-BBUC

76. Economists refer to this as the 'cost of switching' and have demonstrated the resulting inefficiencies: Paul Klemperer, 'Competition when consumers have switching costs' (1995) 62(4) Review of Economic Studies 515.

77. Jonathan Hall and Alan Krueger, 'An analysis of the labor market for Uber's Driver-Partners in the United States' (2016) NBER Working Paper No. 22843, 16.

78. Eric Newcomer and Olivia Zaleski, 'Inside Uber's auto-lease machine, where almost anyone can get a car', *Bloomberg* (31 May 2016), http://www.bloomberg. com/news/articles/2016-05-31/inside-uber-s-auto-lease-machine-where-almost-anyone-can-get-a-car, archived at https://perma.cc/6WFZ-SJ88

79. 'Why is the vehicle leasing program for Uber drivers so expensive?', *Quora* (undated), https://www.quora.com/Why-is-the-vehicle-leasing-program-for-Uber-drivers-so-expensive, archived at https://perma.cc/R4XL-NURP; Leslie Hook, 'Uber hitches a ride with car finance schemes', *Financial Times* (11 August 2016), http://www.ft.com/content/921289f6-5dd1-11e6-bb77-a121aa8abd95, archived at https://perma.cc/ULZ7-QGMZ

80. Jia Tolentino, 'The gig economy celebrates working yourself to death', *The New Yorker* (22 March 2017), http://www.newyorker.com/culture/jia-tolentino/the-gig-economy-celebrates-working-yourself-to-death, archived at https://perma.cc/JX8G-37QX

CHAPTER 4

1. Hans C. Andersen, *Keiserens nye klæder* (tr. Jean Hersholt), http://www.andersen.sdu.dk/vaerk/hersholt/TheEmperorsNewClothes_e.html, archived at https://perma.cc/Y7T2-8ML9

2. Matthew Hancock, 'Foreword by Minister of State for Business, Enterprise and Energy', in Debbie Wosskow, *Unlocking the Sharing Economy: An Independent Review* (BIS 2014), 5.

3. Steve Case, *The Third Wave: An Entrepreneur's Vision of the Future* (Simon & Schuster 2016).

4. Erin Barry, 'Uber, Lyft effect on economy show work "innovation": case', *CNBC* (17 April 2016), http://www.cnbc.com/2016/04/15/uber-lyft-effect-on-economy-show-work-innovation-case.html, archived at https://perma.cc/LDF5-5Y4E

5. Arun Sundararajan, *The Sharing Economy: The End of Employment and the Rise of Crowd-Based Capitalism* (MIT Press 2016), 69.

6. Ibid., 70.

7. Ibid., 72.

8. Ibid., 73.

9. Ibid., 77.

10. Ibid., 172.

11. Ibid., 173.

12. Putting out might appear to be a particularly curious label to Anglophone audiences. It is probably a translation of the German *Verlagssytem* ('putting-out system').

13. Duncan Bythell, *The Sweated Trades: Outwork in Nineteenth-Century Britain* (St Martin's Press 1978).

14. Matthew Finkin, 'Beclouded work, beclouded workers in historical perspective' (2016) 37(3) Comparative Labor Law & Policy Journal 603, citing Prabin Baishya, 'The putting out system in Ancient India' (1997) 25 Social Scientist 51.

15. See Matthew Finkin, 'Beclouded work, beclouded workers in historical perspective' (2016) 37(3) Comparative Labor Law & Policy Journal 603; Susan Kitchell, 'Tonya, the Japanese wholesalers: why their domination position' (1995) 15(1) Journal of Macromarketing 21; J Lautner, *Altbabylonische Personenmiete und Erntarbeiterverträge* (1936) 164.

16. Select Committee on Homework, *Reports of the Select Committee on Homework* (HC 290-IV, 1907–8), xxv. The parallels are by no means limited to history: think, for example, of twentieth-century outsourcing and global supply chains.

17. Arun Sundararajan, *The Sharing Economy: The End of Employment and the Rise of Crowd-Based Capitalism* (MIT Press 2016), 159–75.

18. Consider, for example, this dizzying description of clothing manufacture:

> [T]he middleman fixes the garment, and passes it on to the tailor or 'maker' to baste for fitting; from this it passes to the 'machiner' to machine the main seams; again back to the fixer to fix the shoulder seams, collars and sleeves; back again to the tailor to put in the stitching; and a last to the whom to fell in the lining and stitch buttons and buttonholes. The garment is then ready to go out to the 'presser', and after a final inspection from the middleman 'fixer', the finished article is returned to the shop.
>
> (Barbara Drake, 'The West End tailoring trade', in Sidney Webb and Arnold Freeman (eds), *Seasonal Trades* (Constable 1912), 78–9)

19. Select Committee of the House of Lords on the Sweating System, *Reports of the Select Committee on the Sweating System* (HL 361-XX, 1887–88), Q 1772 (Mr Lewis Lyons).

20. James Schmiechen, *Sweated Industries and Sweated Labor* (Croom Helm 1984), 56–7.

21. For a graphical illustration, see the picture plates, ibid.

22. Henry Mayhew, *The Morning Chronicle Survey of Labour and the Poor, Vol. 2* (Routledge 2016), 95, 143–5.

23. Anne-Sylvaine Chassany, 'Uber: a route out of the French *banlieues*', *Financial Times* (3 March 2016), https://www.ft.com/content/bf3d0444-e129-11e5-9217-6ae3733a2cd1, archived at https://perma.cc/78JC-EP7Z

24. Hannah Curran, 'How a mom found professional success while staying at home with a newborn', *Fiverr* (21 February 2017), http://blog.fiverr.com/how-a-dallas-mom-found-professional-success-while-nursing-a-newborn-baby/, archived at https://perma.cc/J2SK-4N3H

25. Ibid.

26. Henry Mayhew, *The Morning Chronicle Survey of Labour and the Poor, Vol. 2* (Routledge 2016), 71.

27. Ibid., 72.

28. Ibid., 73.

29. Arun Sundararajan, *The Sharing Economy: The End of Employment and the Rise of Crowd-Based Capitalism* (MIT Press 2016), 159–75.

30. Duncan Bythell, *The Sweated Trades: Outwork in Nineteenth-century Britain* (St Martin's Press 1978), 18–19.

31. Vernon Jensen, *Hiring of Dock Workers and Employment Practices in the Ports of New York, Liverpool, London, Rotterdam, and Marseilles* (Harvard University Press 1964), 21–2.

32. See, e.g., the story of 'blue eyes', the preferred men in the port of Liverpool: ibid., 163.

33. Ibid., 164.

34. Duncan Bythell, *The Sweated Trades: Outwork in Nineteenth-Century Britain* (St Martin's Press 1978), 78.

35. James Schmiechen, *Sweated Industries and Sweated Labor* (Croom Helm 1984), 56.

36. Juliet Stuart Poyntz, 'Introduction', in Sidney Webb and Arnold Freeman (eds), *Seasonal Trades* (Constable 1912), 60–1, citing Mr Cyril Jackson and Rev. J. C. Pringle, *Report of the Royal Commission on the Poor Laws and Relief of Distress on the Effects of Employment or Assistance Given to the 'Unemployed' Since 1886 as a Means of Relieving Distress outside the Poor Law* (Appendix, Vol. XIX, Cd 4795, 1909), 31.

37. Ibid., 60.

38. Sidney Webb and Beatrice Webb, *Industrial Democracy, Vol. II* (Longmans 1897), 435.

39. 'The wages actually received by the workmen...differ from the price of their work...[s]uch difference being occasioned by deductions...[and] other charges made by the "middleman"': Select Committee on the Stoppage of Wages (Hosiery), *Report from the Select Committee on Stoppage of Wages (Hosiery)* (HC 421-XIV, 1854–5), iii. The Parliamentary Committee on Stoppages also identified the apparently widespread practice of trying to sign up as many workers as possible to charge frame rents, rather than limiting the number of frames to the amount of work actually required, which left all workers with a mere part-time allocation of work: ibid., iii–iv. See also Commissioner Muggridge, *Reports of the Royal Commission on the Condition of the Framework Knitters* (vol. XV, HC 609, 1845), 83.

40. Vernon Jensen, *Hiring of Dock Workers and Employment Practices in the Ports of New York, Liverpool, London, Rotterdam, and Marseilles* (Harvard University Press 1964), 25; Henry Mayhew, *The Morning Chronicle Survey of Labour and the Poor, Vol. 2* (Routledge 2016), 102–3, 117. This was linked to the practice of paying in truck as an anti-competitive move designed to undercut standard wage rates. The 'cuts' mentioned were often made indirectly by providing certain 'benefits' as a substitute for wages.

41. James Schmiechen, *Sweated Industries and Sweated Labor* (Croom Helm 1984), 103.

42. Roger Lloyd-Jones and Mervyn Lewis, *Manchester and the Age of the Factory* (Croom Helm 1988), 75.

43. Barbara Drake, 'The West End tailoring trade', in Sidney Webb and Arnold Freeman (eds), *Seasonal Trades* (Constable 1912), 81.

44. Select Committee on Homework, *Reports of the Select Committee on Homework* (HC 290-IV, 1907–8), iii. See also Sidney Webb and Beatrice Webb, *Industrial Democracy, Vol. II* (Longmans 1897), 758.

45. James Schmiechen, *Sweated Industries and Sweated Labor* (Croom Helm 1984), 59.

46. Friedrich Engels, *The Condition of the Working Classes* (1845), as cited by Duncan Bythell, *The Sweated Trades: Outwork in Nineteenth-Century Britain* (St Martin's Press 1978), 10—although note that this was not, back then, an argument in favour of equal pay. It took more than a century for challenges to the underlying inequalities to gain real traction.

47. Duncan Bythell, *The Sweated Trades: Outwork in Nineteenth-Century Britain* (St Martin's Press 1978), 163.

48. Ibid., 165, shows how these efforts sometimes succeeded in convincing the workers themselves, too. Again, this is a clear parallel with on-demand work today.

49. Erin Hatton, 'The rise of the permanent temp economy', *The New York Times* (26 January 2013), https://opinionator.blogs.nytimes.com/2013/01/26/the-rise-of-the-permanent-temp-economy/, archived at https://perma.cc/2D7S-B68Z. Kalanick subsequently apologized: 'Travis Kalanick's Uber-apology', *The Economist* (3 March 2017), https://www.economist.com/news/business-and-finance/21717810-many-woes-ubers-boss-travis-kalanicks-uber-apology, archived at https://perma.cc/NMN9-UV4X

50. Duncan Bythell, *The Sweated Trades: Outwork in Nineteenth-Century Britain* (St Martin's Press 1978), 168, and sources cited there.

51. James Schmiechen, *Sweated Industries and Sweated Labor* (Croom Helm 1984), 102–3, 189.

52. W. B. Crump, *The Leeds Wollen Industry 1780–1820* (The Thoresby Society 1931), 25, as cited by Duncan Bythell, *The Sweated Trades: Outwork in Nineteenth-Century Britain* (St Martin's Press 1978), 178.

53. Izabella Kaminska, 'The sharing economy will go medieval on you', *Financial Times* (21 May 2015), https://ftalphaville.ft.com/2015/05/21/2130111/the-sharing-economy-will-go-medieval-on-you/, archived at https://perma.cc/GL9K-L7WZ

54. International Labour Office (ILO), *Non-Standard Employment around the World: Understanding Challenges, Shaping Prospects* (ILO 2016), 2.

55. David Weil, *The Fissured Workplace: Why Work Became so Bad for so Many and What Can Be Done to Improve it* (Harvard University Press 2014); David Weil, 'How to Make employment fair in an age of contracting and temp work', *Harvard Business Review* (24 March 2017), https://hbr.org/2017/03/making-employment-a-fair-deal-in-the-age-of-contracting-subcontracting-and-temp-work, archived at https://perma.cc/H4VG-QP59

56. Ibid.

57. Valerio De Stefano, 'The rise of the "just-in-time workforce": on-demand work, crowdwork, and labor protection in the "gig economy"' (2016) 37(3) Comparative Labor Law & Policy Journal 471.

58. Ursula Holtgrewe, 'Working in the low-paid service sector: what is to be learned from the analogue world?', in Werner Wobbe, Elva Bova, and Catalin Dragomirescu-Gaina (eds), *The Digital Economy and the Single Market* (FEPS 2016), 100, argues that this is true both as regards:

    the devaluation of some forms of work as 'not a proper job' or something done for love or 'pin money' or both, and an idea of employability that renders labour market access contingent on an uncertain and possibly limitless amount of upfront investments by workers.

59. Matthew Finkin, 'Beclouded work, beclouded workers in historical perspective' (2016) 37(3) Comparative Labor Law & Policy Journal 603, 608.

60. James Schmiechen, *Sweated Industries and Sweated Labor* (Croom Helm 1984), 187.

61. Jill Rubery and Frank Wilkinson, 'Outwork and segmented labour markets', in Frank Wilkinson (ed.), *The Dynamics of Labour Market Segmentation* (Academic Press 1981), 115.

62. As cited in Recruitment and Employment Confederation (REC), *Gig Economy: The Uberisation of Work* (REC 2016), 48.

63. As cited in Vernon Jensen, *Hiring of Dock Workers and Employment Practices in the Ports of New York, Liverpool, London, Rotterdam, and Marseilles* (Harvard University Press 1964), 122–3.

64. Jacob Hacker, *The Great Risk Shift: The Assault on American Jobs, Families, Health Care, and Retirement—and How You Can Fight Back* (Oxford University Press 2006).

65. Ibid. See also Daniel Hemel, 'Pooling and unpooling in the Uber economy' (2017) University of Chicago Legal Forum, forthcoming.

66. Jennifer Smith, ' "I'm ashamed": Uber CEO Travis Kalanick issues grovelling memo to staff admitting he needs to "grow up" after video surfaces of him yelling at one of his own drivers', *Daily Mail* (28 February 2017), http://www.dailymail.co.uk/news/article-4269350/Uber-CEO-Travis-Kalanick-lashes-driver-video.html, archived at https://perma.cc/5F8F-WWCD

67. Christine Lagarde, 'Reinvigorating productivity growth', *IMF* (3 April 2017), http://www.imf.org/en/news/articles/2017/04/03/sp040317-reinvigorating-productivity-growth, archived at https://perma.cc/84CC-9TCH

68. 'Are we adapting instead of innovating?', *Flip Chart Fairy Tales* (3 May 2012), https://flipchartfairytales.wordpress.com/2012/05/03/are-we-adapting-instead-of-innovating/, archived at https://perma.cc/XQR2-7QPB

69. Martin Sandbu, 'The problem is not too many robots, but too few', *Financial Times* (4 April 2017), http://www.ft.com/content/bcb600d4–1870–11e7-a53d-df09f373be87, archived at https://perma.cc/QCX5-4K6N

70. See, e.g., Paul Krugman, 'Robot geometry (very wonkish)', *Financial Times* (20 March 2017), https://krugman.blogs.nytimes.com/2017/03/20/robot-geometry-very-wonkish, archived at https://perma.cc/KGF7-YKRS; Robert Gordon, *The Rise and Fall of American Growth* (Princeton University Press 2016).

71. Uber contests these allegations: Mike Isaac, 'How Uber deceives the authorities worldwide', *The New York Times* (3 March 2017), http://www.nytimes.com/2017/03/03/technology/uber-greyball-programme-evade-authorities.html?_r=1, archived at https://perma.cc/G48X-RUV7; Julia Carrie Wong, 'Greyball: how Uber used secret software to dodge the law', *The Guardian* (4 March 2017), http://www.theguardian.com/technology/2017/mar/03/uber-secret-programme-greyball-resignation-ed-baker, archived at https://perma.cc/CVR6-BR3R; Amir Efrati, 'Uber's top secret "Hell" program exploited Lyft's vulnerability', *The Information* (12 April 2017), http://www.theinformation.com/ubers-top-secret-hell-programme-exploited-lyfts-vulnerability, archived at https://perma.cc/7TQX-UJ4M; Julia Carrie Wong, 'Uber's secret Hell program violated drivers' privacy, class-action suit claims', *The Guardian* (25 April 2017), http://www.theguardian.com/technology/2017/apr/24/uber-hell-programme-driver-privacy-lyft-spying, archived at https://perma.cc/35ZK-DVKC

72. I am grateful to Professor Jack Balkin, participants at an ideas seminar at Yale Law School's Internet and Society Project (ISP), and students on the ISP's law and innovation course for discussions that fleshed out this point. There is, as

usual, plenty of historical precedent: the frame rental system was one early example of 'lock-in' practices, designed to keep a surplus of workers available to benefit platform operators. As a UK parliamentary committee noted in 1855:

> [A] much larger body of persons are committed to and detained in the manufacture, through successive generation, than can be adequately supported by it, while the gradual working of the ordinary remedy by the withdrawal of superfluous hands is intercepted and frustrated.
>
> (Select Committee on the Stoppage of Wages (Hosiery), *Report from the Select Committee on Stoppage of Wages (Hosiery)* (HC 421-XIV, 1854–5), iv)

73. Ryan Avent, 'The productivity paradox', *Medium* (16 March 2017), https://medium.com/@ryanavent_93844/the-productivity-paradox-aaf05e5e4aad, archived at https://perma.cc/TFE8-7X8N

74. Select Committee on the Stoppage of Wages (Hosiery), *Report from the Select Committee on Stoppage of Wages (Hosiery)* (HC 421-XIV, 1854–5), iv. Duncan Bythell agrees:

> So long as outwork labour remained plentiful and its price fell ever lower, manufacturers had little incentive to turn to alternative means of production... contemporaries often believed that the very cheapness of hand-labour actually delayed the adoption of newly invented labour-saving machines.
>
> (Duncan Bythell, *The Sweated Trades: Outwork in Nineteenth-Century Britain* (St Martin's Press 1978), 177)

The example given is the development of power looms in the textile industry in the 1830s and 1840s, with manufacturers reporting before parliamentary committees that low labour cost made it unnecessary to invest. There are also more recent examples, such as agricultural innovation in California in the 1970s: Eduardo Porter, 'Revisiting a minimum-wage axiom', *The New York Times* (4 February 2007), http://www.nytimes.com/2007/02/04/business/yourmoney/04view.html, archived at https://perma.cc/5JG4-F22A. See also Julia Tomassetti, 'Does Uber redefine the firm? The postindustrial corporation and advanced information technology' (2016) 34(1) Hofstra Labor and Employment Law Journal 1, 36–7, who argues that: 'In the postindustrial corporation, the norm of maximizing profits through the resourceful and innovative management of production and marketing has atrophied.' See also James Flannery, *The Glass House Boys of Pittsburgh: Law, Technology, and Child Labour* (University of Pittsburgh Press 2009).

75. David Z. Morris, 'Uber sharply lags competition in self-driving progress', *Fortune* (18 March 2017), http://fortune.com/2017/03/18/uber-self-driving-car-progress/, archived at https://perma.cc/6GAT-LRQA. The company has also been subject to a lawsuit disputing its ownership of key underlying technology: Mike Isaac and Daisuke Wakabayashi, 'A lawsuit against Uber highlights the rush to conquer driverless cars', *The New York Times* (24 February 2017), http://www.nytimes.com/2017/02/24/technology/anthony-levandowski-waymo-uber-google-lawsuit.html, archived at https://perma.cc/YW9E-B3SU

76. Izabella Kaminska, 'Do the economics of self-driving taxis actually make sense?', *Financial Times* (20 October 2015), https://ftalphaville.ft.com/2015/10/20/

2142450/do-the-economics-of-self-driving-taxis-actually-make-sense/, archived at https://perma.cc/P65L-SCLD

77. Duncan Bythell, *The Sweated Trades: Outwork in Nineteenth-Century Britain* (St Martin's Press 1978), 176.

78. Ibid.

79. Viral Acharya, Ramin Baghai, and Krishnamurthy Subramanian, 'Wrongful discharge laws and innovation' (2012) NBER Working Paper No. 18516, 2. See also 'Does employment protection encourage innovation?', *Flip Chart Fairy Tales* (7 November 2012), https://flipchartfairytales.wordpress.com/2012/11/07/does-employment-protection-encourage-innovation/, archived at https://perma.cc/83ED-NCGM

80. 'What will the gig economy do for innovation?', *Flip Chart Fairy Tales* (11 December 2015) https://flipchartfairytales.wordpress.com/2015/12/11/what-will-the-gig-economy-do-for-innovation/, archived at https://perma.cc/8E2C-XKVA

81. Izabella Kaminska, 'The taxi unicorn's new clothes', *Financial Times* (1 December 2016), https://ftalphaville.ft.com/2016/12/01/2180647/the-taxi-unicorns-new-clothes/, archived at https://perma.cc/YNT5-AH3D

CHAPTER 5

1. Niccolo Machiavelli, *Il Principe* (Oxford University Press 1891).

2. Ronald Coase, 'The nature of the firm' (1937) 4(16) Economica 386. Coase suggested that the main advantage of hierarchical employment relationships over contracts with independent contractors was the entrepreneur's degree of control and the resulting decrease in transaction cost, whether in the search, selection and training of workers, or the employer's tight control over the production process.

3. Simon Deakin and Frank Wilkinson, *The Law of the Labour Market: Industrialization, Employment, and Legal Evolution* (Oxford University Press 2005); Mark Freedland, Alan Bogg, David Cabrelli, Hugh Collins, Nicola Countouris, Anne Davies, Simon Deakin, and Jeremias Prassl (eds), *The Contract of Employment* (Oxford University Press 2016).

4. Further problems arise, including, notably, jurisdictional issues when platforms are incorporated in a country different from their workers' and/or customers' jurisdiction. In reality, however, this appears to be less frequent a scenario than assumed (remember, for example, Amazon's long-time insistence that all new Turkers reside in the United States). A detailed system of legal norms deals with such 'conflicts of law': Louise Merrett, *Employment Contracts in Private International Law* (Oxford University Press 2011).

5. 'TaskRabbit, 'Terms of service' (1 June 2017), http://www.taskrabbit.com/terms, archived at https://perma.cc/S6ZM-VXUS. The UK equivalent (http://www.taskrabbit.co.uk/terms, archived at https://perma.cc/XTH7-Q8V4) isn't capitalized, but attempts to set up functionally equivalent legal structures.

6. *Street v Mountford* [1985] AC 809, 819, HL *per* Lord Templeman.

7. *Autoclenz Limited v Belcher and ors* [2011] UKSC 41, [35], *per* Lord Clarke. For a comprehensive overview, see Alan Bogg, 'Sham self-employment in the Supreme Court' (2012) 41(3) Industrial Law Journal 328.

8. *Alexander v FedEx Ground Package System*, 764 F.3d 981, 998 (9th Cir. 2014). It is important to note that not all decisions in the *FedEx* litigation came to the same conclusion. Given the wide range of tests used for employment classification across different US states and statutes, this is not necessarily surprising.

9. International Labour Organization (ILO), Recommendation 198 of 2006, Art. 9. For a detailed guide, see ILO, *Regulating the Employment Relationship in Europe: A Guide to Recommendation No 198* (Geneva 2013), 33*ff.*

10. Miriam Cherry, 'Beyond misclassification: the digital transformation of work' (2016) 37(3) Comparative Labor Law & Policy Journal 577.

11. Jane Croft, 'Uber challenged on UK drivers' status', *Financial Times* (20 July 2016), http://www.ft.com/content/2bedda7a-4e7e-11e6–88c5-db83e98a590a, archived at https://perma.cc/3BB7-LDZG

12. *Aslam and Farrar v Uber*, Case No. ET/2202550/2015, [87]–[89] (London Employment Tribunal, Judge Snelson), http://www.judiciary.gov.uk/wp-content/uploads/2016/10/aslam-and-farrar-v-uber-reasons-20161028.pdf, archived at https://perma.cc/44Z9-UBC4

13. *Uber v Aslam and Farrar*, Case No. UKEAT/0056/17/DA, [116] (Employment Appeal Tribunal), https://assets.publishing.service.gov.uk/media/5a046b06 e5274a0ee5a1f171/Uber_B.V._and_Others_v_Mr_Y_Aslam_and_Others_UKEAT_0056_17_DA.pdf, archived at https://perma.cc/Z4C3-57Y2. At the time of writing, Uber has announced its intention to bring a further appeal against this finding.

14. *Dewhurst v Citysprint UK Ltd*, Case No. 2202512/2016, [49] (London Employment Tribunal, Judge J. L. Wade).

15. 'L'Urssaf poursuit Uber pour requalifier ses chauffeurs en salariés', *Le Monde* (17 May 2016), http://www.lemonde.fr/economie-francaise/article/2016/05/17/l-urssaf-poursuit-uber-pour-requalifier-ses-chauffeurs-en-salaries_4920825_1656968.html, archived at https://perma.cc/7W9E-JDGN

16. This guidance was withdrawn under the Trump administration, but an archived version is available at http://www.blr.com/html_email/AI2015-1.pdf. See, e.g., Biz Carson, 'The US government just reminded companies like Uber why they could be in serious trouble', *Business Insider UK* (15 July 2015), http://uk.businessinsider.com/us-department-of-labor-reminds-companies-of-1099-classification-rules-2015–7, archived at https://perma.cc/LZJ4-UGGQ. These interpretations were promptly repealed by President Trump's administration: https://www.natlawreview.com/article/donald-trump-s-labor-secretary-revokes-obama-era-dol-joint-employer-and-independent, archived at https://perma.cc/U5P6-QV6Z

17. Simon Goodley, 'Deliveroo told it must pay workers minimum wage', *The Guardian* (14 August 2016), http://www.theguardian.com/society/2016/aug/14/

deliveroo-told-it-must-pay-workers-minimum-wage, archived at https://perma.
cc/2DC7-DCVP

18. Miriam Cherry, 'Beyond misclassification: the digital transformation of work'
(2016) 37(3) Comparative Labor Law & Policy Journal 577.

19. *Berwick v. Uber Techs Inc.*, Case No. 11–46739 EK (Cal. 2015), http://www.scribd.
com/doc/268980201/Uber-v-Berwick-California-Labor-Commission-
Ruling#scribd, archived at https://perma.cc/7YT2-QDK3. Miriam Cherry,
'Beyond misclassification: the digital transformation of work' (2016) 37(3)
Comparative Labor Law & Policy Journal 577, points out that administrative
bodies in other states, including Florida, have sided with the platform.

20. Travis, 'Growing and growing up', *Uber Newsroom* (21 April 2016), https://
newsroom.uber.com/growing-and-growing-up/, archived at https://perma.
cc/9ALX-YR8P. Employment classification was not accepted on Uber's
part.

21. *Douglas O'Connor et al. v Uber Technologies Inc.*, Case No. 13-cv-03826-EMC
(ND Cal.) and *Hakan Yucesoy et al. v Uber Technologies Inc.*, Case No. 15-cv-
00262-EMC (ND Cal. 2016) Order denying plaintiffs' motion for preliminary
approval (18 August 2016), 21, 25, 29.

22. Readers familiar with English employment law will wonder about a further
criterion that has become increasingly prominent in determining employment
status both for workers and employees: mutuality of obligation. Given the
importance of rating algorithms and other lock-in systems as discussed in
Chapter 3, however, it appears likely that that criterion (which has been characterized as a 'fresh emphasis on a form of personal control': Simon Deakin and
Gillian Morris, *Labour Law* (6th edn, Hart 2012), 164) would be met in many
situations—if it is relevant at all: Jeremias Prassl, 'Who is a worker?' (2017) 133
Law Quarterly Review 366.

23. Oxford Professors Paul Davies and Mark Freedland have long criticized the
'constant and increasing counter-factuality' of the traditional approach: Paul
Davies and Mark Freedland, 'The complexities of the employing enterprise', in
Guy Davidov and Brian Langile (eds), *Boundaries and Frontiers of Labour Law*
(Hart 2006), 274. In a world of fissured work, outsourcing agencies, and, now,
on-demand platforms, it can be difficult to identify a single employer exercising
control over its employees.

24. The five employer functions are: (1) hiring and firing (which category includes
all powers of the employer over the very existence of its contract with a worker,
from initial vetting to dismissal); (2) work (when working, employees owe
duties to their employer, including, in particular, a duty to provide labour and
its results); (3) pay (one of the employer's fundamental obligations, this also
includes social security and pension contributions); (4) control (employers tell
their workers what to do—and sometimes how to do it); and (5) profits and
losses (employers are entrepreneurs—they are in the business of making a profit,
whilst also being exposed to any losses that may result from the enterprise). For
details, see Jeremias Prassl, *The Concept of the Employer* (Oxford University Press

2015), 32. I was not the first to attempt such classification; much of my work in this area was inspired by Mark Freedland, *The Personal Employment Contract* (Oxford University Press 2003), 40. It is important to note that direct customer–worker interaction will not usually count as the exercise of an employer function: if I order a meal in a restaurant, for example, I am in some sense telling the waiter what to do—but I am not doing so as part of my management of what Coase would understand to be the restaurant's enterprise-internal market. See further Einat Albin, 'A worker–employer–customer triangle: the case of tips' (2011) 40(2) Industrial Law Journal 181.

25. Jeremias Prassl and Martin Risak, 'Uber, TaskRabbit, and Co.: platforms as employers? Rethinking the legal analysis of crowdwork' (2016) 37(3) Comparative Labor Law & Policy Journal 619.

26. This guidance was withdrawn under the Trump administration, but see archived version at available at http://www.blr.com/html_email/AI2015-1.pdf, section II.B.

27. If the latter deliberately deceives workers as to the length of a task, on the other hand, only the client will be responsible.

28. *Jungheinrich*, C. Cass. soc., 30 November 2011, no. 10–22.964; see also *Molex*, Cass. soc. 2 July 2014, no. 13–15.208.

29. Case C-242/09 *Albron Catering BV v FNV Bondgenoten and John Roest*, ECLI:EU:C:2010:625.

30. For a recent illustration, see Alexia Elejalde-Ruiz, 'Why should McDonald's be a joint employer? NLRB starts to provide answers', *The Chicago Tribune* (10 March 2016), http://www.chicagotribune.com/business/ct-mcdonalds-labor-case-0311-biz-20160310-story.html, archived at https://perma.cc/ST85-CXZY

31. Jeremias Prassl, *The Concept of the Employer* (Oxford University Press 2015), 166ff.

32. The proposed reforms' impact on platforms, however, might be initially more dramatic: costs will rise to reflect employer responsibilities—although this may well be a justified correction. We explore these questions in detail in Chapter 6.

33. Mia Rönnmar, 'The managerial prerogative and the employee's obligation to work: comparative perspectives on functional flexibility' (2006) 35(1) Industrial Law Journal 56, 69.

34. *Bristow v City Petroleum Ltd* [1987] 1 WLR 529, 532, HL. The provisions are today contained in sections 17 et seq. of the Employment Rights Act 1996.

35. Platforms would also become subject to a host of related obligations, from withholding tax at source to contributing to social security and pension payments. In the short term, this might result in individual workers being left with less money in their pocket; in the longer term, however, they would be protected against the vicissitudes of working life. Platforms are also much better equipped to organize central accounting and tax compliance than individual workers, who might not have enough money left at the end of each tax year to comply with their legal obligations.

36. Seth Harris and Alan Krueger, *A Proposal for Modernizing Labor Laws for Twenty-First Century Work: The 'Independent Worker'* (Hamilton Project 2015).

37. Ibid., 13.

38. Anne Davies forcefully makes this point when she argues that:

> It is the employer's responsibility to use its managerial prerogative to gain the max-
> imum benefit…[from workers' standby time]. If the employer chooses not to exer-
> cise that prerogative…that choice should not operate to the disadvantage of the
> worker.
> (A. C. L. Davies, 'Getting more than you bargained for? Rethinking the meaning
> of "work" in employment law' (2017) 46 Industrial Law Journal 30, forthcoming)

39. *Aslam and Farrar v Uber*, Case No. ET/2202550/2015, [100] (London Employment
    Tribunal, Judge Snelson), http://www.judiciary.gov.uk/wp-content/uploads/2016/
    10/aslam-and-farrar-v-uber-reasons-20161028.pdf, archived at https://perma.cc/
    44Z9-UBC4

40. Rachel Hunter and Jeremias Prassl, 'Worker status for app-drivers: Uber-rated?',
    Oxford Human Rights Hub (21 November 2016), http://ohrh.law.ox.ac.uk/worker-
    status-for-app-drivers-uber-rated/, archived at https://perma.cc/7Y54-QF42

41. Many rights, such as unfair dismissal protection, were designed with a 'qualifi-
    cation' threshold requiring a certain period of time with a particular employer
    (up to 24 months in the UK) before a right becomes available. Another prob-
    lem relates to enterprise size thresholds: see my note in 'Les seuils sociaux en
    Europe: Royaume-Uni' [2015] Revue de Droit du Travail 215 and other com-
    parative articles in that issue.

42. Robert Reich, 'The share-the-scraps economy' (2 February 2015), http://rober-
    treich.org/post/109894095095, archived at https://perma.cc/V3PH-U7DY

43. Ibid.

44. Another model can be found in the French 'Prime' or 'Indemnité de précarité',
    a price uplift of 10 per cent on fixed-term contracts: see art. L1243–8 of the
    Code du Travail. There is also historical UK precedent in the Catering Wages
    Act 1943. On wage uplifts more generally, see Einat Albin, *Sectoral Disadvantage:
    The Case of Workers in the British Hospitality Sector* (PhD thesis, University of
    Oxford 2010).

45. http://www.fairwork.gov.au/employee-entitlements/types-of-employees/casual-
    part-time-and-full-time/casual-employees, archived at https://perma.cc/WPW2-
    8WBP. Today, the system is generally implemented through a series of so-called
    Awards—but this technical aspect of Australian labour law isn't directly relevant
    to the present discussion. Similar provisions could easily be translated into domes-
    tic mechanisms, from individual (minimum) wage legislation through to col-
    lective agreements. I am grateful to Dr Tess Hardy of Melbourne Law School
    for extensive help with background materials for this section.

46. General Retail Industry Award 2010 (MA000004), clause 13.2, http://award-
    viewer.fwo.gov.au/award/show/MA000004, archived at https://perma.cc/
    N43Z-N3RF

47. Andrew Stewart, Anthony Forsyth, Mark Irving, Richard Johnstone, and Shae
    McCrystal, *Creighton and Stewart's Labour Law* (6th edn, The Federation Press
    2016), 247.

48. Rosemary Owens, Joellen Riley, and Jill Murray, *The Law of Work* (2nd edn,
    Oxford University Press Australia & New Zealand 2011), 188.

49. For further economic analysis, see, e.g., Joan Rodgers and Iris Day, 'The premium for part-time work in Australia' (2015) 18(3) Australian Journal of Labour Economics 281.

50. Australia and New Zealand have developed a system under which casual workers' minimum wage rates can be 'loaded' under the award system, with additional penalties of up to 50 per cent depending on when work takes place (for example on Sundays). See ibid.

51. See also *The Australian Workers Union v Irvine* (1920) 14 CAR 204, 215, in which it was found that a regular wage:

> assures to the employee reasonable certainty of provision for his family and dependents... the waste of time is a serious interference with a wage based on the cost of living; and if one has to provide a living wage for these workers they should get something more to cover the lost time.
>
> (Cited in Rosemary Owens, 'Women, "atypical" work relationships and the law' (1993) 19(2) Melbourne University Law Review 399, 410)

52. HL Deb., 6 February 2013, vol. 743, col. 265.

53. HL Deb., 20 March 2013, vol. 744, col. 611. The notion of a 'commodification of employment rights' should not be confused with the commodification of labour as such: cf. Simon Deakin, 'Conceptions of the market in labour law', in Ann Numhauser-Henning and Mia Rönnmar (eds), *Normative Patterns and Legal Developments in the Social Dimension of the EU* (Hart 2013), 141, 150; Alain Supiot, 'Grandeur and misery of the social state' (2013) 82 New Left Review 99, 104.
The entire saga of the so-called employee shareholder status is recounted in Jeremias Prassl, 'Employee-shareholder "status": dismantling the contract of employment' (2013) 42(4) Industrial Law Journal 307. The UK government has announced its intention 'to close the status itself to new entrants at the next legislative opportunity': Department for Business, Energy & Industrial Strategy, 'Employee shareholders', https://www.gov.uk/guidance/employee-shareholders, archived at https://perma.cc/57JE-TGSE

54. Lisa Heap, *Striving for Decent Work to End Insecurity in Australian Workplaces* (Australian Institute of Employment Rights 2012), 80 (citations omitted), http://economicdevelopment.vic.gov.au/__data/assets/pdf_file/0007/1311388/Submission-AIER-Attachment-1.pdf, archived at https://perma.cc/4LQH-LK2X. This report also highlights important issues regarding enforcement:

> In reality many casual workers do not receive the casual loading. Alternatively they work in circumstances where it is difficult to find a permanent equivalent worker with who to compare rates of pay in order ascertain whether a casual loading has in fact been applied. Enforcement is an issue. The Fair Work Ombudsman has a role to play here, however given the difficulties in definition described in the paragraphs above it may be a difficult task to ascertain the appropriate benefits accruing to casuals in a range of circumstances.
>
> (Ibid., 81)

55. Act of 10 October 2001 on Minimum Wage for Work (Consolidated Text), art. 1 et seq. (Journal of Laws 2016.1265), as amended. See further http://www.roedl.

com/pl/en/hot_news/labour_law_and_social_insurance_in_poland/new_regulations_on_the_minimum_hourly_pay_under_contracts_of_mandate_and_contracts_for_services.html, archived at https://perma.cc/6HLD-KN9W. There are numerous flaws and drawbacks in the legislative design—notably, as regards significant carve-outs and other avoidance opportunities. I am grateful to Professors Joanna Unterschuetz and Marcin Wujczyk for discussions on this point.

56. Abi Adams, Judith Freedman, and Jeremias Prassl, 'Different ways of working' (14 December 2016), https://abiadams.com/research/different-ways-of-working/, archived at https://perma.cc/J2NK-LUAK. Another major set of concerns relates to the enforcement of gig-economy workers' rights—that is, that low claim values can dramatically reduce incentives to litigate: Abi Adams and Jeremias Prassl, 'Vexatious claims: challenging the case for employment tribunal fees' (2017) 80(2) Modern Law Review 412.

57. Andrei Shleifer and Lawrence Summers, 'Breach of trust in hostile takeovers' (1987) NBER Working Paper No. 2342.

58. For a detailed discussion, see Bob Hepple, 'Workers' rights in mergers and takeovers: the EEC proposals' (1976) 5(1) Industrial Law Journal 197.

59. Regulation (EU) 2016/679 of the European Parliament and of the Council of 27 April 2016 on the protection of natural persons with regard to the processing of personal data and on the free movement of such data, and repealing Directive 95/46/EC (General Data Protection Regulation) [2016] OJ L119/1, Art. 20(1). For updated implementation information, see http://ec.europa.eu/justice/data-protection/index_en.htm, archived at https://perma.cc/4CYX-7YEH. For an explicit call for portable ratings, see Resolution of the European Parliament of 15 June 2017 on a European Agenda for the collaborative economy (2017/2003(INI)).

60. Simon Deakin, 'Shares for rights: why entrepreneurial firms need employment law too', FT Economists Forum (12 February 2013), http://blogs.ft.com/economistsforum/2013/02/shares-for-rights-why-entrepreneurial-firms-need-employment-law-too/, archived at https://perma.cc/YNV6-BXHM

61. Sally Guyoncourt, 'Why Uber drivers' loo breaks are going out the window—literally', The Independent (10 June 2015), http://www.independent.co.uk/news/uk/home-news/why-uber-drivers-loo-breaks-are-going-out-the-window-literally-10311620.html, archived at https://perma.cc/KXW3-G6X4

62. Jonathan Owen, 'Uber driver "threatened" by senior manager after establishing union', The Independent (3 November 2015), http://www.independent.co.uk/news/business/news/uber-driver-threatened-by-senior-manager-for-establishing-union-a6720146.html, archived at https://perma.cc/KXW3-G6X4

63. Courts will, however, look at the reality of the underlying relationship to determine whether the workers in question are genuinely independent entrepreneurs. See, for an example before the Court of Justice of the European Union, Case C-413/13 FNV Kunsten Informatie en Media v Staat der Nederlanden, ECLI:EU:C:2014:2411.

64. Independent Workers Union of Great Britain, 'How we began', https://iwgb. org.uk/how-we-began/ archived at https://perma.cc/CMW9-UDCA

65. Anna Patty, 'Airtasker and unions make landmark agreement to improve pay rates and conditions', *The Sydney Morning Herald* (1 May 2017), http://www. smh.com.au/business/workplace-relations/airtasker-and-unions-make-land-mark-agreement-to-improve-pay-rates-and-conditions-20170427-gvtvp0. html, archived at https://perma.cc/R8GP-6FVW

66. 'Council unanimously adopts first-of-its-kind legislation to give drivers a voice on the job', *Seattle Gov* (14 December 2015), http://www.seattle.gov/council/ issues/giving-drivers-a-voice, archived at https://perma.cc/2VW4-QHRB. At the time of writing, the Ordinance had been put on hold by the US Court of Appeals of the Ninth Circuit, pending a case brought by the US Chamber of Commerce: https://perma.cc/288N-EK5U

67. Ibid.

68. Code du Travail, arts L7341-1–L7342-6; http://www.legifrance.gouv.fr/affich-Code.do;jsessionid=477C7170C222AE05ECF8817BB26DFA0E.tpdila17v_2?i dSectionTA=LEGISCTA000033013020&cidTexte=LEGITEXT00000607205 0&dateTexte=20170531, archived at https://perma.cc/FAU9-LPUS

69. Lilly Irani and M. Six Silberman, 'Turkopticon: interrupting worker invisibility in Amazon Mechanical Turk' (CHI 2013, Changing Perspectives, Paris, France), https://hci.cs.uwaterloo.ca/faculty/elaw/cs889/reading/turkopticon.pdf, archived at https://perma.cc/Q32W-6MB6

70. FairCrowdWork, 'Home', http://www.faircrowdwork.org/en/watch, archived at https://perma.cc/DNZ9-SKU2

71. For further collective ideas, see Rebecca Smith and Sarah Leberstein, *Rights on Demand: Ensuring Workplace Standards and Worker Security in the On-Demand Economy* (NELP 2015).

72. Robert Booth, 'Uber appeals against ruling that its UK drivers are workers', *The Guardian* (14 December 2016), http://www.theguardian.com/technol-ogy/2016/dec/14/uber-appeals-against-ruling-that-its-uk-drivers-are-employees, archived at https://perma.cc/AH9S-ERGN

73. 'ORB/Uber Poll, 2016: flexibility identified as key benefit', *ORB International* (10 October 2016), https://perma.cc/H983-VE3Z

74. Work and Pensions Committee, *Oral Evidence: Self-Employment and the Gig Economy* (HC 847, 2016–17), Response to Q188 (Heidi Allen MP), http://data. parliament.uk/writtenevidence/committeeevidence.svc/evidencedocument/ work-and-pensions-committee/selfemployment-and-the-gig-economy/ oral/47653.pdf, archived at https://perma.cc/UN7F-F9LZ

75. Chartered Institute of Personnel and Development (CIPD), *To Gig or Not to Gig? Stories from the Modern Economy* (CIPD 2017), 32.

76. Ibid., 32.

77. Ibid., 33.

78. Vanessa Katz, 'Regulating the sharing economy' (2015) 30(4) Berkeley Technology Law Journal 1067, 1092.

CHAPTER 6

1. Patricia Marx, 'Outsource yourself', *The New Yorker* (14 January 2013), http://www.newyorker.com/magazine/2013/01/14/outsource-yourself, archived at https://perma.cc/RN4K-RKUM

2. Bhrmie Balaram, Josie Warden, and Fabian Wallace-Stephens, *Good Gigs: A Fairer Future for the UK's Gig Economy* (RSA 2017), 41.

3. 'Disappointed with Deliveroo, have I been unlucky or are they no good?', *Reddit* (21 March 2016), http://www.reddit.com/r/london/comments/4bbbjp/disappointed_with_deliveroo_have_i_been_unlucky/?st=is7ap77e&sh=b2f8c793, archived at https://perma.cc/32DN-YRTX

4. Julie Downs, 'Are your participants gaming the system? Screening Mechanical Turk workers' (Carnegie Mellon University 2010) http://lorrie.cranor.org/pubs/note1552-downs.pdf, archived at https://perma.cc/RGA6-MRQ8; 'The myth of low cost, high quality on Amazon's Mechanical Turk', *TurkerNation* (30 January 2014), http://turkernation.com/showthread.php?21352-The-Myth-of-Low-Cost-High-Quality-on-Amazon-s-Mechanical-Turk, archived at https://perma.cc/6S5H-6RKA

5. Yanbo Ge, Christopher R. Knittel, Don MacKenzie, and Stephen Zoepf, *Racial and Gender Discrimination in Transportation Network Companies* (2016) NBER Working Paper No. 22776; Joshua Barrie, 'This CEO says he has a 3.4 rating on Uber because he's gay', *Business Insider UK* (16 February 2015), http://uk.businessinsider.com/gay-businessman-low-uber-rating-london-2015-2, archived at https://perma.cc/ANN3-DD5F. Other passengers feel that the relative anonymity provided by ride-sharing platforms is an improvement on taxis: see Jenna Wortham, 'Ubering while black', *Medium* (23 October 2014), https://medium.com/matter/ubering-while-black-146db581b9db#.2c0efltcr, archived at https://perma.cc/FMU3-L5D3; Nick Grimm, 'Uber apologises over discrimination against blind customer, human rights activist Graeme Innes', *ABC News* (15 April 2016), http://www.abc.net.au/news/2016-04-15/uber-driver-refuses-blind-customer-ex-commissioner-graeme-innes/7328984, archived at https://perma.cc/B25F-DCUU; Sarah, 'Settlement with the National Federation of the Blind', *Uber Newsroom* (1 March 2017), https://newsroom.uber.com/nfb-settlement/, archived at https://perma.cc/YK2V-KPVP

6. Who's Driving You?, ' "Ridesharing" incidents: reported list of incidents involving Uber and Lyft', http://www.whosdrivingyou.org/rideshare-incidents, archived at https://perma.cc/V4TM-YJMV. When UK tabloid *The Sun* investigated Uber-related complaints in 2016, it found that, over the course of the previous year, 32 sexual assault allegations in London had involved Uber drivers—with leaked internal screenshots suggesting that the number might be much higher. After a Delhi Uber driver was found guilty of raping a passenger in 2015, the service was temporarily banned from the city—and when operations resumed, the platform emailed the survivor alongside other users to inform them that 'We're back, to serve you and get you moving once again': Mike Sullivan

and Scott Hesketh, 'Uber drivers accused of 32 rapes and sex attacks on London passengers in last year alone', *The Sun* (18 May 2016), http://www.thesun.co.uk/archives/news/1205432/uber-drivers-accused-of-32-rapes-and-sex-attacks-on-london-passengers-in-last-year-alone/, archived at https://perma.cc/NXH8-RDZP; Charlie Warzel and Johana Bhuiyan, 'Internal data offers glimpse at sex assault complaints', *BuzzFeed News* (6 March 2016), http://www.buzzfeed.com/charliewarzel/internal-data-offers-glimpse-at-uber-sex-assault-complaints?utm_term=.xvEz2M9E8#.yvN4R8Q1N, archived at https://perma.cc/9N3T-W7H2; Geeta Gupta and Sumegha Gulati, 'We are back to serve you: Uber sends email to Delhi rape victim', *The Indian Express* (24 January 2015), http://indianexpress.com/article/india/india-others/uber-emails-rape-victim-we-are-back-in-delhi/, archived at https://perma.cc/6CZU-J5LP

7. Caroline O'Donovan, 'Postmates customers are frustrated with delivery costs estimates', *BuzzFeed News* (26 May 2016), http://www.buzzfeed.com/caroline-odonovan/st?utm_term=.usQm6ron1#.vn99mYQ35, archived at https://perma.cc/9HDN-BKJZ

8. Once publicity was drawn to this fact, Uber offered refunds and free rides out of the city: Brian Ries and Jenni Ryall, 'Uber intros surge pricing during Sydney hostage siege, then backtracks after outcry', *Mashable* (15 December 2014), http://mashable.com/2014/12/14/uber-sydney-surge-pricing/#Q6LCbuUtvSqL, archived at https://perma.cc/CWZ3-Y9SZ; Alison Griswold, 'Uber isn't getting rid of surge pricing—it's just hiding it', *Quartz* (23 June 2016), http://qz.com/715092/uber-isnt-getting-rid-of-surge-pricing-its-just-hiding-it/, archived at https://perma.cc/96FK-XRHJ; Alison Griswold, 'Uber's sweeping price cuts usually don't work', *Quartz* (3 March 2016), http://qz.com/629783/ubers-sweeping-price-cuts-usually-dont-last/, archived at https://perma.cc/4FMU-HPH7; Amit Chowdhry, 'Uber: users are more likely to pay surge pricing if their phone battery is low', *Forbes* (25 May 2016), http://www.forbes.com/sites/amitchowdhry/2016/05/25/uber-low-battery/#5578c4ef6f1d, archived at https://perma.cc/6L6Y-SS3Z. This tendency to try to make problems go away appears to be confirmed by a series of internal Uber policy screenshots obtained by news website Buzzfeed. When faced with complaints pertaining to confirmed driver alcohol or drug use, support logic instructions suggest that 'if rider does not want to escalate with LE [law enforcement] or media, follow strike system, issue warning, and resolve without escalating': 'Internal data offers glimpse at Uber sex assault complaints', *Buzzfeed* (7 March 2017), https://www.buzzfeed.com/charliewarzel/internal-data-offers-glimpse-at-uber-sex-assault-complaints?utm_term=.kwrmerQ3MG#.fwNnogvPrD, archived at https://perma.cc/XG76-C6RV

9. TaskRabbit, 'Terms of service', clause 12, https:/www.taskrabbit.co.uk/terms, archived at https://perma.cc/S7CY-FK9S. Users may also be liable for a host of other obligations: see further Vanessa Katz, 'Regulating the sharing economy' (2015) 30(4) Berkeley Technology Law Journal 1067, 1102, n. 193.

10. Vanessa Katz, 'Regulating the sharing economy' (2015) 30(4) Berkeley Technology Law Journal 1067, 1103; Joe Fitzgerald Rodriguez, 'Uber settles wrongful death lawsuit of Sofia Liu', *San Francisco Examiner* (14 July 2015), http://www.sfexaminer.

com/uber-tentatively-settles-wrongful-death-lawsuit-of-sofia-liu/, archived at https://perma.cc/5MWE-Z3AL

11. Grace Marsh and Josh Boswell, 'Deliveroo drivers are accused of causing mayhem "riding against the clock" ', *The Sunday Times* (5 June 2016), https://www.thetimes.co.uk/article/deliveroo-cyclists-cause-road-mayhem-riding-against-the-clock-0m3l3rvod, archived at https://perma.cc/F6XH-MLV7

12. Ibid.

13. Emily Badger, 'The strange tale of an Uber car crash and what it means for the future of auto', *CityLab* (10 September 2013), http://www.citylab.com/commute/2013/09/real-future-ride-sharing-may-all-come-down-insurance/6832/, archived at https://perma.cc/6XEJ-EMZC

14. Ryan Calo and Alex Rosenblat, 'The taking economy: Uber, information, and power' (2017) Working Paper, 23.

15. Ibid., 28, 39.

16. Shu-Yi Oei and Diane Ring, 'Can sharing be taxed?' (2016) 93(4) Washington University Law Review 989, 994.

17. Ibid., 995.

18. Ibid.

19. Gov.uk, 'Businesses and charging VAT', http://www.gov.uk/vat-businesses, archived at https://perma.cc/V7N4-SSEM

20. Robert Booth, 'Tax barrister plans to take Uber to court over alleged £20m black hole', *The Guardian* (21 February 2017), http://www.theguardian.com/technology/2017/feb/21/tax-barrister-uber-uk-high-court-alleged-20m-vat-black-hole, archived at https://perma.cc/4P3L-B2SZ

21. Jane Croft and Madhumita Murgia, 'Uber faces legal challenge on paying VAT', *Financial Times* (20 March 2017), http://www.ft.com/content/190f12c4-0d92-11e7-a88c-50ba212dce4d, archived at https://perma.cc/5U8F-JZZB

22. Jolyon Maugham, 'That's one UberVAT problem', *Waiting for Tax* (20 December 2016), https://waitingfortax.com/2016/12/20/thats-one-uber-vat-problem/, archived at https://perma.cc/QU7M-2TR9

23. Shu-Yi Oei and Diane Ring, 'Can sharing be taxed?' (2016) 93(4) Washington University Law Review 989, 1019.

24. Philip Hammond, 'Spring Budget 2017' (Speech delivered to Parliament, 8 March 2017), http://www.gov.uk/government/speeches/spring-budget-2017-philip-hammonds-speech, archived at https://perma.cc/74YS-XXLJ. The self-employed is a larger category than the gig economy, of course.

25. Mounia van de Casteele, 'Operation de l'Urssas chez Uber', *La Tribune* (29 March 2017), http://www.latribune.fr/technos-medias/innovation-et-start-up/operation-de-l-urssaf-chez-uber-674075.html, archived at https://perma.cc/8595-8WME

26. See, e.g., 'The taxman has strong grounds to test Uber's business model', *Financial Times* (22 December 2016), http://www.ft.com/content/94738c64-c83d-11e6-8f29-9445cac8966f, archived at https://perma.cc/U3AW-HRR5

27. IRS forms 1099-MISC are also to be used to report 'fish purchases for cash'(!): Justin Fox, 'The rise of the 1099 economy', *Bloomberg* (11 December 2015),

http://www.bloomberg.com/view/articles/2015-12-11/the-gig-economy-is-showing-up-in-irs-s-1099-forms, archived at https://perma.cc/9LZ5-2JEW

28. Caroline Bruckner, *Shortchanged: The Tax Compliance Challenges of Small Business Operators Driving the On-Demand Platform Economy* (Kogod Tax Policy Center 2016), 15.

29. Elizabeth Warren, 'Strengthening the basic bargain for workers in the modern economy' (Speech delivered at the New America Annual Conference, 19 May 2016), http://www.warren.senate.gov/files/documents/2016-5-19_Warren_New_America_Remarks.pdf, archived at https://perma.cc/TWH4-PQVB

30. Mailin Aasmäe, 'ETCS and Uber collaborate in seeking solutions for the development of the sharing economy', *Republic of Estonia Tax and Customs Board* (9 October 2015), http://www.emta.ee/eng/etcb-and-uber-collaborate-seeking-solutions-development-sharing-economy, archived at https://perma.cc/47YA-Z49P; Jurate Titova, 'Uber signs MoU with the City of Vilnius', *Uber Newsroom* (2 November 2015), https://newsroom.uber.com/lithuania/uber-vilnius-memorandum-with-the-city-of-vilnius/, archived at https://perma.cc/RV4R-HN7X

31. Ina Fried, 'Gig economy companies like Uber are helping the Feds spread the word about Obamacare', *Recode* (25 October 2016), http://www.recode.net/2016/10/25/13389860/gig-economy-uber-obamacare-burwell, archived at https://perma.cc/P6S8-JYDS

32. Work and Pensions Committee, *Written Evidence: Self-employment and the Gig Economy* (HC 847, 2016–17), Uber, Hermes and Deliveroo workers questioned on challenges of self-employment, http://www.parliament.uk/business/committees/committees-a-z/commons-select/work-and-pensions-committee/news-parliament-2015/self-employment-gig-economy-evidence-16–17/, archived at https://perma.cc/R7CX-GWCG; Sarah Butler, 'Uber driver tells MPs: I work 90 hours but still need to claim benefits', *The Guardian* (6 February 2017), http://www.theguardian.com/business/2017/feb/06/uber-driver-mps-select-committee-minimum-wage, archived at https://perma.cc/Z2D5-SCW3

33. Even platforms themselves might profit. Take competition law as an example: an increasing number of lawsuits allege that if gig-economy workers are genuinely independent contractors, then their use of an app to determine prices would be a clear violation of competition or antitrust law. (See, for an overview, Julian Nowag, 'Uber between labour and competition law' (2016) 3 Lund Student EU Law Review 94.) Employers, of course, are free to coordinate prices amongst their employees and to charge a standardized price for their product.

34. Paula Giliker, *Vicarious Liability in Tort: A Comparative Perspective* (Cambridge University Press 2010).

35. See now the Opinion of Advocate General Szpunar in Case C-434/15 *Asóciacion Profesional Elite Taxi v Uber Systems Spain SL* (11 May 2017). My initial analysis can be found at Jeremias Prassl, 'Uber: the future of work…or just another taxi company?', *Oxford Business Law Blog* (16 May 2017), http://www.law.ox.ac.uk/business-law-blog/blog/2017/05/uber-future-work…-or-just-another-taxi-company, archived at https://perma.cc/NER8-3CY7

36. Simon Deakin and Frank Wilkinson, *The Law of the Labour Market: Industrialization, Employment, and Legal Evolution* (Oxford University Press 2005), 15. Strictly speaking, their model is focused on the role of the *contract of employment* in British employment law; the underlying analysis, however, can easily be extrapolated to most employment law systems around the world.

37. Ibid., 109.

38. Ibid., 86–7.

39. Alain Supiot, *Beyond Employment: Changes in Work and the Future of Labour Law in Europe* (Oxford University Press 2001), 10, as cited in Simon Deakin and Frank Wilkinson, *The Law of the Labour Market: Industrialization, Employment, and Legal Evolution* (Oxford University Press 2005), 14.

40. Simon Deakin and Frank Wilkinson, *The Law of the Labour Market: Industrialization, Employment, and Legal Evolution* (Oxford University Press 2005), 16.

41. Harry Markowitz, 'Portfolio selection' (1952) 7(1) The Journal of Finance 77; Harry Markowitz, *Portfolio Selection: Efficient Diversification of Investments* (2nd edn, Blackwell 1991).

42. Simon Deakin and Frank Wilkinson, *The Law of the Labour Market: Industrialization, Employment, and Legal Evolution* (Oxford University Press 2005), 16.

43. Larry Summers, 'Some simple economics of mandated benefits' (1989) 79(2) The American Economic Review: Papers and Proceedings of the Hundred and First Annual Meeting of the American Economic Association 177, 180; cf., in favour of redistribution, Louis Kaplow and Steven Shavell, 'Why the legal system is less efficient than the income tax in redistributing income' (1994) 23(2) The Journal of Legal Studies 667.

44. Larry Summers, 'Some simple economics of mandated benefits' (1989) 79(2) The American Economic Review: Papers and Proceedings of the Hundred and First Annual Meeting of the American Economic Association 177, 181.

45. Ryan Calo and Alex Rosenblat, 'The taking economy: Uber, information, and power' (2017) Working Paper, 40.

46. Shu-Yi Oei and Diane Ring, 'Can sharing be taxed?' (2016) 93(4) Washington University Law Review 989, 1056ff.

47. Miriam Cherry, 'Beyond misclassification: the digital transformation of work' (2016) 37(2) Comparative Labor Law and Policy Journal 577, 586 (citations omitted).

48. Chris, 'DUI rates decline in Uber cities', *Uber Newsroom* (6 May 2014), https://newsroom.uber.com/us-illinois/dui-rates-decline-in-uber-cities/, archived at https://perma.cc/GN7W-YLNN. Drink driving became one of the key arguments used by ride-sharing advocates once Uber and Lyft ceased to operate in Austin, Texas: Lindsay Liepman, 'DWI arrests spike after Uber/Lyft leave Austin', *CBS: Austin* (23 June 2016), http://keyetv.com/news/local/dwi-arrests-spike-after-uberlyft-leave-austin, archived at https://perma.cc/E5A3-9KAP

49. Noli Brazil and David Kirk, 'Uber and Metropolitan traffic fatalities in the United States' (2016) 184(3) American Journal of Epidemiology 192, 192. Politi-Fact Texas rated Uber's claims in Austin as 'mostly true', noting that 'different

time frames for making statistical comparisons suggest a range of results—
even, in one slice, more DWI collisions than before. It's worth repeating that
Uber is referring to correlations between ride-sharing's availability and collisions, not necessarily causation': W. Gardner-Selby, 'Uber says drunk-driving
crashers down in Austin since advent of ride-sharing services', *Politifact* (16
December 2015), http://www.politifact.com/texas/statements/2015/dec/16/
uber/uber-says-drunk-driving-crashes-down-austin-advent/, archived at https://
perma.cc/4X3U-ZEP6

50. Franklin D. Roosevelt, *Statement on the National Industrial Recovery Act* (16 June
1933), http://docs.fdrlibrary.marist.edu/odnirast.html, archived at https://
perma.cc/7H7V-W9S8. Roosevelt consistently argued in favour of basic labour
standards: see Teresa Tritch, 'FDR makes the case for the minimum wage', *The
New York Times* (7 March 2014), http://takingnote.blogs.nytimes.com/2014/
03/07/f-d-r-makes-the-case-for-the-minimum-wage/, archived at https://
perma.cc/6WPQ-DYWU

51. Simon Deakin and Frank Wilkinson, *The Law of the Labour Market: Industrialization,
Employment, and Legal Evolution* (Oxford University Press 2005), 109.

EPILOGUE

1. John Maynard Keynes, 'Economic possibilities for our grandchildren', in *Essays
in Persuasion* (Palgrave Macmillan 2010), 21.

2. Ibid., 325.

3. President John F. Kennedy, News Conference 24 (14 February 1962), https://www.
jfklibrary.org/Research/Research-Aids/Ready-Reference/Press-Conferences/
News-Conference-24.aspx, archived at https://perma.cc/LDS6-Y8X7

4. John Maynard Keynes, 'Economic possibilities for our grandchildren', in *Essays
in Persuasion* (Palgrave Macmillan 2010), 325.

5. Carl Frey and Michael Osborne, *The Future of Employment: How Susceptible Are
Jobs to Computerisation?* (Oxford Martin School 2013).

6. Ibid., 38, 42.

7. Eric Brynjolfsson and Andrew McAfee, *The Second Machine Age: Progress and
Prosperity in a Time of Brilliant Technologies* (W.W. Norton & Co. 2014), 10.

8. Cynthia Estlund, 'What should we do after work? Automation and employment law' (2017) New York University Public Law and Legal Theory Working
Papers No. 578, 21.

9. Ibid., 23.

10. David Autor, 'Polyani's paradox and the shape of employment growth' (2014)
NBER Working Paper No. 20485, 129.

11. Ibid., 136.

12. Eric Brynjolfsson and Andrew McAfee, 'Human Work in the robotic future:
policy for the age of automation', *Foreign Affairs* (13 June 2016), https://www.
foreignaffairs.com/articles/2016-06-13/human-work-robotic-future, archived
at https://perma.cc/VJ57-4WU8

13. Justin McCurry, 'South Korean woman's hair eaten by robot vacuum cleaner as she slept', *The Guardian* (9 February 2015), https://www.theguardian.com/world/2015/feb/09/south-korean-womans-hair-eaten-by-robot-vacuum-cleaner-as-she-slept, archived at https://perma.cc/86YB-RF49; Aarian Marshall, 'Puny humans still see the world better than self-driving cars, *Wired* (5 August 2017), https://www.wired.com/story/self-driving-cars-perception-humans/, archived at https://perma.cc/B8L9-7K32; Marty Padget, 'Ready to pay billions for self-driving car roads?', *Venture Beat* (17 May 2017), https://venturebeat.com/2017/05/17/ready-to-pay-trillions-for-self-driving-car-roads/, archived at https://perma.cc/ZJ9K-LSXF. There is, furthermore, an important distinction between jobs that could be automated and those that actually are: see David Kucera, *New Automation Technologies and Job Creation and Destruction Dynamics* (International Labour Organization 2016).

14. Although I struggle to see how a robot could do the job of the TaskRabbit organizer we encountered in Chapter 1: coming up with a bespoke beach party, and keeping parents and children happy, strikes me as pretty much impossible to automate.

15. Jane Croft, 'Artificial intelligence closes in on the work of junior lawyers', *Financial Times* (4 May 2017), https://www.ft.com/content/f809870c-26a1-11e7-8691-d5f7e0cd0a16, archived at https://perma.cc/MH5X-UBVU

16. David Autor, Frank Levy, and Richard Murnane, 'The skill content of recent technological change' (2003) 118(4) Quarterly Journal of Economics 1279. The authors note that the work left for humans will fall into two categories:'abstract tasks', requiring high-end skills, from creative design to experienced project management; and low-skilled 'manual tasks'. Both, however, can easily be out-sourced, even if different platforms might be required.

Acknowledgements

Nearly three years ago, I was invited to speak at the International Labour Organization in Geneva. It was a long, sunny day and I had been looking forward to sneaking off to the *Bains de Pâquis* for a swim and fondue. But a session on crowdwork organized by Valerio De Stefano caught my eye: I trundled along, and was fascinated by discussions of algorithmic bosses, historical putting-out models, and crowdsourced work.

To say that I was hooked is an understatement: having recently completed a book on multilateral employment, I was both embarrassed by knowing so little about these emerging developments, and excited to see how traditional employment law discussions would play out in a novel context. On my way back to Oxford, I decided to pitch a new chapter on crowdwork for the paperback edition of *The Concept of the Employer* (Oxford University Press, 2015) to my editor, Alex Flach. He came up with an exciting counter-proposal: why not write a different book, exploring the gig economy in depth?

And so I set off to work on *Humans as a Service*. Writing these lines as we are about to go to print gives me an opportunity to acknowledge all those whose work and support have been invaluable in finishing the book, inspiring and shaping many of its ideas along the way—in particular, Janine Berg, Miriam Cherry, Valerio De Stefano, Martin Risak, and Six Silberman. In the autumn of 2015, we enjoyed a fascinating gig-economy workshop organized by Valerio, Matt Finkin, and Janice Bellace at the Wharton School, University of Pennsylvania, other attendees at which included Abi Adams, Antonio Aloisi, Cynthia Estlund, Steven Greenhouse, Sarah Lewis, Wilma Liebman, and Steven Willborn.

My fellow law dons at Magdalen College, Oxford—Katharine Grevling, Roderick Bagshaw, and Roger Smith—have been the most supportive colleagues a junior academic could wish for, and I am deeply grateful for Mark Freedland's thoughtful engagement and support over the years. I continue to be in the debt of friends and colleagues in the broader labour law community: Einat Albin, Saphieh Ashtiany, Lizzie Barmes, Catherine Barnard, Alan Bogg, David Cabrelli, Hugh Collins, Nicola Countouris, Anne Davies, Paul Davies, Simon Deakin, Ruth Dukes, Sandy Fredman, Judy Fudge, Virginia Mantouvalou, Tonia Novitz, and others have all been patient sounding boards as I slowly came to the realization that whilst the technology enabling gig work was new, nearly all of the fundamental issues involved had been traversed for many years.

Most of the actual writing was done in two long spurts at Yale Law School, where I am grateful for the kind welcome extended by Harold Koh and Mary-Christy Fisher, Guido Calabresi, Al Klevorick, Robert Post, Roberta Romano, David Schleicher, Alan Schwartz, Steve Wizner, Georganne Rogers, and Maria Dino. Henry Hansmann twice lent me his study for a term, and Jack Balkin, Rebecca Crootof, Ignacio Cofone, and B. J. Ard invited me to come along and discuss the work at the Yale Internet and Society Project.

Given the fast-moving subject matter, I was extremely lucky to have the support of some truly stellar research assistance. Jennifer Ho and Rachel Hunter in particular gathered materials on different platforms; Gillian Hughes and David Rowe worked through and fact-checked the final manuscript in painstaking detail. Zoe Adams provided insights and assistance with historical research for Chapter 4, and the librarians at the Lillian Goldman library at YLS dug up nineteenth-century materials to support my historical quests, which my Magdalen colleague Siân Pooley kindly read and commented on. Other colleagues helped with access to foreign materials, including Elisabeth Brameshuber, Tess Hardy, Marcin Wujczyk, and Joanna Unterschuetz.

As my work progressed, I was grateful for invitations to present emerging ideas at over 40 workshops and lectures around the globe. Space limitations prohibit a full list, but I am exceptionally grateful for the discussions, industry insights, and challenges offered by government officials, international organizations, employer representatives, trade unions, academics, and gig-economy platforms—including in particular Uber's Amit Singh and Guy Levin.

I was fortunate to receive feedback on a first draft of the book from a large number of friends and colleagues, including George and Imogen Adams, Einat Albin, Diamond Ashiagbor, Lizzie Barmes, Eirik Bjorge, Craig Becker, David Cabrelli, Paul Linton Cowie, Wolfgang Däubler, Hitesh Dhorajiwala, Luca Enriques, Matthew Finkin, Michael Ford QC, Charlotte Garden, Jacob Hacker, Max Harris, Hubert Horan, Ben Jones, Vijay Joshi,

Miriam Kullmann, Vili Lehdonvirta, Jan Marco Leimeister, Jose Maria Miranda, Guy Mundlak, Ulrich Mückenberger, Rahel Nedi, Kalypso Nicolaidis, Tom Norman, Kate O'Regan, Aidan Reay, Diane Ring, Brishen Rogers, Benjamin Sachs, David Schleicher, Andreja Schneider-Dörr, Adrian Todoli Signes, Tom Slee, Gary Spitko, Sandy Steel, Vanisha Sukdeo, Andy Summers, Julia Tomassetti, Malcom Wallis, Steve Wilborn, Fred Wilmot-Smith, and several others from industry, the judiciary, and government who have asked to remain anonymous. An extended stay at the Hong Kong University Faculty of Law courtesy of Des Voeux Chambers allowed me to rewrite the manuscript into the final version before you today. I have attempted to state the law as of September 2017, with more recent updates included at proof stage where possible; the usual disclaimers apply.

At Oxford University Press, Alex Flach and Emma Taylor were superb editors, encouraging the project from the start and providing guidance and feedback throughout. It is rightly customary to thank everyone in the production team for their hard work in putting the final product together, but especially so in the context of this book: Hannah Newport-Watson coordinated a team of 'gig workers' to copy-edit, proofread, and index the final text: thank you, Vanessa Plaister, Jeremy Langworthy, and Yvonne Dixon! Kiryl Lysenka (hired through upwork) came up with the cover design.

Last, but by no means least, I owe a large debt of gratitude to friends and family for their support over the past few years. Trying to renovate a house from scratch has taught me everything a labour lawyer (never) wanted to know about personal dependence and subordination. We would not have made it without the kindness and wisdom of Sebastian Butschek, Katharine Grevling, our parents, and Elizabeth Macfarlane and Emma Smith.

Central to everything was the love and support of Abi Adams. There isn't a page in this book which hasn't been discussed with and challenged and improved by her, or a day of its writing which went by without stimulating discussion and crucial input. I am incredibly lucky to have found a soulmate and co-conspirator. This book is dedicated to Abi with my deepest love and admiration.

J.F.B.B.P.
Magdalen College, Oxford
Hilary Term MMXVIII

Index